9-23-8

Books by Catherine Drinker Bowen

FRIENDS AND FIDDLERS

BELOVED FRIEND
The Story of Tchaikowsky and Nadejda von Meck
(*In Collaboration with B. von Meck*)

FREE ARTIST
The Story of Anton and Nicholas Rubinstein

YANKEE FROM OLYMPUS
Justice Holmes and His Family

JOHN ADAMS AND THE AMERICAN REVOLUTION

THE LION AND THE THRONE
The Life and Times of Sir Edward Coke

ADVENTURES OF A BIOGRAPHER

FRANCIS BACON
The Temper of a Man

MIRACLE AT PHILADELPHIA
The Story of the Constitutional Convention,
May to September 1787

BIOGRAPHY
The Craft and the Calling

FAMILY PORTRAIT

Family Portrait

My brothers aboard the GEE WHIZ, *about* 1908. *Left to right: Jim,*
Harry, Philip, Cecil.

Family
Portrait

Catherine Drinker Bowen

"I speak truth, not so much as I
would, but as much as I dare; and I dare
a little the more, as I grow older."
— MONTAIGNE

with illustrations

An Atlantic Monthly Press Book

Little, Brown and Company • Boston • Toronto

LIBRARY OF CONGRESS CATALOG CARD NO. 75–105569

SECOND PRINTING

ATLANTIC–LITTLE, BROWN BOOKS
ARE PUBLISHED BY
LITTLE, BROWN AND COMPANY
IN ASSOCIATION WITH
THE ATLANTIC MONTHLY PRESS

Published simultaneously in Canada
by Little, Brown & Company (Canada) Limited

PRINTED IN THE UNITED STATES OF AMERICA

FOR MY SISTER

Ernesta

Contents

ix

CONTENTS

List of Illustrations

xi

Foreword

This book is a celebration and a mourning. Perhaps I have been writing it all my life. Even with biographical subjects as remote from my domestic experience as Sir Edward Coke, John Adams, Francis Bacon, Justice Holmes, I think my brothers looked over my shoulder, seldom approving but always challenging. Four brothers, older than I, inhabited a world that I could never enter and about which — I know it now — I was possessed of an unremitting curiosity from the age of eight. The conventions of our family would not let me ask questions about my brothers' world. What they did away from home, their private likes and dislikes, could only be thought about, imagined. I have never been able to undertake the biography of a man who was small-minded or ignoble. Were all four of my brothers, then, heroes to me? And were these biographies an attempt to reduce the hero to manageable terms?

People ask why I never wrote about a woman. I have had to invent answers. The real answer, "But I did, six times," would be incomprehensible. None of my biographical subjects were to me "all man." My sister inhabited and as it were informed the spirits of my heroes as my brothers did, as I did myself. Ernesta's beauty, like my brothers' superior age, put her in another category from me; she too resided in a place apart, I could not equal her. Yet she was never an enigma as my brothers were. I "understood" Ernesta, knew what she was thinking and was seldom surprised by what she did or elected to do. Henry James, at thirty-six, at fifty-five, wrote intimately and authentically about a young girl, Daisy Miller, and about an even younger boy in *The Turn of the Screw.* His biographer, Leon Edel, explains that in both stories James was writing about himself, in a desperate attempt to resolve an old, old conflict, placate the furies by acknowledging and accepting what he had undergone in his youth. Studying the human condition, a writer uses such enlightenment as comes to hand. And as for the sexes, artists in every field have been able to cross that line; it is common knowledge that witches can change their sex at will.

In *Family Portrait* I meet my brothers not obliquely but head on. Together we skate on the Lehigh Canal; the black ice rushes beneath our feet and across the river at the steel works the open hearth fires glow red and high as any imagined hell. Together we sail our boats on Jersey waters; in the old parlor in Bethlehem Harry and I make music with piano and violin. Always, in real life, my brothers were teaching me; they looked down from their heights and pulled me along. "Go forward, Katz, with that right skate. Don't just slide, *push out!* Get your whole body into it." In this book they teach me still, yet in it I am at long last their equal: my eyes are level with theirs and I see them whole.

Nothing but time can bridge the awful distance. Before one can know that the elders too have been young and vulnerable one must be old oneself. I did not attempt this book until both parents had died and two brothers, Harry and Cecil, also the aunts and uncle whom the reader meets on west Spruce Street. There existed much to help my memory, the family were great keepers of records. They wrapped old letters in bundles, noting on the outside, "Letters of intense interest, relating to those *gone hence*." They signed their letters, "Double love," or they began, "Darling Sister, You missed *three days* writing to me. Pray don't do it again." The family archives yielded eight diaries, reaching from 1758 to 1964. My mother's mother, aged six, opened her journal with the confident statement that she intended to write in it all her life. Ernesta was sixteen and I eleven when we began our diaries. In 1917, one of Ernesta's was published, a full-length book entitled *An Uncensored Diary from the Central Empires* — a vivid, lighthearted account of wartime adventures undergone by herself and her husband, William C. Bullitt, who seemed to have *entrée* to the most exalted circles. Aunt Cecilia Beaux's autobiography came out in 1930: *Background with Figures*. My father and my brother Harry left unpublished autobiographies.

There has never been a doubt in my mind that ancestors are part of every biography. Usually I put them at the beginning, on the periphery, and move inward to my characters. This time the plan would not do, though I tried it. There exist musical compositions that need their coda, need a rounding out, a filling in; without a coda the music would trail off, loose-ended. Following sixteen chapters, I put the Drinker ancestors in a coda, where I think they belong.

It has been written that one does not celebrate in rhyme one's daily bread — and the very words are, as the poet well knew, a celebration. Another poet, John Hall Wheelock, at eighty-odd wrote lines which for me acted as final impulse toward this family portrait: —

> *And not in grief or regret merely but rather*
> *With a love that is almost joy I think of them,*
> *Of whom I am part, as they of me. . . .*

Family
Portrait

I

Prelude to Bethlehem.
A dominance of males.

W HEN MY SISTER Ernesta heard we were going to move to Bethlehem, Pennsylvania, she sat up in the cherry tree and cried for three days. My father had been named president of Lehigh University. I was eight and Ernesta thirteen, her life already established in suburban Philadelphia — her friends and her hopes and what I afterward learned were her ambitions. At this time, 1905, we lived on the campus of Haverford College, twenty minutes from town by the Paoli Local, on the Pennsylvania Railroad's main line to Pittsburgh. My parents still used the old phrase, they were "going to town on the cars."

People today call this region the Main Line and it has acquired a reputation for snobbishness and solid affluence which it did not have in my youth, certainly not our campus, which was inhabited by the Quakers who ran the college and taught in it. The Morley

3

Ernesta at ten, by Cecilia Beaux.

family lived not far from us; when their son Christopher grew up he wrote a poem about the Paoli Local, full of loving nostalgia, though by the time he wrote it Christopher was a famous author, moving in New York literary circles, about as far from Quakerdom as a man could travel:

> *Along that green embowered track*
> *My heart throws off its pedlar's pack*
> *In memory commuting back*
> > *Now swiftly and now slowly —*
> *Ah! lucky people, you, in sooth*
> *Who ride that caravan of youth*
> > *The Local to Paoli!*

The college gateway, a handsome stone affair, led to Lancaster Avenue. We were the first house inside it. The avenue, now a roaring concrete thoroughfare, was then a country road with a meadow opposite where a tethered cow grazed in what I recall as a perpetual springtime of buttercups. My father was not on the Haverford faculty but the college had built a house for him to rent. I don't know why they accorded him this favor. As a lawyer, perhaps he had rendered service to the college; at any rate he was a friend and fervent admirer of Isaac Sharpless, the president. Also my father was by descent a Philadelphia Quaker of many generations, though he had outwardly relinquished all Quaker habits and did not like to be reminded that a Quaker great-grandfather, his namesake, had been exiled to Virginia in 1777 for refusing to bear arms in the Revolution.

My parents had moved out from the city for the sake of their four sons, three of whom eventually were graduated from Haver-

5

ford Grammar School, on the other side of the College Lane from our house. When the school bell rang, the boys would simply run across the road and a wide grassy playing field to the school building; in the afternoons we could see them busy at baseball or cricket or football as the season demanded. The field had big goalposts at each end; I thought they spelled H for Harry, my oldest brother, but the other boys said no, it was H for Haverford.

My parents could not, I think, have devised a more secure existence for their sons. And it was in his sons that my father's interest centered. I wonder indeed that he found time to notice Ernesta and me at all, though notice us he did in a manner at once magisterial and affectionate. Until I was twelve or thirteen he used to call me to him where he sat reading. He would smile, his hand on my shoulder. "Well, Kitty," he would say, "who loves you?"

"*You* do, Pa," I would reply according to schedule, and he would kiss me and give me a pat of dismissal. I never questioned the truth behind this little ritual, but neither did I question the fact that my brothers were of far more importance than I. It was a man's world; women were to be loved and tolerated. I think my father knew of his daughters' comings and goings, their progressive triumphs and failures, only through my mother, whose interest in us remained passionate and unflagging. On rare occasions when I appealed to my father for parental permission he merely said, "Ask Mamma," with accent on the last syllable. I think too that as my sister grew older and her extraordinary physical beauty became manifest, my father was uncomfortable in her presence, a little shy. Such beauty confers a power and a status not quite suitable; a woman's career should be keyed to a lower register.

My mother was a person in no way inferior to her husband in character or brains. But in those early Haverford days, with a

6

Cecilia Beaux and Harry, about 1892.

house full of six obstreperous young, I believe her energies were drained in household management. Also she made our clothes, saw to our music and read aloud to us; she could say by heart the entire rhymed story of the Three Little Pigs, as well as Mr. Daddy Long Legs and Mr. Floppy Fly from the Edward Lear book. When we were sick she dosed us with sugar pills, being a staunch homeopathist.

Later on, in my teens, when the others were grown and my mother had more time, she became my intimate friend and protector; even at eleven I wrote in my diary that I could not live without her. But that was in Bethlehem. At Haverford I was still relegated to the nursery and to Mattie, our nurse, or to the downstairs·schoolroom with Miss Anna, the governess who taught most of us to read and write. Actually I remember Mattie and Miss Anna in those days better than I do my mother — I saw more of them. My brother Phil and I ate our supper early, in a room adjoining the pantry. A table let down from the wall and we had little armchairs to sit in. When Mattie came with the dessert tray Philly used to sing out on a rising note of interrogation: "Applesauce, prunes or baked ap-puls?"

Below my bedroom was the parlor, as we called it, with the piano. At night going to sleep I could hear my brother Harry practicing Chopin waltzes, Schubert songs. I came to know this music intimately, especially the hard places where Harry stumbled. When I grew up and heard the pieces played correctly I thought the pianist had left out something when he did not go twice over those passages. At a college concert one spring Harry played two Grieg pieces and a Chopin waltz. I knew them phrase for phrase as I knew my nightly prayers, which were elaborate and as lengthy as Miss Anna would permit, the purpose being to delay her departure.

A big pond lay near us on the College Lane. When I was about five my father persuaded President Sharpless to fence it in for skating and charge a small admission to the public for upkeep (my father protested in vain the sign CLOSED ON SUNDAYS). A small cabin, built on the bank, had a stove where we could warm up, stamping in on our skates. My first skates had each, for safety's sake, two runners, which turned up in front like Hans Brinker's in the picture. They were called boat skates and I was immensely proud of them, though Phil, three years my senior, said they were sissy skates, "for babies." This particular gibe I was already learning to ignore, though perhaps I never became truly immune to it.

The hierarchy ran from Harry at the top down through Jim, Cecil, Ernesta and Philip. Between Harry and me lay sixteen years, an impenetrable wall. Harry was tall, over six feet, well made, with black hair, a high color and an air of authority which I think must have come to him with his first breath. He seemed more uncle than brother. Indeed the three older boys were remote as if they inhabited some other, grander sphere. They patronized and ordered me about, sent me to their third-floor rooms on errands and addressed me always as Katz, after the Katzenjammer Kids in the funny papers.

Actually I was devoted to all three, especially Cecil, the third one, who in the course of a long life was destined for adoration or hatred from everyone who knew him. With Cecil there could be no gentler medium. Phil of course was my contemporary, to be followed or fought with but certainly not adored.

9

Ernesta, aged two, with Nurse Mattie, by Cecilia Beaux, 1894.

When Harry, at sixteen, entered Haverford College my father began keeping a scrapbook in which were pasted references to the Drinker boys. I have the books; to open them is to be transported to an era very far away, when there was time for everything and metropolitan newspapers reported schoolboy doings as if these counted in the world's affairs. The first entry is from the *Philadelphia Inquirer*, at the height of the college football season of 1897: "HAVERFORD TUNING UP. The scrub did not fare so well. Tatnall wrenched his knee badly, and Drinker, after a magnificent game at end, was laid off with a sprained ankle."

The headlines were notable. "Special to the *Public Ledger*," they said grandly. "Special Telegram to the *Philadelphia Times*." (The telegrams had all of fifteen miles to travel.) "Bright Outlook for Haverford," the lead would be, or "Haverford Improving." In his sophomore year Harry made the first team and my father began underlining these metropolitan notices: "The end positions are being well looked after by Sharpless and Drinker. They are both well built, and are not only very good on the defensive, but are good ground gainers when given the ball, particularly Drinker." Fred Sharpless was the son of President Sharpless, he became my brother's friend for life. As a physician, Fred would attend my mother in her last illness, at eighty-six. But what Fred really cared for his life long was athletics and athletic prowess. Perhaps male aggression found a legitimate Quaker outlet on the playing field; at any rate the Friends pounded one another unmercifully. "After a Bitter Battle the Team Fails to Score," says the *Philadelphia Press* for October 23, 1898. . . . Following an elaborate headline concerning the Haverford-Swarthmore game, one paper announces that "although outplayed and outweighted the Quakers stuck everlastingly to it. Fine work for Drinker, Lowry and Fox."

College football, then as now, was a rough game. At the end of the 1898 season the *Philadelphia Evening Bulletin* summed up football injuries across the country, remarking with fine literary verbiage that "the sport so dear to the college boys is one fraught with danger to life and limb," and going on to columns of fearful statistics about "Collar bones broken, shoulders broken, noses broken, legs broken, ruptured kidneys, ligaments torn, concussion of the brain, internal injury . . ." I wonder that my father could endure it. He was always nervous over the family's health, much more so than my mother with her sugar pills. None of my brothers broke any bones, though Harry wrenched a knee that continued to trouble him for years. Phil butted head-on into a boy named Pier Hazard and knocked out Pier's two front teeth, occasioning frantic apologies from our side; Jim dislocated an elbow.

It was a small price to pay for glory, which the clippings testify continued while Jim and Cecil in their turn ran and batted and fenced and punted their way through grammar school and college. Playing against the University of Pennsylvania in 1902, "Drinker," says the *North American*, "standing on the 25 yard line, dropped a beautiful goal which both sides applauded." This must have been Jim, who as a junior went to England with the college cricket team and played such schools as Harrow, Rugby and Cheltenham. When Harry was a senior and Jim a sophomore, the *Philadelphia Times* described a fencing exhibition between "H. S. Drinker Jr. and J. B. Drinker, both clever foilsmen who displayed splendid activity."

All these exploits with their attendant slips at the wicket and failures at the goalpost were fervently replayed at the supper table. So-and-so had fumbled a punt in the third quarter, resulting in a touchdown for Swarthmore. Somebody dropped an easy fly in the slips at cricket or the umpire gave an out L.B.W.* on a ball that was plainly wide. The fury that went into all this held energy enough to build a battleship. My father at the head of the table encouraged the talk, convinced beyond shadow of doubt that Waterloo had indeed been won on the playing fields of Eton. And besides, he was passionately interested. But he would permit no arguments or shouting — I think because of his Quaker upbringing. "I will not have strife in my house," he said and the boys obeyed him, careful to stage all serious fights beyond his sight and hearing. I grew up believing that to yell at somebody in anger partook of sin, like lying.

My father's role was not that of athletic adviser; I doubt if he had ever played on a team in his hardworking life. He listened. Nor did he compliment his sons. Had he not read aloud to us from *The Jungle Books* that it is unlucky to praise the cubs to their faces? What I remember Pa saying, and he must have said it frequently, was that a man must learn to *lose*. One morning after a disastrous ball game Cecil got into a fight on the fieldhouse porch with his opponent; next day Papa made him go and apologize. Cecil's face turned so black going through the front door I thought he would surely strangle getting the words out. I always wondered if he really did apologize; I know my father never asked him.

As for *girls* learning to lose, it was never mentioned. I think Ernesta and I were supposed to pick up these immutable principles, these enormous life secrets simply from the male contagion. Men ran the world, men must make the rules. Oddly enough

* Leg before wicket.

there was at this early time little talk of lessons and textbooks. That came later, when my brothers were in graduate school. With their undergraduate studies my brothers pursued a course every bit as competitive as on the playing field. To fail an examination was on a par with missing a field goal; it let the team down. Years later, when my turn came, I never received praise for getting good marks at school. I was simply expected to get them — a gruesome responsibility but one a person learns to accept.

Fortunately the five of us possessed what were called active brains. I say five because Ernesta, except for a brief unhappy interval at Baldwin School in Bryn Mawr, had lessons at home until she went to what Phil and I called scornfully "that fancy school in Paris." My brother Harry from the first showed himself a brilliant student, which must have been a trial to Jim, two classes down, who was easygoing and liked to play the mandolin. My father did not keep Harry's report cards; there is not one in the scrapbook. But he kept Jim's, also certain of Jim's examination papers. A paper in Greek composition brought me up short when I saw it: "Question 3. Translate, 'It happened that his mother cared more for Cyrus than for his brother.'" No doubt all siblings wonder which child their parents love the best. For my mother I am not sure, though I have my suspicions. But in my opinion Papa cared most of all for Jim, perhaps because this second son, less competitive, was friendly and funny and said things that made my father laugh. Jim had soft brown eyes, a snub nose, a wide grin, and he got into scrapes. There is a letter from President Sharpless, dated June of 1900:

"Dear Friend, I am informed that thy son James, with other Freshmen, has been a party to invading and disorganizing the rooms of the members of the Sophomore Class. . . ."

A self-governing board of upperclassmen — including brother Harry — at once took the matter in hand and meted out suitable penalty. Quaker schools have always been forward at instituting self-government, a procedure which would serve them well in future days of serious undergraduate revolt. My father wrote back to President Sharpless that he agreed with the penalty imposed and would "express to James disapproval of what he has done." Jim redeemed himself by winning what was called a "corporation scholarship," duly noted in the scrapbook together with a letter from Uncle Will of west Spruce Street, Philadelphia, in the best Teddy Roosevelt style. "*Hello!* Hel*lo!* Jem Drinker! Bully for you, old boy! We're most glad, the aunts and all of us, as if you had batted a century. "

> *Nunc opus dimittitur!*
> *Nunc otium tibi est.*
> *Nunc coelum ad ludendum invitat. Ludamus!"* †

At the time we moved to Bethlehem, Harry was twenty-five, finished with Haverford College and law school and established in a Philadelphia law firm. Jim too had been graduated from Haverford and worked in a Philadelphia bank called the Girard Trust Company. When I asked Jim what he did there he said he stood behind a barred window and handed out money. I thought this generous and altogether fitting, Jim being by far the best-natured

* A century is a high score in cricket.
† Now the work is dismissed!
  Now leisure time is thine.
  Now the heavens invite to sport. Let us play!
Lilly Ross Taylor, the eminent classicist, told me that if the Latin was a quotation she had not found it. She said Uncle Will must have made it up, and if so he wrote good Latin.

of my brothers. Actually I cannot believe they made him teller; he probably ran around in a back office emptying baskets.

Cecil was then eighteen, thin, wiry, quick-moving, with stiff brown hair, a cowlick, and ears that stuck out. A sophomore at Haverford, he showed fierce ambition as to his place on various athletic teams, determined to reach a collegiate position as glittering as that won by his own older brothers. He ended as president of the senior class. By now it must be apparent that the condition known as sibling rivalry raged rampant in our family, the situation being at the same time heightened and mitigated by the fact that the three boys were strong, healthy and bursting with life. Phil was too young to come into it, though later he would run neck and neck with Cecil in a race more bitter than anything we saw in youth.

My father always explained that he left his law business and accepted the presidency of Lehigh University because his three older sons were grown and he needed boys to look after. Of these, Lehigh offered some five hundred. For my father, Bethlehem and the Lehigh Valley had become almost a natural habitat; he was a graduate of Lehigh. Uncle Henry Drinker of Montrose, Pennsylvania, up in the coal country, had paid for the Lehigh education, my paternal grandfather being long since dead and no money in the stocking. My father, born in Macao, China, had been only seven when Grandpa, a merchant captain, died suddenly and his widow sailed home all but penniless, bringing my father and a daughter of sixteen whom I would one day know as Aunt Kate.

At Lehigh my father belonged to the first entering class after the university's founding in 1865. Lehigh is an engineering school, expediently located at the heart of Pennsylvania's steel, coal and zinc regions. My father enrolled as an Engineer of Mines, "being incited thereto," he wrote, "by a passion for collecting minerals." But in his senior year he found himself the only Mining student left, the other three having dropped by the way. Dr. Coppée, president and formerly professor of belles lettres at the University of Pennsylvania, sent for my father and told him they could not keep the course going for only one student; Harry had better change to the School of Civil Engineering. Papa replied that having spent three years at Mining he wanted his Mining degree — a statement in which Dr. Coppée, a benign gentleman with a flowing white beard, acknowledged the justice. My father procured three heavy tomes entitled *Crookes' and Röhrig's Metallurgy*, studied them and made notes on which Dr. Coppée, who knew nothing at all of the subject, daily quizzed him.

In June of 1871 my father received a diploma: Engineer of Mines. His graduating thesis, "Mines and Works of the Lehigh Zinc Company," must have had merit because it was read that summer at a meeting of the Institute of Mining Engineers, and duly published in their *Transactions*. Things may have been simpler in those days, or perhaps my father learned more by his lonely struggles than he would have in class. Possibly also it was this experience which led him to tell me in later life that if you really wanted to you could learn everything from the books themselves and there was no sense putting out time and money taking courses.

The year after graduation my father spent as clerk in a colliery. Then at his own request he was transferred to the Lehigh Valley Railroad as part of a surveying corps working on construction of the Musconetcong Tunnel, between Easton and New York. After a few weeks my father became chief engineer. The tunnel, a mile long, was looked on as an important engineering feat; it seems surprising that a mere fledgling should be given such a position. Half a century later when I remarked to Cecil that Papa must always have been brilliant, Cecil said no, Pa wasn't brilliant, he just had all this energy, he worked harder than other people.

At any rate I have a photograph of that engineering team, eight young men with hats on their heads, each holding his instrument. My father, then in his middle twenties, is posed in front, sitting on the ground, a surveyor's chain in his hand. His hat is pushed back, showing a high forehead and thin face, and giving him a rakish look that seems altogether foreign to the father I knew. The man next him has a corncob pipe in his mouth, no doubt in order to look tough. Lehigh engineers, as I would one day discover, were supposed to be tough and rugged.

When the tunnel lines came together, east to west after three years' work, there was a big celebration, with champagne. My father heard himself publicly congratulated, the lines having met within three eighths of an inch and the grade within half an inch. My father then proceeded to write an enormous book called *Tunneling, Rock Drills and Explosive Compounds,* 1028 pages not counting the appendices, starting with Hindu rock-cut temples and coming down through Agricola to the lake tunnels at Chicago and Cleveland. It was handsomely illustrated with engravings and dedicated to Lehigh University. When the book came out my father was twenty-eight — wiry, indefatigable, wonderful I am told at getting on with men and according to my later observation entirely without understanding of women, including my mother, to whom he was a devoted husband for sixty years.

The tunnel book was barely published when my father suddenly turned to law as a profession. He said engineering hadn't enough future, by which I think he meant money to support a

*The Musconetcong Tunnel Engineering Corps, 1875. Papa is center
front, trying to look tough.*

family. He studied law in Mr. James Gowen's Philadelphia office, was admitted to the bar, and at once found himself busy as mediator in legal-engineering problems of the Lehigh Valley Railroad. Before too long he had been made general solicitor and assistant to the president and had a locomotive named after him. I have a picture of it, labeled *H. S. Drinker, 1888.* Meanwhile there had been the marriage to my mother, Aimée Ernesta Beaux, whom my father carried off triumphantly from a house in West Philadelphia which had a mansard roof, porches, bay windows, a vegetable garden and inhabitants named Uncle Will, Uncle Charlie, Grandma, Aunt Eliza, Aunt Emily, and my mother's sister, Cecilia Beaux. The three boys came along in due season and then to my mother's joy a girl — her namesake, Ernesta. "Not more than a foot long," reported Jim, aged ten. "She has black hair and iberows and very red cheeks like Mama and we are very glad."

II

Bethlehem, 1905

THE TOWN of Bethlehem lies northward above Philadelphia, no more than an hour and a half from the Reading Terminal at 13th and Market Streets. Yet in spirit, in tone and general ethos the Lehigh Valley at that time represented another place and planet, a Wild West of its own. There was vitality here, a basic industrial thrust, a roaring go-ahead get-ahead atmosphere of America on the move. The circus was not more different from the meetinghouse than this town from Haverford, Pennsylvania.

When we moved there, Bethlehem had a population of about twenty-five thousand people, divided down the middle by the Lehigh River and the old Lehigh Canal which ran alongside. North of the river lay the Moravian settlement with its church, sister house and parochial school, the ancient tree-shaded graveyard and the Seminary for Young Ladies which I would one day attend. Southward the steel company's great sheds, belching fire and smoke, stretched beside the water for nearly a mile. Lehigh University perched serenely on a hillside — we called it the mountain — far above the river, the steel mills and the tangled railroad tracks where three lines met. In my teens I would know those tracks well; every morning I would cross them walking to school, every afternoon wait while the long freights clanked by, carrying coal and iron ore from the west or transporting the finished steel to faraway city markets. Already, Bethlehem bought iron ore from Africa and shipped its product to South America.

Between steel company and university the bloodlines were close. The men who had founded the college — Asa Packer, Eckley B. Coxe, Robert H. Sayre, John Fritz the steelmaster — these, with the Wilburs and Hartshornes and Lindermans, had been railroad builders, owners of coal and iron mines, contractors, presidents of zinc plants, cement plants, textile mills which sprang up in the company towns that grew and ringed us round: Catasauqua, Emmaus (we called it Ee-maus), Lititz, and the rest. Bethlehem, with Easton and Allentown, was indeed the focus of an industrial complex that reached into the mountains as far as Drifton, Wilkes-Barre and Scranton. From these towns came the entrepreneurs, the management men, most of them self-made, out for profits and frank about it in a booming laissez-faire economy that put no limits on a free marketplace. And into South Bethlehem, on our side of the river, poured the immigrant laborers, ignorant, unorganized, fated to be blocked for years in any attempt at union or betterment.

Nobody talked about conditions in the foreign part of town, or suggested they be improved. What people talked about was *opportunity*. Had not Asa Packer been a poor boy, and Charles Schwab begun as a stake-driver? Eugene Grace, future president of Bethlehem Steel, the morning after Lehigh commencement, was to put on overalls and climb into the cab of a big electric crane. This, people said proudly, was America, where every poor boy had his chance. The university fed these plants and companies with their graduates. Lehigh seniors went down the mountain, diploma in hand as my father had done, to jobs on the railroad or in the steel company sheds.

Iron and the H-beam dominated our town. Mill whistles waked the valley at early morning, blew the noon hour and closed the shops at sundown. Imperious, relentless, they called the tune. Steel money, coal money built the college on the mountain and paid the professors. My mother knew it and early sensed she would not feel at home on this campus and in this town with its rough, wide-open atmosphere. She had visited Bethlehem years before with my father when one of his railroad friends had married. At the reception the bridesmaids slid down the banisters, pink taffeta dresses, flowered hats and all. My mother, paralyzed with shyness, stood and watched. Not so had life been conducted in the house on west Spruce Street with the mansard roof where she and her sister sang Mendelssohn duets as they dried the dishes in the pantry. My mother was not shocked or offended. Simply, she would not be able to live up to such jovial standards. "I didn't know how to talk to these people," she said, telling me the story.

Certainly our house at Haverford had not lacked gusto. But family ceremonies in Bethlehem took a different turn, more interesting perhaps but less decorous. For instance, the matter of the Myers funeral. There were four sons in their thirties and early forties, known locally as the Myers boys, and four daughters. When the last parent died the big house was to be broken up and the furniture distributed. The Myers arranged things by holding a

Mamma, by Cecilia Beaux, 1891.

big party after the burial. Then the eight lined up inside a gate facing the house and at the crack of a pistol raced to the front door while the crowd cheered — the game being that what you grabbed first belonged to you. One heard also about the affair of Mrs. Doster's piano. Mrs. Doster was beautiful and talented and played magnificently; my mother used to drive across the river to sit and listen. Sometimes I went along. Mrs. Doster's husband, General Doster, many years older than his wife, had made a considerable fortune in the law, and built a big house behind the beech trees on Lehigh Street. My father spoke of him as a man of ability, my mother said he was a cantankerous old curmudgeon. Whether the general was jealous of his wife's music I did not know, being too young to think about it. But one day Mrs. Doster went out of town to visit, and when she came back, there sat her Steinway grand out on the lawn, where the general had had it carried. "And it was raining!" my mother told my father furiously. "Oh Harry, these people are all border ruffians!"

My father always laughed when my mother inveighed against Bethlehem and the border ruffians. Himself a trifle remote in manner even at his most genial, my father loved Mamma's stories and the way she talked, her excitement, even her outrage. On our side of the river — South Bethlehem — the steel moguls had in the late 1890s built their mansions on Fountain Hill, about a mile across the valley from Lehigh. Bonus Hill, people called it. The houses were mostly wooden and sat high, steeply roofed, their eaves embroidered in gingerbread and crowned with a cupola or glassed-in tower. There were wide lawns, terraces with flights of stone steps leading to the front door, lighted by big white gas globes on poles. Most of the steel barons, again, had moved down from the coal towns and intermarried with their kind: a Frick and a Sayre, a Linderman and a Frick.

Charles Schwab's house was biggest. At forty-three, Mr. Schwab came to town as president of Bethlehem Steel, the same year my father came to Lehigh. Schwab was a tyrant, ruthless, talented, who dealt in millions and would end his life in bankruptcy. "If we are going to go bust," he liked to say, "we will go bust big." He inaugurated a whole new slate of management men, seventeen of them, his "Boys of Bethlehem," whom he predicted would become millionaires, and they did. Mr. Schwab was possessed, not of charm but of a kind of hypnotism; he could walk in anywhere and negotiate a loan for his company and his schemes. Perhaps it was sheer ebullience, the authority of great vitality. In Mr. Schwab's Bethlehem office hung a large painting given him by Andrew Carnegie entitled *The Jolly Monk*. I have seen it often. A fat monk sits laughing beside his meager fare of a raw apple and a glass of wine, his hands contentedly on his stomach. Mr. Carnegie said the picture was a lesson: "Good business can only be done in a cheerful frame of mind."

Every Tuesday Mr. Schwab shuttled to New York and back in his private car, the *Loretto*. A man from the Schwab ménage, Joe Ray, went along. Nobody knew exactly what Joe Ray's duties were; Mr. Schwab called him his majordomo. The two never tired of laying bets, on anything and everything. En route to Pittsburgh one day, Mr. Schwab bet Joe a thousand dollars that Mrs. Ray would try to shoot Joe before nightfall. For Joe this seemed a safe enough risk, seeing he had left his wife at home. But when the train drew in to Pittsburgh there was Mrs. Ray on the platform with a popgun; she fired away. Mr. Schwab had sent her on an earlier train. He collected his money but he never would tell what he paid Mrs. Ray for her trip and her trouble.

All of these people gave parties, big smashing affairs of the kind that had terrified my mother. On holidays there were flag raisings, and mammoth fireworks on the Fourth of July. Mr. Linderman gave a Christmas party never to be forgotten by the children who attended. Dressed as Santa Claus, Mr. Linderman held up his hand and squeezed a red rubber ball, upon which a huge Christmas tree slid magically onto the stage.

Next door to the Episcopal Church lived Ethelbert Talbot, known as the Cowboy Bishop because he came from Wyoming and claimed he had preached to the Plains Indians. Bishop Talbot was big and kind and extraordinarily handsome, with a booming voice to match his size. When he came to our house for a trustees' meeting he always spoke to me and gave me a pat on the head. In his later years the bishop grew notoriously absentminded. Once on the train going upstate he forgot his ticket and his money. The conductor said never mind, he could pay next time. But the bishop confessed to worse trouble; he had forgotten where he was going. The conductor said, "Now Bishop, you just put back your head and take a nap. I'll watch the stations and when I see a welcoming committee I'll wake you." Sure enough, at Wilkes-Barre a committee appeared and the bishop got triumphantly off the train.

But of all the Fountain Hill notables, the one I seem to remember best is Mrs. Skeer. My mother said Mrs. Skeer's husband, long since dead, had owned coal mines around Hazleton. A plump lady with tiny hands and feet, Mrs. Skeer used to call on us, driving up in a shining victoria behind matching bays, with two men on the box in maroon coats, white breeches and high boots. I had never seen such a sight — certainly Haverford held nothing so fine. Mrs. Skeer was given to lace parasols and white glacé kid gloves which she owned "by the dozens." She ordered her underwear from Paris — "handmade" — and so fragile it could not be washed but must be sent to the cleaners. She kept it in glass cases around her "boudoir," where it could be viewed on request. Mrs. Skeer collected porcelain. One afternoon she told a visitor that the teacups they were using came from a museum in Europe; she had paid a fortune for them. Of course the visitor dropped hers and broke it, whereupon Mrs. Skeer dashed her own cup to the floor and said what did it matter and she never liked this china anyway.

All these stories, these heroines and heroes were accepted by me uncritically as part of my new life, part of Lehigh and the men and women who flowed in and out of our house: the students who streamed uphill past my bedroom window when the bell rang for classes in the morning; the trustees who met around our dining room table, shut off by big sliding doors from the room where we sat — men from Scranton, Pittsburgh, Hazleton, Mauch Chunk, who knew coal mines and switchback railroads and drank their whiskey straight. Mauch Chunk, a mining town up in the mountains, soon became as familiar to me as Bryn Mawr was to my sister. Our three housemaids came from Mauch Chunk: Bridget Murphy the cook, Tessie the parlormaid, and Mary McClafferty, who would be with us till she died fifty years later. "My brother Clancy drives the fast freight," Mary told Phil and me. "Maybe on the way to school one day ye'll see him while you wait for the trains to go by. Leanin' out the cab window with his cap on his head. I'll tell 'em to wave to you," Mary said.

The glory of this was overpowering; for years one shouted hopefully to every freight engineer on the Lehigh Valley and Reading roads. From the first I loved Bethlehem and everything about it. My sister did not, though she never said so once we made the move. She simply lived through the week, studying her lessons at home with various tutors and escaping on Fridays to Haverford, Bryn Mawr, Philadelphia and her friends. The tutors came from the lower ranks of the Lehigh faculty; my mother recruited them. Also a Frenchwoman arrived twice a week before school to take Ernesta and me for French walks, something my best friend from next door, Marion Thornburg, thought too queer for words. I excused Mamselle illogically if truthfully by saying that my mother's father had been a Frenchman who never did learn to speak proper English. All I remember about the walks is that I nearly froze and that Mamselle tweaked my nose and called me *"Petit nez rouge."*

I don't know how my sister escaped going to school in Bethlehem. Perhaps she simply refused, and my mother, who sympathized with Ernesta's genuine grief at leaving "home," as the two of them called Haverford, interceded and won the point. To the degree that my father ignored our social life he showed interest in our education — certainly he showed it in mine. My sister could be very stubborn, a trait I think now she shared with my father. The two of them had a tight-lipped way of simply turning from what offended them. And unlike myself, Ernesta did not hesitate to defy Papa when the occasion warranted. To avoid this horrible contingency my mother would do almost anything. She did not fear my father but she adored him; to cause him pain was a sin against the Holy Ghost. When a domestic storm threatened be-

29

tween Pa and Ernesta, my mother would raise her hands in a large propitiatory gesture. "We must have peace in this house," she would say. "Peace, peace, and the olive branch waving."

I do not remember what subjects my sister studied with the tutors. But in English literature she was a hungry reader, taking herself through Thackeray, Dickens, Scott, George Eliot and the rest, sitting absorbed on the library sofa, her black hair falling round her shoulders, lids down over the glorious dark eyes, her long legs tucked under her. Afterward she wrote résumés and criticisms which she liked to show me. My brother Phil went for a year to the Moravian Parochial School across the river, until he was banished to St. George's in New England, where he stayed for six years, returning in the holidays. The three older brothers, Harry, Jim and Cecil, came from Philadelphia for weekends, sometimes bringing their girls. One autumn Saturday Cecil turned up with the entire Haverford College football team. I don't know where they slept but my mother managed to feed all eleven of them.

There was no question about my going to school, right away the first year, at the age of eight. A Miss Kellogg kept what was called a dame school, in the parish house of Bishop Talbot's cathedral on Fountain Hill. I walked there or rode my bicycle every day. I think my parents and Professor Thornburg, my best friend's father, must have started the school in despair of what to do with us; the Thornburgs had eight children.

Miss Kellogg I remember in a gray wool dress that came down to her shoes, belted and long-sleeved; her high collar had white ruching around it. A wooden pointer seemed to grow to Miss Kellogg's right hand; I cannot remember her without it. The room

where we sat had two long tables, one for the big children like
Lewis Thornburg and one for the rest of us, and two blackboards,
a big one and a little one. On these we did our sums and wrote
compositions. My father insisted that I learn Latin; when Miss
Kellogg said I was too young, Papa said *he* began Latin at seven. I
cannot recall any nonsense about coloring and crayons and cutting out pictures. I think of a room full of sunlight and myself at
the blackboard, the dry chalk in my fingers, doing subtraction, the
subsequent pleasure of wiping off the board with a felt eraser.

I stayed two years at Miss Kellogg's; I think it was then the
virus of competitiveness first infected me. At home there had been
no use competing, everybody being too far beyond and ahead. But
at Miss Kellogg's I found myself for the first time with my equals,
my fellows. I could run as fast, spell as well when we stood up for
a spelling bee. We spelled by syllables, rhythmically, like a chant
— a method that ensured a word once learned could not be forgotten: "V-i, vi; v-i-o, vio; l-e-t let, violet." What I particularly
enjoyed was parsing sentences on the blackboard. The diagrams
fitted together like a puzzle, a game, with lines slanting down for
the adjectives and adverbs, and smaller lines branching out for
prepositions.

On weekends when my brothers came from Philadelphia, life
resumed the family pattern from which even the dame school,
modest though it was, had begun slightly to estrange me; I cared
greatly for these new friends of my own age. But on Friday evenings the sibling hierarchy reestablished itself, strong and clear.
From the time I could walk I think this difference in ages was
sharp in my mind, fixed and irretrievable as the space between
the planets and the stars: Harry-Jimmy-Cecil-Ernesta-Philly-
Kitty. I would never catch up. I would always be smallest and

dumbest (I would have said), though I recall no chagrin at the notion and nothing of what would today be called an inferiority complex.

Actually I think the hardest position was not mine at all but Jim's, wedged between two brothers of quite extraordinary mental and nervous intensity, not to mention ambition. Fortunately for Jim he seemed to have been born good-natured; at graduation from Haverford he received a traditional trophy that signified the best-liked all-round man in the class. It was a big, long-handled wooden spoon, tied with the college colors, red and black. My father had it copied in a silver brooch for my mother; she loved to wear it. It was impossible to make Jim fight, though I have seen his brothers bait him. As big as they were and as strong, Jim simply would not quarrel. "Oh, what's it matter?" he would drawl. "Keep your shirt on, you old beefsteak!" I heard him say it to Harry and I was petrified; it was like talking back to God.

On Sundays after midday dinner, Jim always invited me — and Phil when he was home — into the poolroom and told us a story. The poolroom was left over from Haverford; the reason we possessed so exotic a furnishment was because my father thought it would help to keep the boys home at night. Actually I think it did. And the sound of pool balls clicking still means Saturday night to me — an odd enough circumstance considering the general moral austerity of our bringing up. The poolroom walls were hung with the stuffed and mounted heads of animals my father and brothers had shot on expeditions to Colorado and Wyoming: a moose head, a six-point buck, two mountain sheep with curly horns. This had been in Haverford days, when my father was still with the Lehigh Valley Railroad; I think they traveled free. Jim said Pa taught them to shoot by cracking away at telephone poles while they sat on the observation platform.

The story that Jim told us continued in serial form from Sunday to Sunday. Its hero was a dragon that lived entirely on fried egg sandwiches, a benign beast whose adventures all turned out happily and who spent a large part of his time snoozing in the sun. His name, for no explained reason, was Cabayanus, and he used to fall hopelessly in love with princesses and follow them about. (Jim, too, was forever in love.) I was enthralled with Cabayanus, but Phil used to grow restless. "I thought dragons were for *fighting*," he told Jim. "I thought they breathed fire and smoke and ran after people and killed them with their thrashing tails, and Saint George thrust his spear therein all bloody."

At this time Phil was thirteen and much intrigued with blood and battles. On Sundays it was my mother's custom to call the six of us to her bedroom after dinner, read aloud a chapter from the Bible and then hear each of us recite a verse. My father never attended these sessions, but Harry came, had his verse by heart and led off, the rest of us following in turn. And no matter what pleasant psalm the others had chosen, Philip always came out with three or four savage lines about Saul slaying his thousands, the Egyptians being overwhelmed in the Red Sea, or the babes slain with the sword by Herod. Ernesta and I used nearly to burst, suppressing giggles during these recitations. But my mother never changed expression, and when Phil was through she merely nodded, her mouth prim, and turned to me for my contribution.

33

III

The President's House

FOR A CHILD, a girl of eight, ten and onward, the life at Lehigh offered a marvelous freedom. The president's house was the third one uphill from Packer Avenue, a big old-fashioned place with high ceilings and considerable grounds of its own. We inherited a grass tennis court — all weeds and bumps, woods, a brook, and a large stable inhabited solely by Ernesta's pony, Taffy, imported from Haverford. Behind our house, South Mountain stretched limitless. Marion Thornburg and I roamed at will through the woods, climbed the big rock at Lookout Point where we could see smoke pour from the chimneys of the steel works far below along the river. In the autumn we hunted chestnuts.

To me, the Lehigh campus was a world in itself; I knew and loved every foot of it. Just up the hill from our house stood the huge granite building called Packer Hall, a monstrosity of Railroad Gothic with a pointed steeple. My father had his office in the

"Don't hurry the eighth notes," Harry said.
Catherine Drinker.

building, at the head of a long, wide flight of wooden stairs. Marion and I used to climb to the top and slide down the banisters, sitting upright and facing the bottom, no hands, our arms spread wide. Jim Myers, the old janitor, said we'd better not let my father catch us at it. Or we would venture further, up the dark belfry tower, crawling under beams and over dirty boards, then jump to catch the bell clapper, hoping it would swing, which luckily it never did. Packer Hall bell rang the hours day and night. Every morning at a quarter to eight it announced chapel, and my mother, gloved, hatted, solemn as if it were Sunday, walked down across the campus with my father. Sometimes I went with them, when my music practicing had been done early enough. We sat in the first pew; it seemed odd to see my father in his gown, throned in the pulpit high above the students. This was the only church service, on or off campus, my father went to except the baccalaureate sermon in June. The famous Bethlehem Bach Choir met in Lehigh Chapel; my father accepted the presidency, he said, on condition that he never be expected to attend a concert.

As for the Packer Hall bell, its voice from the first established order and told me, in dream and waking, that this was home. The first night we were at Lehigh the bell pealed at 9:30. My father, alarmed, hurried up the hill, thinking there must be a fire or some kind of trouble. "Why Doctor," Jim Myers said, "don't you remember curfew from the old days?"

In Bethlehem everyone called my father "Doctor," by virtue I suppose of various honorary degrees that came to him as president. My mother never got used to it. "*Doctor!*" she would call out from her end of the supper table. "Mary says there's a student asking for you at the door" — and she would giggle. Actually a student at the door seemed a perennial condition. They came

37

when they were in trouble or needed money, a scholarship, a supplementary job to help them through. I used to hear about it. "Young Kowalsky says his father is sick and can't work and he will have to leave college. He's that boy from the mining district. We'll have to do something." In those days people still came down frequently with typhoid fever. My father was forever fussing about the drinking water on campus, harassing the mayor and the city fathers, achieving new filters, bringing in chemists and plumbers.

At home my father's study was close to the front door. Students came to talk over class business and athletic affairs; my mother said plaintively they always came at suppertime. The engineering clubs held their evening meetings in our library, with the furniture pushed back and folding chairs set up: the Civil Engineers, the Miners, the Electricals, the Chemicals. After the papers were read my mother provided what she called a collation in the dining room, with Bridget's fried oysters, coffee and homemade ice cream. My bedroom adjoined my parents'. I can remember my father coming in very late one night; the door was open. I woke and heard him tell my mother he had been down to the saloon on New Street to bring young Hillman home to the fraternity. The boy had been drunk for three days. My mother demurred. Surely somebody else could have rescued Hillman, it was two in the morning! "Etta," my father said, "suppose it had been Jim or Cecil."

I don't know how my father achieved his trusted relationship with the Lehigh students. I do not think he worked at it, as the phrase goes. Rather, it came naturally to him; instead of four sons he had indeed five hundred. I do know that the students responded in kind. After a successful football game, or the evening before, when the "smoker" let out, there would be a crowd of boys

My father as president of Lehigh.

on the road by our house, directly below my bedroom window. "Rah rah rah!" they shouted. "Dr. Drinker, Dr. Drinker, DR. DRINKER!" On the night of the annual freshman-sophomore "rush," when the two classes battled up and down the steep terraces below Packer Hall, Papa had an ambulance from St. Luke's Hospital waiting at our kitchen steps. By that same token my father nourished a cordial friendship with Dr. Estes, head of the hospital, with Mayor Sweeney of Bethlehem, the police chief, and Father Toohey of the Roman Catholic Church on East Fourth Street. On more than one evening when I asked what Pa was doing in the dining room with the sliding doors shut, my mother said, with her especial Presbyterian sniff of disapproval, "He's in there with Mr. Sweeney and *that Father Toohey*, drinking whiskey and talking about the Lehigh boys." My mother said Papa was a Machiavelli. When I inquired what it meant she said he got his way by devious means.

On the campus everybody spoke to me; I knew all the faculty by name: Professor Meaker, whom I met each morning on the path leading down to Packer Avenue — a tall man in a blue suit with bicycle clamps around his ankles. He would doff his hat to me solemnly, to my profound satisfaction; the youngest of six looks for condescension but not for bows. There was also Professor Franklin in the physics laboratory, who showed me the sensitive flame and let me test it across the room — showed me, too, how sand forms patterns on a steel plate when a violin bow is drawn down the edge. I took to hanging round the laboratory door; once I blew some glass and took it home. When my father remarked that college professors were hardworking, busy men, my mother cut him down. "Now, Papa," she said, "the professors *like* Kitty. I am sure she doesn't bother them one bit."

The pains my mother took on occasion to declare that people liked me must have been due to the fact that I was at the time quite bitterly shy. Small wonder my diary at eleven declared that I would die without Mamma. "It is a terrible misfortune to be born shy," I wrote just after my twelfth birthday, in a thick school notebook labeled *Vol. 3, dedicated to Mamma.* "You can't talk to anybody because you don't know what to say. You get embarrassed all the more if you don't talk and altogether it is a *terrible* micksup to be shy and tonguetied when you are with strangers. I would love and adore to be popular. Sometimes my shyness makes me so furious that I just X — X!"

The sign meant I just cursed, words failed me. There is little doubt that what made me so shy was a consciousness of my looks. My mother's sister, Cecilia Beaux, a portrait painter, had years ago begun using my sister as a model, my brother Harry also. In our big square front hall hung full-length portraits of Ernesta, Harry, Cecil, and one of Phil as a small child. When Beaux, as we called my aunt, came to visit there was much talk about bones, measurements, the distance from brow to ear, the advantage — in fact the absolute necessity — of having one's eyes placed far apart. This stressing of the right kind of bones had early convinced me that mine were very wrong indeed. A forehead too high, a chin too long were not going to alter themselves. My aunt said bones *stayed;* they stayed till you were ninety.

I hated Beaux for this, nor did I love her more when I heard her tell a caller that when she first saw her niece Kitty in the cradle she knew that wasn't a forehead to paint. "There's a forehead that will go to Bryn Mawr and write a *book.*"

It was a fate too dreadful for contemplation and I put it from me, or thought I had. My two oldest brothers said Bryn Mawr

Ernesta and Phil at Haverford, by Cecilia Beaux, 1887.

Cecil at four, by Cecilia Beaux.

College girls knew too much and talked too much; my sister said they let their skirts hang all wrong. Ernesta, of course, had no intention of going to college; she was headed for school abroad. The diary spoke often of shyness and lined up the enemy in categories: "I don't mind old gentlemen, above 45. I don't mind old ladies, above 45. I don't mind young ladies, under 30 much. I *do* mind young gentlemen under 30." There were particulars, after which *Vol.* 3 announced, as in all true confessions, a therapeutic result: "When I first started to write I was in the dumps but now I feel excellent."

I had reached my teens before I began going to Lehigh football games and watching baseball and lacrosse. But as a child I seldom missed any student activity which took place around the campus, such as the parades after victory (we called them pee-rades), with the college band in brown and white uniforms, tooting and blowing and banging their drums. Each winter after examinations the sophomores burned Old Man Calculus at night in a dazzling ceremony called the Calculus Cremation. Marion Thornburg's father taught calculus; as head of the mathematics department he had a reputation for ruthless flunking and general demolition of the unfit. My mother objected to my presence at the cremation, though she did not forbid it. But she saw something altogether too realistic in that dark gibbet above the pyre, the hooded sophomores dancing round the flames, the stuffed figure swinging. My mother said it even *looked* like Professor Thornburg, with its long legs. But when I told Marion she said stoutly, No! those dumb sophomores wouldn't dare!

On class day in June the Ben Greet Players came to town and performed their Shakespeare on the terrace above our old grass tennis court. No stage needed to be built, and no scenery or wings.

44

The actors simply walked out from a grove of trees and faced their audience. The terrace sloped upward to a backdrop of great chestnuts; from three sides the players could slip offstage into the trees. Mr. Greet told my mother it was the pleasantest stage they ever experienced. Of course they gave *A Midsummer Night's Dream,* and another year *As You Like It.* And of course for weeks afterward Marion and I were Titania, Puck, Rosalind, dancing over the grass in middy blouse and bloomers, trailing my mother's scarves and chanting our lines:

> *Thorough bush, thorough brier,*
> *Over park, over pale,*
> *Thorough flood, thorough fire,*
> *I do wander everywhere . . .*

Modern biographies are filled with the searing traumatic experiences of sensitive young people when first they meet with sex, death, and other inescapable facts of living. From the age of eleven I was in love. The boys were legion; I am sure none of them guessed at my passion. Certainly they did not return it, but they asked me to play tennis or field for them at baseball, much as my brothers did. I enjoyed this, though it became worrisome when boys called me a good sport, seeming to preclude something different and more desirable. I fell regularly for my sister's beaux, kept somebody's picture in a locket hung round my neck and in the diary wrote pages about the current *him* — mushy, romantic and not a little anxious in tone: a dance was coming at school, and would Johnny take me? But as for any serious confrontation, let alone temptation, it simply did not happen. There were indeed incidents when sex in its nakedness stopped fleetingly and moved

45

on, let us say to maidens more receptive or more vulnerable. The incident, for example, of Crazy Franz. The fact that I remember it so vividly may be proof of something; yet I cannot think of it as proof of shock. Like most communities of the day, Bethlehem had its town idiot who wandered about unchecked. Ours went by the name of Crazy Franz. One day as I was walking home from school Crazy Franz stopped me and stood gibbering and making most peculiar gestures. I thought he was asking me to button his trousers and I might have complied had not a student in a Lehigh cap come along. He said something to Franz, then took my arm — I was nine — and led me up the campus and home.

At eleven I first heard the word fuck. By then Marion Thornburg and I had exchanged Miss Kellogg's for Bishopthorpe Manor on Fountain Hill, a school attended by the daughters of the steel and railroad magnates. Marion told me that one of our classmates had fucked behind the Wilburs' hedge with Billy Barth. Marion explained what it meant, but to me the entire program seemed so preposterous I thought she was making it up. In my diary I gave the story as Marion told it, then wrote, "I can't believe civilized people would do such a crazy disgusting thing." The girls at Bishopthorpe used to bait me by saying they bet they could shock Kitty Drinker. When I said defensively they couldn't, it brought on a whole rash of stories about sex. Finally I told my mother, one night after prayers when the light was out. What I said was that Billy Barth had lain down on top of Ellen and peed into her weedles place.

Shortly afterward I was removed from Bishopthorpe to the Moravian Seminary across the river. My parents must have thought the Moravians were not quite so advanced — and from my experience they were right. Perhaps I was emotionally overprotected.

Yet my mother gave me wide latitude. I came and went from the house with much freedom, knowing always that Mamma was there, in her place, ready to receive my confidences but never demanding them. Recalling my shyness with boys, I have wondered, since, if having four older brothers is, for an adolescent girl, more handicap than help. My blood told me plainly enough that boys who attracted me were not my brothers, yet I could not surmount that hurdle. At fourteen I wrote, after a dance, "Toots let all the boys hug her as if they were girls." One night (I must have been sixteen) I was standing at the foot of the bed in my nightgown when my mother came in from her room. "Well, dear," she said, "did you have a nice time at the dance?" I said it had been all right, and that downstairs just now when Frank said good night he tried to kiss me. "Did he?" my mother asked in her light, eager voice. "Did he kiss you, Kitty?" I said no he didn't, because I backed off. My mother paused and then said surprisingly, "Well, goodnight, dear. Maybe next time things will go better." I think my mother knew that a daughter so painfully shy needed not braking but encouragement. At any rate the sense of her unfailing presence allowed one to take what seemed enormous risks and embark on daring journeys into terra incognita.

The fact is that by today's standards I stayed ridiculously innocent until I was married at twenty-two. Sex existed and was plainly important. But also it remained remote. My brothers never spoke of sex, never mentioned it, though there was abundant talk about love, and our house on weekends was filled with their girls, imported from Philadelphia. Perhaps nothing in this family chronicle removes it so far from today's mores and today's social ethos than the statement that my four brothers were all of them virgins when they married. It is hard to remember how prevalent was the notion in certain circles that not only young women but young men did well if they went to the marriage bed without previous experience. Had not the girl in *The Green Hat* remarked, when her young bridegroom jumped out the window on their wedding night, "Boy died for purity"? Few readers of that very popular novel thought it funny at the time.

I found out about my brothers' virginity when Ernesta wanted to marry a man, perfectly eligible in all directions except that he had had syphilis. He told Harry about it, saying the only honorable course would be to tell, and that the doctor certified his health and said it was all right for him to marry. This was long before the days of penicillin; one relied on the mercury treatment. A family conclave resulted in a broken engagement; the young man died afterward of what was then called brain fever. I was not included in the family councils, but according to Ernesta, her brothers demanded why they should "keep themselves clean for marriage" if their sister went off and married a man with syphilis. The whole episode was dramatic and unhappy. I liked Jay. Previous to the revelations and their consequences, he appeared a laughing, generous-minded youth whose family, incidentally, possessed a place in Newport that Cecil said was absolutely tailored for Mrs. Astorbilt — Cecil's name for Ernesta.

I confess that my ignorance of sex as a girl was equaled only by my lack of social conscience. I must have been eighteen before I so much as recognized that poverty was a condition for which not only the poor were responsible. I had never seen the foreign part of Bethlehem where the steelworkers lived. Not only was there no occasion for me to pass through, but I had been given to believe that immigrant laborers in America had their chance at the sun as well as anybody. My father looked on the steel company as Opportunity with a big O, for young men of all backgrounds. Lehigh boys, belonging to families in the mining district that Pa knew from his own youth — these boys, he said, were fortunate to have a college education. It raised them a step, three steps above their background. I am quite sure my father believed this same education would be available one day to the sons of the foreign laborers down by the river.

My father's ambition was to see that his Lehigh boys, as he called them, acquired knowledge besides the technical, some acquaintance with a world beyond the Lehigh Valley, and with literature, the books my father had come to know in his own youth. He instituted courses in English literature and persuaded the faculty to make them compulsory. To my father the steel company stood as furtherance of a young man's education, a sort of graduate course, as indeed the Lehigh Valley Railroad had been for him when he wrote his book on tunneling. And had he not read law in the office of James Gowen, the man who broke open the case of the striking Molly Maguires up in the coal mines around Wilkes-Barre? My father was not himself interested in money; he would have been disappointed had any of his sons embraced a purely moneymaking career. Yet he believed in hard work as a challenge, almost as a religion. Hard work was indicative of American manhood, it was part and parcel of the U.S.A. and its "development," boom and bang.

I grew up, therefore, believing the steel company offered splendid openings for vigorous young men and that Charles Schwab, Mr. Carnegie, Mr. Frick, Eckley Coxe and the rest were benefactors to mankind. It might be said also that we ourselves were by no means rich people. My father's salary at Lehigh when we went there was $8000 a year. I am quite sure he had no backlog of

49

savings; he had been poor himself. We paid our maids from three to five dollars a week, which was considered generous. Bridget in the kitchen could neither read nor write. My mother kept saying we must teach her, but Bridget would have none of it; she said her recipes were in her head-like and she didn't want all that bother. Mattie, our former nurse, and Miss Anna the governess had been left at Haverford with other perquisites of my father's successful legal career. In Bethlehem when we had to go off campus we sent to the railroad station for a cab — my father called it a hack — or we drove in the buggy behind Taffy, our pony. I wore my sister's hand-me-downs and thought them stylish enough; a seamstress came from time to time and cut the skirts to fit. The seamstress was French; her name must have been Mathé but to me she was Madamatty, all in one word. (Forty years later I thought of Madamatty when I read in the English *State Papers Domestic* for 1603 that the Spanish ambassador to London spelled Sir Walter Ralegh's name always as Wattawally.)

Concerning the fervent absorption in my own affairs, it was a state of mind shared by my brothers and sister — a condition I look on now as no accident. If my mother had any principle of child rearing it was love and setting an example. But if my father had one it was to keep us busy. "Give young people plenty to do and then let them alone," he said. At Haverford a Mr. Doyle had come every day to give my brothers boxing lessons before breakfast; if they didn't box in college, never mind. At Lehigh there was a large greenhouse on the president's grounds; my father's predecessor, Dr. Drown, had been an ardent rose grower. My father converted the greenhouse to a gymnasium by clearing out the plant benches, putting down a floor marked for games, and lining the glass with heavy wire against breakage. We had parallel bars, a tumbling mattress, rings to swing on and a stuffed leather object to vault over, called a horse.

When my brothers came for weekends they instructed me quite seriously in the use of these contraptions. I learned to do an uncertain backflip and walk on my hands. But I never became proficient, though my brother Jim could do a whole series of backflips and told me I could too if I wasn't such a chicken. All four of my brothers were forever telling me there was nothing to be scared of. "Go ahead, Katz, go ahead!" The total effect of my three older brothers upon me became stronger at Lehigh than at Haverford, even though their physical presence perforce grew scarcer. Phil and I quarreled and yelled; one day in the rose garden I bit Philly on the wrist and ran to the front porch for shelter. When we made a fuss Harry seemed always on hand to bring us to order. He did it by simple roaring. "Stop it, kids! Katz, you and Philly quit, now! Come on in the house. And get those bikes off the driveway."

It was the voice of God in the tumult and we heeded it. I doubt if my father even guessed at Harry's role in my life, certainly not of its extent. "Harry tells me you are doing quite well on your violin," Papa would say, smiling vaguely, when I was twelve or thirteen. My father's office with the desk and telephone lay only one room away from the parlor where the piano stood and where I practiced. The sounds must have been excruciating but my father bore with it. If Harry and Mamma believed the girls should have music, well then, let them have it and make the most of their opportunity.

Ernesta's piano practice was halfhearted; she never cared for it though she learned to accompany herself when she sang. "*O solé mio*," she would warble in a small, clear treble, "*Sta'n fronte a te.*"

Neither of us knew what it meant. But with me as with Harry music became a passion, almost a way of life, though as performers we never, for all our practicing, were to achieve more than respectable amateurism. In Harry's early boyhood my mother had met a superb piano teacher, a Polish woman who went by the name of Miss Emery. She was tiny and voluble and played Chopin so as to break your heart. I knew her only as an old lady, but she still was master of her instrument. At my mother's invitation Miss Emery spent her summers in our house. My Aunt Beaux had painted Harry as a boy, his legs dangling from the piano bench, his hands on the keys. I have the picture. And there was a family story of Harry practicing in summer beside the open window, with his friends outside batting balls and shouting until he put his hands over his face in misery. "Oh, Ma!" he moaned. "I wish I didn't love music so much!"

I was eight when Harry brought to Bethlehem for a weekend one Kathleen Coolidge, from Boston. Kathleen was perhaps twenty, and she played the violin. The two of them did the Kreutzer Sonata, over and over, working at the hard parts while I sat on the sofa in the corner or crawled under the piano, crouching with my head on my knees, as close to the sound as I could manage. When Kathleen had gone I went to my mother and told her I wanted to play the violin. She took my hands — I remember exactly where she was sitting — and told me that was not an easy thing to do, it would take courage. Did I think I was up to it?

Up to it? Flags waved, banners flew. Harry, however, declared I would have to take piano lessons first, to learn the keyboard and "see if you really mean it." Like Jacob who labored seven years for Leah and seven years for Rachel I did my stint and had my reward. Harry found a violin teacher in Philadelphia, Charlton

Harry at the piano, by Cecilia Beaux, 1889.

Murphy, and my mother collected enough pupils to make a trip to Bethlehem worth his while. Thereafter, Mr. Murphy arrived every Saturday, fiddle in hand, and sat on a high stool while I had my lesson. Mamma said Mr. Murphy needed the stool because he had a weak heart. (Actually Mr. Murphy's heart must have had its own virtue; he lived long enough to give violin lessons to my second husband.) One of Mrs. Doster's children played violin. We had a little string orchestra that met once a week at the Dosters', despite the terrible-tempered general. Mr. Murphy led us. A big tall boy named Lowell Otis played cello. He always referred to his instrument as the doghouse. On my being unwise enough to ask why, he took his bow and replied with growls and barkings of a convincing and horrid virtuosity.

IV

Harry and Sophie

ON SUNDAY mornings in Bethlehem we went to the Presbyterian Church on Fourth Street, all of us except my father. Down the campus and across Packer Avenue to Vine Street, past the row of houses with the porches to a little church that seemed even smaller as we filed in and took our places. The music was awful — a wheezy organ and a soprano who, while the plate passed, sang sentimental pieces that made Harry flinch. When she got under way he would take his hymnbook and go into a trance. I knew he was multiplying hymn numbers in his head; he told me he could do three-figure ones and asked if I wanted him to prove it.

The moment church let out and we had shaken the minister's hand at the door, Harry and I rushed uphill to the Episcopal Cathedral, arriving in time for the offertory, so we could hear the choirboys sing and Mr. Shields play the organ. This was expensive, it meant two collections in one day, but well worth the nickel. Bishop Talbot used to josh us about deserting the Presbyterians. I remember Harry telling him the Presbyterians didn't know the word B-a-c-h and sang hymns with bad melodic lines that jumped and kicked: "*Jee*sus calls us, *o'er* the *tu*mult . . ."

Sunday afternoon was sacred to a family walk around the mountain, up through Lehigh woods to a country trail that wound by farms and pastures through the crossroads village of Saucon and home. Mamma did not come. My father led with Harry, the rest followed. I was hard put to keep up the long stride, though I did not have to go. I think I went to be with Jim or for want of something better, Sunday not being rife with entertainment. But on winter afternoons when the weather was right we went skating, down the canal and back by the river, flying along for miles, the boys ahead to test the ice for safety. When they struck a rough place we took off our skates — they clamped to the shoe in those days — and walked the towpath. It was always bitterly cold but the deep black ice of the canal, the loneliness of the terrain were exciting and one forgot discomfort. Coming home at dusk we would pass the steel works, row upon row of black sheds and chimneys, and skating toward the open hearth we saw the furnace glowing fiery red. Molten ore poured and hissed, sparks streamed in jets. There was a clang and banging of metal on metal; the figures of men were outlined against the fire as they crossed on girders and catwalks. Long afterward when I saw the Gustave Doré Illustrations of Dante's *Inferno* they seemed tame beside what I knew as hell. When I asked my father if the work wasn't dangerous he said yes, it was, and required great skill and strength, but the open hearth men were proud of their jobs and couldn't be made to wear their helmets.

My Bethlehem friends were not invited on these skating expedi-

tions. As I grew into my teens, Jim was the only member of the
family to whom it occurred that at times I might like — and desperately need — to be with people my own age. On Saturday
nights, supper was scarcely done when Harry sat at the piano
going over Mozart sonatas, calling me to come on, didn't I want to
try Number 10 in G major, or was that too hard and had we better
stick to Papa Haydn? But if Harry by chance had not come home
and there was a dance at school, Jim would summon me as I ran
through the hall on my way out. "Take off your coat, Katz, and
let's see your dress. . . . My, that's pretty. Is it new?" I would
reply that well, kind of, Madamatty fixed it up. Jim said fine, and
give 'em hell and don't forget to hold your head up; girls look
awful when they slump and was that Johnny in the hall, the boy
with glasses? On such occasions Jim took to calling me Beautiful
Bianca, the Belle of Bethlehem. I knew he was being funny but I
liked it, and laughed, and went off feeling admired.

With Harry at home, Jim escaped to the poolroom when the
music began. Through open doors I could hear the click of balls
when we stopped for a minute. My brother Harry at the piano
was like one possessed. His hands with the black fuzz of hair on
them devoured the keys. He never tired. "Don't hurry the eighth
notes!" he would shout, above the music. "It's sloppy. Here, wait,
see how it sounds?" And he would imitate me. "Don't hurry *anything*," he said. "In this kind of music every note should sound.
Come on now, start at letter A and don't miss that F natural again.
Papa Haydn was laughing when he wrote this one. Hear that joke
at the end, in the coda? Haydn did it on purpose."

The hours of playing with my brother held another dimension
than music. Our performance was a game, a challenge exciting
and hazardous, calling on one's deepest effort of muscle, brain and

57

spirit. I loved and feared it at the same time — loved the sound, the hint and promise of what this music could be if Harry and I got it right — feared because, young though I was, I sensed that the whole program might in the end defeat me. The more I learned, the plainer this became. What if I never could play the music as it should be played, never achieve those opening chords in the Kreutzer Sonata, no matter if I practiced all day and all night? At this time I had no slightest notion of music as a profession or that violin playing might be a "career." Neither Harry nor Mamma mentioned such a thing; I am sure it did not cross their minds. Harry and I played because the music existed, there on the stands before us. Papa Haydn invited us to his feast, bade us dance, sing, mourn with him.

When Mr. Murphy, my violin teacher, began giving me parlor pieces to practice, Harry grew impatient. "*Humoresque,* ugh!" he growled. "*Melody in F, Melody on the G String. The Bee.* Buzz buzz. Sugar candy. Get Ernesta for these piano parts. Let's not bother with transposed pieces and doctored-up Bach, eh, Katz? Tell Mr. Murphy you're headed in another direction." Of course I told Mr. Murphy no such thing. He was coaching me to play in a pupils' recital at the Acorn Club in Philadelphia, and though the notion of public performance filled me with horror I simply went along with instructions and hid the pieces from Harry when he came home. Eventually Harry told Mr. Murphy, in my hearing, that it was all nonsense Kitty performing at the Acorn Club, and if she had to do it, couldn't she play something worthwhile? Mr. Murphy removed his pince-nez, stared icily at my brother and declared that he would manage his pupils, thank you, in his own way.

Violinists traditionally study concertos, for the technique.

Harry did not care for these, either. The reduced orchestral scores gave the piano too little to do, and besides, Viotti and de Bériot were looked on as inferior stuff. Years later, when I was a student at the Damrosch Institute* in New York, I played the Brahms D minor Sonata for my final examination before Franz Kneisel. I had studied it for months, with Harry coaching me at home. But when Kneisel entered the examination room and saw the music on the stand he frowned, picked it up and struck it with his knuckles. "You are supposed to play a concerto," he said, and his Slavic *r*'s rolled menacingly. "Surely you were told? Why have we this Brahms sonata?"

I said my older brother liked to practice the Brahms with me on the piano, and Kneisel asked if my brother was a musician. I replied that Harry happened to be a lawyer but he loved music and he said most concerti were just for show-off, so we usually played sonatas — Mozart and Bach and Haydn and Beethoven. "This part after G," I said, "where the bow goes over and back on the open D string — my brother says to make it mysterious, as if we were under water. Is that a good idea, Mr. Kneisel?"

Something in Mr. Kneisel's face had made me bold, or I never could have asked the question. Mr. Kneisel looked at the music and looked at me and then he put back his head and laughed. "Under water?" he said. "Yes, yes, a good idea. Proceed, Miss R-Rhine-maiden, with your Brahms. We will forget the rules this time."

By now I was well aware that my brother liked best to work on music which had in it an elemental vigor. I could not persuade him to any enthusiasm for Ravel, or even Debussy. The *Images*

* Now the Juilliard.

59

and *Fêtes*, for instance, he dismissed by saying they sounded as if Greuze wrote them. Except for Mamma and me, no Drinker could abide Greuze. I never saw men who were more in need of gentleness, finesse and the power to yield and change their course. Yet all of the Drinker men but Jim professed instant scorn of anything that hinted of "feminine weakness," by which I think they meant turning from the task at hand. To persist in spite of obstacles was a masculine virtue; my father liked to use the word manly. Womanly of course meant pusillanimous, sissy. A show of emotion was not sissy, as long as one didn't cry openly after losing. In my seventeenth year an incident occurred, small in itself yet wonderfully characteristic of Harry. We were practicing, at the time, the Brahms F minor Clarinet Sonata; I played the wind part on the viola. The first movement is marked *Appassionato*. One evening, tuning my instrument, I noted that Harry had crossed out *Appassionato* in his part with a heavy black line and substituted above it *Energetico*.

I giggled and asked if he had done it to be funny. Characteristically, Harry did not hear me. "What's the matter?" he demanded. "Of course it ought to be *energetico!* Can't you feel the vigor in that theme? Come on, quit talking! Take the long repeat and don't hurry at letter C the way you did yesterday. Clarinets can't hurry and Brahms knew it."

From the first, my father had been uneasy about his son's absorption in playing the piano. Should a rising young lawyer allow himself to be so preoccupied with one of the arts? True, Harry was doing well enough in his profession. At law school in spite of piano practice he had been graduated at the head of his class and had won the coveted Sharswood Prize for an essay on the term *res gestae*. Harry's graduation, both from college and law school, had in fact been spectacular with prizes and honors. His law degree came from the University of Pennsylvania. But he took his second-year law at Harvard so he could study with Dean Ames and Professor Williston, though he had a hard time persuading not only the dean but his father to this. Ames said Harry could do it if he took both the first and second year courses together. This he did. Since childhood, Harry had had the use of only one eye for reading; the doctors told him he must not study by artificial light. At night he hired a student to read law to him, and trained himself so he could repeat entire pages from memory. He developed a system of making digests, after the eighteenth-century fashion, reviewing every Saturday, he later told me, "all the material since the beginning of the year." He said this meant he never had to cram for exams but went into them "fresh and eager."

Nevertheless, Harry's piano playing continued to worry his father. This periodic immersion in music had in it something uncomfortable, not quite in the American pattern for males. Papa said it must be the French blood coming out, from Mamma's side. Pa said also that when he was in college he had sung in the glee club and thought he was musical until he married into a musical family — by which he meant the aunts and uncles on west Spruce Street. Harry however told his father not to worry, that he was holding up his end at Dickson, Beitler and McCouch and anyway, Sophie would keep him on an even keel.

Sophie was Harry's lately acquired fiancée, a young woman born to keep a husband straight. Sophie's face in repose was not pretty, and had a sulky look. But when she smiled her eyes lit up; two dimples appeared, and small, even white teeth. She was not bony or rangy like the Drinkers but dainty, of medium height with long yellow hair, a neat figure and small hands and ankles.

All her movements were deliberate and she was quiet-spoken, though she possessed, we were afterward to learn, a formidable temper. Her full name was Sophie Lewis Hutchinson and she was cousin to half of well-bred Philadelphia, where she made her début the autumn after she left boarding school in Maryland. Harry had courted her by playing the piano with her, four hands.

My mother was shy with Sophie; the two never really got on. I think Mamma was jealous of her firstborn. Also, Sophie had a decisive manner and a way of planning ahead that was not part of Mamma's nature. Many years later, I heard Mamma tell Sophie one day, "Oh no, dear, we can't have the porch painted now, as you suggest. The cherries are ripe and we'll be going to Beach Haven." That we had always timed our annual hegira to the Jersey beaches "when the cherries are ripe" could be no part of Sophie's tradition. Remarks like that made Sophie feel hopeless, she said, as if she were lost in a mist.

Harry and Sophie had got engaged at Aunt Beaux's summer place, Green Alley, in Gloucester, Massachusetts. When Beaux heard the news, she told Harry indiscreetly that it was "dangerous to marry a woman who is always right." Harry adored van Eyck's painting of the young married couple standing hand in hand, and Beaux had promised that when Harry became engaged she would paint him, hand in hand with his fiancée. This she did, *prompter*, before the two left Gloucester — perhaps in partial expiation for her remark. But the picture did not come out right. Indubitably it is one of Beaux's failures; there is about it something false, very far from Beaux's best style.

Harry and Sophie were deeply in love when they married, and remained so for more than fifty years. My brother's feeling for his wife was overwhelming, and ruled him all his life. At eighty he wrote that when during business hours he met Sophie accidentally on Chestnut Street he still went weak at the knees, and that she had never ceased to interest him. Yet on the surface it seemed a strange alliance and people often so remarked. The big red-cheeked, black-haired man who bore always a hint of wildness, even of brutality — what was there that held him to this conventional, deliberate woman who prided herself on what she called her practicality?

Once the two were married and settled, my brother could not bear to have his wife away from him, even for a night. One time when Sophie went for two weeks to Arizona with their sick child, Harry said to me, pacing the room and all but shouting the words, "Sister, do you realize that only a line divides us from *hell?*" He flung out an arm and pointed downward; plainly, the devils reached up for him, all Sophie-less as he stood. On Sophie's train coming from Arizona (this was before World War II), Harry arranged for orchids to be delivered at every big station. Sophie told me afterward it had embarrassed her when the porter came with those big boxes, paging through the cars: "Mrs. Drinker, Mrs. Drinker!" It seemed crazy, Sophie said, adding that all the Drinkers were sentimental.

To Sophie, sentimental was a bad word, one of the worst in the language. I am not quite sure what she meant by it, but I believe she used the word in defense against a swarm of too energetic, too volatile in-laws who were often in danger of losing control, of shouting with joy or bursting into tears. The boys kissed their father goodby at railroad stations; Sophie had seen them weep at the sad scenes in books they had known since childhood. Papa choked up when he gave Mamma some especially good news about Lehigh University, such as a big donation from an alumnus, or a boy coming through successfully who had been expected to flunk. Harry was perhaps the worst. He cried quite frankly for joy — a loud sniff, a blowing of the nose, a whack on the shoulder of the person nearest him. I saw him do it when his last child was married from church and, quite as fervently, the ensuing day when a crate arrived containing fifty-odd big volumes of the Bach Gesellschaft edition that Harry had bought in Germany the previous summer. He sat on the floor turning the leaves and wiping his eyes.

These manifestations, shared by the entire family, no doubt kept us from getting ulcers, but to Sophie they never ceased to be trying. Underneath I believe she was a woman of truly stormy emotions, but something in her upbringing made it bad taste to let go. She once told me I could always be counted on to cry at family funerals. Ironically, in her sixties, Sophie developed a disease of the eyes that would not let tears form; she had to drop them in periodically from a bottle.

Together Sophie and Harry taught music to their four children. Yet Sophie often said she did not want her daughters to grow up taking music too seriously, or become overly intense about it. Warped, was the word Sophie used. "Such women are unhappy in later life," she said. "They don't make good wives."

No doubt she was right; I happened to be in the middle of a divorce when she said it. By this time we were all in middle life. But my brother Cecil had hated Sophie on sight and for some fifty years managed to treat her with a rudeness bordering on savagery. "She makes things *safe* for Harry," Cecil said, spitting on the word. "But why should that big black-haired bozo be safe? Harry was born for something better than safety."

What life would later teach us was that Cecil of all men needed a wife who could make him safe, make him behave — one of those dainty, feminine, steel-spined Sophies with a nose for danger ahead.

Harry's worldly ambition I think was no ordinary youthful eagerness to "succeed at the law." Rather it seemed a ferocity, an obsession, though quite obviously it gave its victim intensest pleasure, which obsessions are not supposed to do. Harry's sons would one day suffer from their father's single-minded pursuit of his interests. The second time I saw my brother look down into hell was when one of his boys, at eighteen, broke down and a doctor told my brother he had neglected his sons. "It's true," Harry said, and his eye as he said it had again that hunted look. "It's true what they say. I have cared too much for the law and music." No sooner was the trouble resolved, however, than my brother was at it again. I must have reached forty when he made another of those family confessions that seem so startling when they occur. It was on the occasion of my son Ezra's entering the Navy in World War II. Before he enlisted, Ezra said he wanted to change his name and put Drinker into it: Ezra Drinker Bowen. When I asked Harry how to go about the proper legal steps he was astonished. He said he had suffered all his life from the name. "The only thing that rhymes with it is stinker, I found that out in grammar school. I had fights before I got rid of it. At college I told myself I was going to do something to make Drinker a name to be proud of instead of embarrassed about."

Harry arranged the matter of my son's name. But I thought of the *summa cum laude*, the Sharswood Prize, the volumes on the Interstate Commerce Act. What is it that drives men, propels them along their path? People think the goad is glory, ambition —

*Harry in the uniform of the Philadelphia City Troop,
about 1904.*

called emulation by the eighteenth century. And then half the time it turns out to be a clubfoot or bad eyesight or a name that rhymes with stinker. I thought also of the sickness that came to Harry as a young man. The family called it a nervous breakdown. It lasted for months, until Cecil, even more crazily ambitious than Harry, stopped what he was doing and went off with his brother on a trip. Harry never mentioned this illness until in my fifties I broke down myself, toward the end of a long, six-year book I was writing. Harry came to see me, where I lived a mile or so up the road, and asked why I couldn't drive the car or come and play the *Forellen Quintet* next week. I tried to tell him the reason, stumbled and merely said I was scared — scared to drive the car or be in the room with a lot of people.

Sophie, I knew, did not hold with psychiatry or sympathize with nameless fears and vapors. I thought therefore that Harry would say something scornful, or tell me to quit this nonsense and tend to business. To my surprise he did nothing of the kind. He fell silent a minute and then said the same thing had happened to him in his twenties when he was writing about the Interstate Commerce Act. He went up to Gloucester and stayed with Aunt Beaux, just sitting round, doing nothing; he thought he had "heart disease." A doctor came out from Boston, examined Harry's heart, then took him down to the beach and pointed to a buoy, well out, and asked if Harry could swim to it under water. He said if Harry had a weak heart he'd never come up.

"I made it," Harry finished. "I made it joyfully." He put his hand on my shoulder. "Take it easy, Katz. And don't let anyone kid you about this, or bully you. You'll get over it."

V

Beach Haven

THERE was a special smell to the cottage at Beach Haven, indigenous, I think, to the Jersey shore. The minute one opened the front door one met it — a combination of dampness, beach sand, old wicker furniture, oil from the guns that stood racked with the fishing rods in the little west room off the hall. Whatever the mixture, to my nostrils it was very sweet. This whiff, this musty breath meant running barefoot on the beach, bathing in the foam of the breakers. It meant sailing on the bay, crabbing from the dock, riding one's bicycle on the wide yellow-pebbled streets, easy and free.

Yet there was more to these summer months than a vacation. We worked hard at what we did. Both parents saw to that, whether it was learning to shoot or swim or manage a sailboat or even to clean fish before we brought them to Bridget at the back door. It was here also that the family came together and stayed together; when my brothers were in college and graduate school

At Beach Haven: Mamma, Harry and Jim, by Cecilia Beaux.

they spent much time at Beach Haven, studying, working on a thesis or a projected book such as Harry's volumes on the Interstate Commerce Act.

As years passed the cottage became for us a kind of homestead. Our parents might move from Philadelphia to Haverford to Bethlehem and back again. But always that creaky cottage door with the painted glass panels opened to home. . . . The stuffed curlew over the mantel spread its gray-brown wings, the mounted drumfish stared blindly from its board above the sofa. Upstairs the painted iron beds waited with their hard hair mattresses, and in a corner of the dining room the wooden water cooler dribbled from its spigot.

Beach Haven lies at the south end of Long Beach Island, twenty-five miles above Atlantic City. My father bought the cottage in 1888. Before that he had belonged to a gun and fishing club which kept an old schooner, the *Novelette,* as headquarters in Barnegat Bay. Harry was nine when he boarded the *Novelette* on his first trip for ducks. Already he owned a gun; by the time he was twelve Papa let him go alone up the beach for shore birds, though Mamma strongly disapproved. All four brothers possessed guns at an early age and were trained to look on their weapons with respect. Oddly enough Papa never let them go gunning with a friend or even a brother. He said when two boys got together they began fooling and there might be an accident. Harry told me that when he wanted to get up at 2:30 to shoot reedbirds Ma restricted him to three mornings a week; he would wear himself out, she said. Downstairs in the dark kitchen he used to cook six eggs for breakfast and be at the inlet, three miles away, by sunrise. The boys shot plover, snipe, willet, curlew. Yellowlegs flew over the dunes with their clear strong cry; we used it as a family whistle: phew-hew; phew-hew-hew-hew.

Today the whole gunning program seems wicked — and it was wicked, none the less so because of our bland innocence. To no one of our acquaintance did it occur that we were in a way of ruining and rifling our domain, nor that America's pioneer days were gone forever and with them the philosophy of natural abundance. Theodore Roosevelt, one of the first public conservationists, himself was celebrated as a big game hunter. All over America, game still abounded; if there existed wildlife preserves or sanctuaries we did not know it. And there was no limit on the shoot. A man could bring home a bag of ninety birds — and this at a time when Europe had long cared for its game by breeding and replacement. At Beach Haven Inlet the snipe flew in close white formations, swerving and skimming the water. They would come in for clamshells on sticks, no decoys needed.

Paradoxically, my father was to be a founder of the national conservation movement, working with Gifford Pinchot in Pennsylvania and elsewhere. But in these early days, before the First World War, the sky indeed remained the limit, though Pa would not permit a bigger bag than we could eat at table, and to shoot at any but a game bird partook of serious offense.

Curlew Cottage, my mother named our house; she was immensely proud of it. "As a young woman on west Spruce Street," she told me, "I never thought I would have a summer cottage, and neither did Papa, I guess." Curlew Cottage was a frame house, painted a drab olive brown and perfectly hideous. A wide porch ran all round. A captain's lookout crowned the roof, enclosed in colored glass, bright greens and reds and yellows; you reached it by a ladder from the boys' dormitory. Only one cottage lay between us and the dunes, so that the sound of the surf came loud all day, and at night we went to sleep by it. Not counting the third-floor dormitory, there were seven bedrooms, always occupied — and one bathroom with a tin-lined tub, the inside of which I painted white every summer, receiving ten cents for the job.

Before the First World War — and the automobile — the island remained quite isolated, wholly unspoiled, though in my childhood there were already two hotels, the Baldwin and the Engleside. Mr. Engle, a Quaker, would not permit liquor sold on his premises; when the Baldwin eventually opened a bar it was considered fast. No yacht club existed; we moored our boats off the captain's dock. The captain's big catboats had no engines; it was pretty to see them on Saturdays and Sundays maneuver five or six at a time, coming home down the narrow channel.

For us children the trip to Beach Haven each June was a fête, a picnic, though for my mother it must have been something else, with at least six trunks to be packed and dispatched, Papa's cat in a basket, the two dogs to go in the freight car and Bridget, Mary or Tessie forever losing a ticket or a suitcase. Much later, when we possessed a Ford car, I remember Bridget one summer howling with anguish on arrival at the cottage. Dry-eyed and furious, she screamed that she had lost all her money. Mary McClafferty found it on a mudguard where Bridget had put it while packing the car. All those rattling miles the little leather purse had clung. It held five hundred dollars; Bridget was never one to put her faith in banks.

But in earlier days the trip down began for us in a ferryboat from Philadelphia to Camden, then the dusty, cindery cars, very stuffy until we reached the bridge and the bay, when a life-giving

73

air came suddenly, as if someone had opened a door. When we smelled the sea we used to break into hallelujahs. Each child had his lunch in a paper bag; a hard-boiled egg, a sandwich and a banana, to be eaten on the train. So settled did this habit become with the years that when at eighteen I set off from Bethlehem for a dance at Phil's sacred club in Princeton, I carried my paper bag with the usual ingredients. The sophomore who met me at Trenton Junction asked what was in the package and reacted with horror. "You're not going to eat that stuff right out here in *public*, are you?" he said.

Beach Haven was the end of the railroad line. Mount Holly — Barnegat — Tuckertown — West Creek: the conductor sang out the names. Mamma always took a cab from the Beach Haven station with the maids, the rest of us walked or ran the few blocks to home. The town then boasted two cabs for hire — surreys, roofed and fringed; the horses had tasseled string coverings against the flies. A horsecar ran on rails from our house, which was the end of the line, to the sailing dock. I loved to ride and considered it very grand to sit on the hard seat, waving to friends *en passant*. But the cost being five cents — my weekly allowance — I usually walked instead, half a mile across the marshes, slapping at mosquitoes and green flies.

My father came down every Saturday night and left Sunday. I have a poem of his about Beach Haven. He wrote it on Mamma's best notepaper with the curlew engraved at the top, standing with its long bill extended. There are two pages of verse in the slanting vigorous script I knew so well; Papa must have felt strongly indeed to break out thus. The paper is dated August, 1890, when he was forty. His three older sons, Harry, Jim, and Cecil, ranged from ten to two; the rest of us were not born. The verses, un-

Papa at forty-eight, with his yellow cat, by Cecilia Beaux, 1898.

rhymed, contain every conceivable cliché, including seabirds that wing their flight, the rhythm of the sounding wave and even an Ah! Me! in upper case with two exclamation points. Yet to read it is for me like a hand clutching at the heart. A refrain opens each verse:

> *I love my home, my home beside the sea,*
> *Where with pleasures meet, and in accord,*
> *The days drift on with those I love.*
> *Where joy attends my coming,*
> *And my going is but parting for a day.*
> *Ah! Me! I know not why*
> *Life has been made so sweet for me,*
> *Nor need I care — the love is mine*
> *And will endure. No shifting sand is its foundation.*
> *Come well, — come ill*
> *My darling and my boys are mine*
> *Forever and today.*

Does every vigorous man of forty believe that his darling and his sons are his forever and today? Or were the 1890s indeed an age of innocence? When I think of the family feuds and fights that were to come, the drinking and the violence among my brothers, let alone certain noisome divorces in the family, I marvel at that poem. How is it possible that one's father — all-wise, all-knowing, all-protecting — could have enjoyed such a state of artlessness? The notepaper, limp with age, lies in my hand. To hold it there, exposed, makes me feel guilty, like Noah's son in the Bible when he uncovered his father's nakedness. Sir Francis Bacon, extolling friendship, said that a man cannot speak to his son but as a son; to his wife but as a husband; to his enemy but upon terms. What right then has a daughter to raise the veil, peer behind the years and with the easy wisdom of hindsight reconstruct her sire as a young man? To call spirits from the vasty deep is a hazardous procedure; who knows if the spirits will bless or curse the caller. Perhaps our forebears were right to say that witches are for burning.

The memories of Beach Haven run all to smells and sounds and sights; they are physical, of the blood and appetite, as is natural to summertime. At the west end of Coral Street the marshes began, turning soft with color at sunset, pink and lilac and golden green. The ocean beach at low tide lay hard underfoot, wet sand dark below the waterline. On the dunes — we called them sandhills — we played King of the Castle or slid down on our bloomer seats, yelling with triumph and pure joy. The floors of Curlew Cottage, the chairs, even the beds were sandy. Always a lone sneaker sat beneath the hall sofa; by August our city shoes were mildewed in the closets, and towels were forever damp.

Behind our house in the laundry, Mary and Tessie spent their Mondays on two sides of a big ironing table, passing over the sheets an iron heated by a little coal stove. Outside the laundry in a small mosquitoey backyard, bathing suits hung eternally on the line; there was a big coal bin by the fence. One day a black snake was discovered amid a general hubbub and upheaval of coal. Cecil went after him with a club, but Tessie said Cecil could save his trouble, the snake wouldn't die before sundown. Impressed, I noted this bit of natural philosophy in my diary.

At mid-afternoon the maids went bathing with their friends, wading through the surf in full-skirted black suits, joining hands in a row and screaming as they jumped the waves. I never saw one of them go beyond the breakers; Philly told me Irish people couldn't swim and I believed him. It would be hard to exaggerate the meaning these maids had for the family; it went far beyond the services for which they were paid. In Mamma's old age Mary McClafferty was to be her friend and confidant; Mary could make her laugh and forget pain. Mary stayed with us, as I have said, for fifty years; she died in Harry's house. She was a big woman, handsome, and bore herself well. She always had followers; I used to hear their deep laugh in the back sitting room on Saturday evenings, but she refused to marry. Mary knew the name of every Irish prizefighter from John L. Sullivan down, but her great hero when he came on the scene was John L. Lewis. Mary said you had to be born in Mauch Chunk to know what John L. had done for the miners, and that of all them loud talkers in Washington he was the one who got things done. The Big Boy, she called him; she had his picture stuck in her mirror, with his hat on, looking fierce.

Bridget stayed with us nearly as long, a tiny woman, first-generation Irish; she told me she never growed beyond four feet because there wasn't enough potatoes in County Clare. Bridget had a quick temper and we were careful not to try it; she used to swear that if I left the pan dirty after making fudge I'd find it clammy cold in my bed some night, and that I was more trouble to her than all her money. She also told my fortune by tea leaves. I would marry a poor man with brains in his head, not a millionaire like my sister. When I asked how she knew Ernesta would marry a rich man, Bridget said, "Did ye ever see her walkin' out with a poor one?"

In Beach Haven I was always hungry. We all were, though we remained thin as rails. I remember the food vividly, though I cannot recall a single meal in Bethlehem. On Sundays we often had boiled bluefish for dinner, so big the fish's tail reached over the edge of the Ivanhoe platter; Bridget came ceremoniously from the kitchen and passed her egg sauce in a china boat. I don't know where my mother got the Ivanhoe china, of which we owned a full set, bowls and pitchers included. Perhaps it came with the cottage, like the twin paintings of the boy and the lobster that hung in the dining room. In the first picture the boy has caught the lobster and is gloating; in the second the lobster has him by the thumb. But the Ivanhoe plates each carried a story from the novel, boldly etched in black and white, with the legend underneath. The one I liked best was *Rebecca Repulsing the Templar*. Rebecca had long black hair, a sweeping medieval gown, and one bare arm outstretched in horror. I gazed long at this scene over the years, but early concluded that Rebecca was making a mistake; the Templar in his armor looked very fierce and taking.

For dessert on Sundays there would be a huge cold watermelon which my father stood up to carve as if it were a turkey. I remember the reedbirds for supper, tiny and buttery, and Pa saying it was all right to gnaw the bones but for heaven's sake, Mamma, tell that child to wipe her mouth. In August came lima beans, and fresh corn piled steaming on the dish, one's eye hopefully on a certain piece. At table I could have eaten every dinner plateful three times over; if Mamma called a halt I sulked. I sat at her left. When the hot covered dishes were handed through the pantry window, Mary carried them around counterclockwise, which meant I came last. Once — I must have been about ten — I was sent from the table for shrieking when Philly got the part of the roast beef I wanted, the crackly outside piece. I swore at him. My mother left me upstairs to kick the bedroom door till dinner was over, when she appeared and spanked me with the back of her old wire hairbrush.

When my brothers married and brought in turn their wives to Beach Haven, there was apprehension as to how the wives would react. People not accustomed to the island, like New Englanders, were apt to scoff, complaining that they missed the trees and green grass. They asked how we could endure all this sun and sand and didn't we think keels on boats were really superior to centerboards? Sophie however liked it from the first. She went fishing with Harry in her old sneakers and dark blue skirt. She cruised with him on the *Gee Whiz,* which at best offered crowded quarters; she followed him up the beach when the bluefish "came ashore." About once every five years this happened, the most exciting episode in Beach Haven sporting life. Suddenly the waves would sparkle with hundreds of shiners, driven inshore by the big fish; above them gulls hovered thick. The boys would telegraph their father in Bethlehem, then dash for their rods and stand all day in the surf, running as the schools moved, and reeling in the magnificent catch.

At one period my brothers took to shark fishing at the inlet or somewhere outside, with heavy rods. It was a bloody, awful sport. They baited with fresh dogfish; when the shark struck they pulled up anchor and sailed after him until the beast, exhausted, could be drawn alongside, when he was whacked on the head and speared with a lance. Harry killed thirty-six sharks, all over six

feet long, duly weighed and measured. The only way to prove the
size of the catch was to dissect out the jaw and bring it home.
Harry presented one such trophy to a friend at the Philadelphia
Academy of Sciences — the jaw of a brown shark, eight feet six
inches and weighing three hundred pounds. The other thirty-five
jaws hung on the side porch wall at Curlew Cottage, cleaned, polished and grinning. Papa would have nothing to do with any of it,
but Sophie showed no distaste. She said shark fishing was a good
way to keep the Drinker males busy and she could think of lots
worse diversions. Often enough she went with Harry on these expeditions.

Ernesta was not in Beach Haven more than half the time. She
spent her summers at Gloucester with Aunt Beaux, or in Northeast Harbor, visiting what Cecil called her fancy friends. But it
was Ernesta who taught me to sail; the boys of course had taught
her. I was late learning for the reason that I could not swim and
we weren't allowed to take our boats out alone until we could do
twenty yards. Our family fleet consisted of the *Gee Whiz*, which
remained altogether the boys' territory, an eighteen-foot catboat
we called the skiff, and two sneak boxes. By the time I inherited
the skiff she was old and heavy and came about slowly. But I
loved her and spent hours on the bay with my friends, fishing or
crabbing at some cove or just drifting peacefully along. Sailing
was taken seriously by the family. You didn't make mistakes like
jibing in a heavy wind; you were supposed to know the tides and
the weather and come in fast when a squall blew up. To do anything silly on a boat was a mortal disgrace.

The great trick lay in making the dock at the day's end. The
Gee Whiz sat at a mooring, but the little boats tied up every

night. The professional yacht captains who took the summer people sailing kept their big catboats at the main dock; we juniors were down on the attached wooden jetty. When not out sailing the captains sat in rows on their clubhouse porch, smoking their pipes and talking about fish. Sailing in, one faced this formidable audience, which watched one's performance closely, saving its comments until one stepped ashore. "Keep a-goin', young lady, and you may learn somethin'. Ought to have come about sooner though, off that last channel marker. . . . I never seed a girl yet could throw a proper half hitch. Here, let me show you. And didn't Cecil teach you to shake your reefs out before furlin'? If he didn't he shoulda. Go on back now and unfurl."

There must have been fifteen or twenty of these captains. In winter they lived on the mainland, at Tuckertown or West Creek. Every summer my father gave a dinner for them in our house. They trooped up the porch steps, impressive in their dark blue coats and hats with gold anchors above the visors. The dining room could not hold them, and tables were set up in the hall. At each plate was a present of a seaman's penknife. The captains knew bribery when they saw it: they were to keep an eye out should any of us get in trouble on the bay. Yet they plainly liked to come, and enjoyed the party; there was deep laughter and reminiscence about the old days on the *Novelette*. Phil and I used to listen, crouched on the staircase.

Saturday was race day on the bay; I acted as crew for Phil when he couldn't get anyone better. Beforehand we trudged back and forth to the dunes, filling sandbags, then sewed them tight, lugged them to the dock and deposited them forward or astern as commanded. The channels and coves at Beach Haven were tricky, a sailor had indeed to know his tides. For myself I think I spent as much time aground on some reef as I did on blue water. The reason our boats had centerboards became evident almost as soon as one left the dock. Shallows appeared unexpectedly and the sand forever shifted; the charts could not keep up with it.

I have often thought that my father, as his children grew to their teens, considered Beach Haven less as a refuge, where "days drift on with those I love," than as a training ground and education for the young. He had always looked seriously on sports, though never as spectator; I doubt if he ever bought a ticket to a "big game" in his life. Nor did he go sailing with me in the skiff, though my mother did. The notion of myself at the helm of any vehicle, a-sea or ashore, in which my father sat passive would have seemed impossible, a contradiction in terms. Papa left "the girls," as I have said, to Mamma; it was she who kept Ernesta and me in order and wielded the hairbrush when needed. In my entire youth I can remember only one occasion when Papa disciplined me, and that occurred at Beach Haven. So greatly did it impress me that even today I cannot recall the scene without discomfort.

I was fifteen, and due to leave next day for a girls' camp in Maine. I suffered from hay fever, and August saw me shipped off above the ragweed line. That summer I had a heavy crush on the boy across the street; Win Allen, his name was. My train was to leave early in the morning. The night before, we planned to picnic up the beach. I suspect that Win was not nearly so taken with me as I with him. At any rate he never told me so or even said he liked me, though there had been much tennis and sailing together and dancing at the Engleside Hotel on Saturday nights. Perhaps

83

Win was as shy as I. Anyway I counted on the evening picnic, the influence of the moon and my imminent departure to induce some kind of declaration. I wanted it badly.

Up the beach we built a bonfire and sat round it after supper, laughing and talking in the dark. Ernesta was along but she had Hervey, Win's older brother, so I didn't have to worry about *that*. Win remained jolly, attentive but entirely impersonal. In desperation I told myself I could not leave Beach Haven unless this boy said something, I didn't quite know what. I began to figure it so that on the way home we two would walk apart from the others. This would give Win the chance to say he was sorry I was going away, put his arm around me and maybe kiss me goodby. With the trembling passion of fifteen I sat by the embers and laid my plans. . . .

From the darkness beyond the fire I heard my name called, and not in the tones of love. My father's figure loomed out, I remember he had on his old panama hat. "Kitty!" he said. "Come home with me. Now, at once!" I saw that he was angry and I asked no questions but rose and followed him in silence, a full half mile down the beach to the boardwalk lights and home. He led me to the room I shared with Ernesta. "Pack that trunk," he said, pointing to where it gaped open by the window, empty except for a few things at the bottom marked for camp. "Pack it *now!* Your mother has gone to bed, she is tired. It is not your mother's business to pack the trunks of fifteen-year-old girls."

I was so scared I took all the things from the beds, including two dresses of Ernesta's, swept them into the trunk, put the first tray in and emptied my top bureau drawer over all. Set in the top tray were compartments for hats; in panic I took two hats from the closet shelf. One was Ernesta's; we wore them to church on

Sundays, mine had red poppies round the brim. I packed them in tissue paper while my father watched. Then I closed the trunk and he locked it. When I got to Camp Wahgash and unpacked the hats they asked me where I thought I was headed for, Newport or Narragansett?

VI

Cecil

I DON'T KNOW at what age I began to trot after Cecil, watching to see what he would do next. Seesul, we pronounced his name, after the American fashion. Harry it was true led me into music, Jim showed me kindness. Yet of all my brothers it was Cecil, ten years my senior, whom I worshipped and tried to emulate. Whatever Cecil's quality — call it magnetism, fascination, witchcraft — it could not be argued with. I know only that as I grew into my teens, Cecil's approval could make or mar the day. He did not ask what I wanted, as Jim did, or seek to know my ambitions. That was not Cecil's way. He simply took hold and shaped me to his image of what I should or could attain to, given the inescapable drawback of being a girl.

As a young man Cecil was not handsome, but his face, his expression held something arresting. He walked fast, all his motions were quick. There was an intensity about him that seldom let go, and that in later life would serve him both well and ill. When something excited Cecil he had a way of running his fingers through his stiff straight hair, leaving it wilder than ever. His were the thin muscular hands of an artisan and he was always building something. Long afterward, when he had become a research physiologist known on two continents, one of Cecil's colleagues at the Harvard Medical School, Stanley Cobb, told me he had never seen a man so skilful manually. "In the lab it was incredible to watch him," Dr. Cobb said. "He could do anything with those hands." Cecil's comprehension was so quick, Cobb added, that he stayed "miles ahead of the rest of us."

At Haverford the house had seemed filled with Cecil's contraptions. In the cellar sat a rowboat with the ribs showing, on the third floor half a bobsled. What Cecil began, he finished; I think Pa saw to that. Ours was the only yard in the neighborhood that boasted a merry-go-round, a shoot-the-chute and a ferris wheel. The shoot-the-chute ran on wires from two tall trees. The ferris wheel, made of wood and painted red, took four riders; it got under way by a running push. All these devices worked and were in frequent demand. The Presbyterians held their annual Christian Endeavor picnic on our place and charged a nickel a ride for everything, indiscriminately. Afterward Phil and I would spend hours vainly searching for dropped nickels; the Presbyterians were canny with their cash.

Cecil's fascination could not be called charm, certainly it was not good nature. His intensity had in it a febrile quality, compelling, contagious. Once I asked my mother what that crowd of boys wanted, standing round the porch steps; she told me they were waiting for Cecil. Actually what she said was they were waiting for Cecil to tell them what to do. The way she said it troubled me. Her tone held something grim, sarcastic. I think now it was foreboding; about Cecil Mamma possessed what amounted to a prescience. But the first time I saw a picture of the Pied Piper with all the children and rats following after, I thought the Piper's hair should be light brown and that his ears ought to stick out. As Cecil grew into his teens I believe my mother became a little afraid of him. There was a latent violence here, and though as a child I never saw it erupt, I knew of it, we all knew. One day this trait would break and ruin him.

After the rowboat had proved itself on the Haverford College pond, Cecil wanted to build a cruising yawl, twenty-six feet long. He said he could do it in the stable, cart her to the Delaware River and live on her in vacations. For a boy of eighteen this was an expensive proposition, entailing, I afterward learned, an initial outlay of five hundred dollars. My father produced the money, and Cecil never forgot it. (Ernesta said, later on, that Pa kept that hellcat so busy he never had *time* to get into trouble.) Years afterward, when I was in my thirties, with two small children, a divorce and no money, Cecil came to me where I lived with my parents. "Katz," he said, "do you want to do anything crazy that costs money? Because I'll stake you to it. I don't care what it is. Pa did it for me when I wanted to build the *Gee Whiz.* He couldn't know she would even float. My God!" Cecil said. "When we slid her onto the river at Essington she sank like a stone. We'd forgotten to put in the deck plugs." They hauled her out and for some thirty years the *Gee Whiz* served us nobly. As for doing something crazy, I told Cecil I wanted to go to Russia for material to write a biography of two musicians named Rubinstein, but that I had said nothing about it to the family. This was 1937, a bad year to visit the Bolsheviks; moreover I would have to leave the children in care of my parents. I did not need money because I had already borrowed it from my publisher. But I needed moral support. Cecil never questioned my motives or if the book showed prospects of success. "I'll talk to Ma and Pa and Harry," he said. "But don't forget, the money's there if you want it."

Ernesta was five years younger than Cecil. And almost from the first, something about her irritated Cecil quite beyond reason. He could not look at Ernesta without turning mean. Harry on his part would not put up with this eternal teasing of his sister. One day when Cecil would not stop, Harry picked him up and threw him bodily across the pool table. The boy landed with nothing worse than a barked shin. But the incident made not the slightest dent in his attitude toward Ernesta; next day he went at it again.

What maddened Cecil was Ernesta's decision, as early as her twelfth year, to speak with a broad *a* and no *r*'s; the rest of us used a flat Philadelphia accent. At Haverford, Ernesta had lessons every day with three or four friends, either in our house with Miss Anna, the governess, or at the house of a girl named Margie where the establishment was large and the female accent fluty. Ernesta spent her summers visiting these various young friends in places like Cooperstown or Northeast Harbor, Maine. After one of these visits she came home with a new voice, markedly different from the family accents. Ernesta was perfectly frank about the whole thing. She said she liked the way her friends talked, and she meant to talk that way herself.

Cecil commenced stationing himself in front of Ernesta when she wished to go through a door. His hair fell over his forehead, his green eyes squinted. When Cecil was angry I used to think he gave off a musty smell like an animal: he hated to wash. "Cahn the cahnary sing?" he would inquire of Ernesta in a high, affected voice. "Oh, plahnt the tomahto, oh deah me, deah me!" Philip joined in when he got the chance and even Jim, easygoing as he was, thought it funny. This went on, not for weeks but for years; my sister's magnificent aloofness never ceased to surprise me. Ernesta did not talk back. She simply managed to look superior, raise those luminous dark eyes and sail by.

As I see it now, this was a notable feat; I myself would never have possessed the stamina to persist. If Ernesta had arrayed herself against the twelve wicked knights who dwelt on the plain of Astolat, she could not have had a doughtier foe. Cecil remained implacable; the broader grew my sister's *a*, the flatter his own became. In the summers at Beach Haven, Cecil was always on the water, sailing, fishing, shooting. He began to talk like the Jersey fishermen and professional yacht captains at the dock, giving two syllables to the words *town* and *round*, and sounding two *r*'s where one would do. "Supper's purt'n near ready," he would call out, through his nose. "Come on dayownstairs!" He was not being funny, he simply talked that way. My mother could mimic him perfectly. "It's purt'n near time, sure 'nuff," she would echo, and she did it so well that in spite of himself, Cecil grinned. But he never let up on Ernesta. "Who's she think she is?" he would ask indignantly. "Mrs. Astorbilt or something?"

I am quite sure that Cecil and Ernesta at one time came to blows over this matter of accent, though I was not present on the occasion. But one Sunday, Cecil sat down to dinner with a cut lip, and that evening I heard my father tell him you don't hit a person smaller than you are, let alone a girl. This seemed to me the most arrant nonsense. What life had made plain to the youngest of six was that if you were in your senses you didn't hit anybody *bigger* than you were. As to the girl part, Ernesta could beat Cecil in a race; she was long-legged and nimble. I had seen her outclimb him on the big pine tree by the gate.

After the cut lip episode, Cecil never permitted Ernesta to enter his sacred log cabin down by the Haverford stable. He had a little coal stove in there, and on Saturdays he and his friends used to make doughnuts. I could smell them where I played by the swing. "*You* can come in, Katz," Cecil would call, loftily. "But leave Mrs. Astorbilt somewhere else."

Actually this was for me no triumph, I felt only embarrassment. Yet the feud persisted. Many years later, when Cecil in his sixties had retired as dean of the Harvard School of Public Health, I stopped to see him where he lived on Cape Cod. He had built a house in a meadow by the sea; his sailboat, a ketch, rigged for swordfishing, lay at her mooring in full sight of the windows. Cecil kept a laboratory in the cellar and went on with his experiments; though I think they were concerned rather with confirmation of former findings than with anything new. His hair was white by now but still thick, and it still stood up any which way. I had been visiting Ernesta at the time, about four hours' drive away. I don't know how long it had been since Cecil had seen Ernesta; by tacit agreement they met seldom. He asked me — still with that South Jersey twang — how I could possibly enjoy staying in the same house with my sister. "Can't stand that broad *a*," Cecil said, pulling on his pipe. "Never could stand it."

When Cecil came to Bethlehem on vacation from college he used to read aloud to me: *Westward Ho!*, Alfred Noyes's *Drake*, Tennyson's ballad "The Revenge" — always some tale of heroes or heroic endeavor. A week or so afterward he would quiz me.

"What did Sir Richard Grenville say when he was wounded in the Armada fight?"

"He said, 'Fight on! Fight on!' " I would reply.

"That's the girl, Katz," Cecil would say, and patting my shoulder briefly he would move along to businesses of his own. He managed to make me care fearfully about all this, perhaps because he cared himself. I wrote in my diary that when Drake had to kill Doughty, his one-time friend, Cecil's voice trembled and he barely got through it. It was Cecil I think who instituted the game at mealtimes: "What did Sam Weller say at Mr. Pickwick's trial, when the judge asked how Sam spelled his name?" Around the table a shout would go up. "He said, 'Spell it with a Wee'!"

My father enjoyed the game but confounded me often. I did not remember what Captain Ahab said when they rescued him from the sea after the whaleboat was smashed: "The eternal sap runs up in Ahab's bones again!" But Phil could answer detail queries about the capture and sanguinary dissection of the whales. There was no mention of symbolism; I think my father and brothers had never heard of it. They read *Moby Dick* for the story, as they read *Treasure Island, The White Company, Captains Courageous* or my Uncle Tom Janvier's *The Aztec Treasure-House.* Papa relished the novels of Rider Haggard and Henryk Sienkiewicz but my mother would have none of these in family conclave. *She* was "not a nice book at all," *With Fire and Sword* fit only for warriors. Mamma showed herself a little annoyed at her husband's appetite for tales of blood and thunder. But Jim said the game as played at table wasn't fit for girls, and why didn't I shoot some questions about *The Little Princess* that he had seen me reading?

Shortly after my sixteenth birthday, Harry and Sophie spent a weekend in Bethlehem, during which a consultation took place between Mamma and Sophie, with Harry, I later learned, a silent witness. Devastating news filtered down. Next autumn I would be sent to boarding school at Catonsville, in Maryland, where Sophie and her sisters had gone. My accent it seems had taken on a Pennsylvania Dutch inflection and I was altogether too involved with friends at the Moravian Seminary. It would be advisable to meet girls of "less provincial background." Even if I never "came out," like Ernesta, surely I ought to be exposed to men other than the Lehigh students with whom I went to dances and football games — young men from places like Wilkes-Barre, Allentown and Mauch Chunk. Even Papa had begun to tease me about my accent. "Ice *cream*," he would say, correcting me. "Not *ice* cream." I heard him tell Mamma, laughing, that Philip seemed to have escaped the contagion. "Does the child *want* to go to boarding school?" Pa asked. "What about her violin lessons, and her Latin? I doubt if they teach Latin in those fancy boarding schools for girls."

My mother replied that St. Timothy's wasn't fancy, it was very plain and strict. "But we aren't sending the child to learn Latin," she told Papa, "or to play Beethoven sonatas. This is what some people call a finishing school."

My father said, "H'm, well, whatever you think right, dear."

To all of this I reacted in violent dissent. I loved Bethlehem and everything about it. Boarding school loomed as a disaster. I told Mamma they could never make me into an Ernesta, not in a thousand years. I wept, stormed, demanded what was wrong with being provincial, said it was a snob word and there was a good chance I'd make the seminary basketball team next year and Micky Jones had already invited me to the sophomore dances at

Lehigh. Mamma remained firm, though she conceded that Papa was not altogether sympathetic with Sophie's ideas; he had inquired if they taught Latin at Saint Timothy's. There comes a time, Mamma advised me, when a young person has to *spread out*, and anyway it wouldn't be forever. "Only for a year, child. Try it. Then we can decide what's best."

Cecil however remained stoutly on my side, though only in private, confessing he didn't know how to counter Sophie's kind of argument, and no use trying. "I don't like any of it, Katz," he said, gloomily. "You'll forget everything I've taught you. You'll forget Sam Weller and Drake and Ralegh and 'Fight on! Fight on!' They want to make a lady of you. But you're headed for something better than that."

To do Sophie justice it should be added that in the end I hurled myself gladly into the life at St. Timothy's, even persuading the family to send me a second year, chiefly because of certain ambitions concerning field hockey. My senior "composition," called "Ralegh Explores the Orinoco," was printed in the school paper, *Tidbits*. (As literary editor I could include pretty much what I pleased.) The piece missed by a hair the school prize for composition, which I much coveted; I had spelled skeleton wrong. I sent *Tidbits* to Cecil, who promptly mailed me a consolation present of *Westward Ho!*. Volume I he inscribed, "Better luck next time, Katz," and Volume II, "Any fool can use a dictionary."

Forty years later, in a book called *The Lion and the Throne*, I wrote two chapters on the trial and execution of Ralegh. I did not think of Cecil as I wrote them. But when the book came out I thought of him and wished that he could see what Ralegh had said on the execution block. Cecil died the year before my book was published.

VII

Grand Tour

MY MOTHER never saw Europe until she reached her middle fifties. In 1908 Papa sent Mamma, Ernesta and me to England and France. I was eleven, Ernesta sixteen. Mamma was overwhelmed at the notion of "going abroad," which had always seemed beyond her means and her dreams. Consequently when we landed in France she saved and scrimped and made us live in flea-ridden lodgings, ride third-class and practice a rigorous economy. We took this in stride as part of the adventure. But Mamma brought home five hundred unspent dollars and dumped them triumphantly in Papa's lap, to his quite evident dismay and vexation.

After this for the next seven years we traveled furiously and extensively; my father's salary was raised and somehow we managed. When Pa could get away he went with us — to Alaska by coastal steamer and to Japan with the Institute of Mining Engineers, some three hundred of them, thence around the world

by way of China, Penang, Aden and India. With the engineers we
went also to the Panama Canal and through it by rail before the
water was put in or the great Culebra Cut completed. Papa had
been a founder of the institute back in the 1870s; now he wrote
home detailed reports on the digging and plans as they progressed. He happened to be a friend of General Goethals, the
chief engineer; the Isthmus teemed with Lehigh graduates working on the dams. Papa looked them up and showed himself immensely proud of their part in the project. Later, when I read his
papers they seemed incredible. Not having heard my father talk
of tunneling or excavation, I had forgotten about his engineering
life. The reports were all measures and weights: "The Gatun Dam
is of earth with a core of impermeable material, 800 feet wide at
bottom. The dam will have 85 feet of pressure, and for only half of
its length the head of water will be 50 feet. From toe to toe the
dam measures. . . ."

The first time the four of us traveled together we headed east-
ward from Bethlehem to Athens, Constantinople, Jerusalem,
Egypt. I had just turned thirteen. We went in winter and came
home by way of southern France; Mamma wanted to see Arles,
where her father, Adolph Beaux, was born, and to meet her
French cousins. She said she had to know if they looked like Ernesta, with black hair and high cheek bones. As it turned out they
didn't; they were plump and fair, as different from my long-legged
quick sister as doves from eagles.

A crowd of cheering students saw us off at Bethlehem station.
They had walked down the hill ahead of time and surprised us.
Mamma wept. Pa made a little speech from the car steps, something about wherever we went he knew he would find Lehigh
men, building bridges and laying rails, and he would write home

and tell them about it. He did, too, in letters to the college paper, the *Brown and White*. He wrote from all over the world, from Japan and Agra and Penang, from the American mission at Jerusalem and from the middle of the China Sea. We were scarcely beyond Trenton on that first trip when the Lehigh letters began. We used to tease Pa and ask how could he see anything in Europe, with his pad forever on his knee and his fountain pen moving — in trains, on the decks of steamers, in hotel parlors at night after supper. I have the letters as duly printed, and the students' occasional editorial replies. "Our beloved President," they called Papa. They said they hoped he would come home rested, and that nobody ever worked so hard for Lehigh as he did.

I set it down because today the relationship seems extraordinary, as if my father had actually achieved his ambition to be a parent to these boys and that they believed in his good faith. The modern world likes to animadvert about simpler times, a simpler era. And indeed in those days one heard much talk on campus of "loyalty" and of pride in what the students quite unashamedly called their alma mater. Perhaps it was a provincial trait, indigenous to this mine-encircled Lehigh Valley. These sons of first-generation immigrants came to Bethlehem poor and serious. Most of them lived in rooming houses off campus, worked hard and considered an engineering education a privilege and a prize. Quite naturally they had warm feelings for the man who helped them toward their end.

It seemed a little out of character that my father was induced to leave the campus at all, on other than on college interests. The next two trips, taken with the mining engineers, were almost in the line of business. But that first jaunt came as a present from the trustees. Charlie Taylor, the Pittsburgh steel man, told Pa one day that the board had discussed the matter and decided they preferred a live president of Lehigh to a dead one and that if Harry Drinker didn't quit work for a while he would be dead — stiff as an H-beam, was how Charlie put it. He reminded my father that he had saved the college from bankruptcy and got rid of a quarter-million-dollar debt; he said that as businessmen the trustees were acting from sound business reasons. ("Of course," my diary noted, "Pa paid for Ernesta and me. Mamma said travel was better than any school and she wouldn't go without us.")

Ever since I grew old enough to be conscious, there had existed a tradition that my father worked too hard; his colleagues said he "drove himself." The locomotive they named after him in his rail-roading days — the *Henry S. Drinker, 1888* — was meant to symbolize this drive, as did the subsequent donation of a gold watch with H.S.D., ON TIME engraved inside the lid. I have a letter from the head of the Lehigh Valley Railroad, written after Papa had accepted the presidency of the college. It pled with the authorities "not to let Harry Drinker work too hard," and said the writer never saw a man "who so abused himself in the interests of his company."

Actually I think the people who forever urged Papa toward a good long rest had the matter wrong end to. My father never suffered a nervous breakdown or anything near it, though my mother did. Pa loved work, he reveled in it. Hard work kept him on his feet, hale and vigorous till the age of eighty; always "his soul enjoyed good in his labour." Nevertheless, in that year of 1910 the whole Lehigh community conspired it seemed to send him off. The faculty ladies gave Mamma a reception and a going-away present. The professors typed out a resolution, signed by twenty men — the heads of departments — wishing us a pleasant voyage (they called it Godspeed) and saying kind things about my father's value to Lehigh and how his health must be preserved. It was a double resolution, signed twice by everybody, the second half being addressed to Mamma. This puzzled me. Whatever could my mother have done to "draw the student body together in closer bonds of sympathy to each other and devotion to their college"? She went to morning chapel, chaperoned the college dances and fed the engineering clubs with Bridget's fried oysters in our dining room. Each season she stood on the athletic field and donated a silver cup to the best lacrosse player on the team. Yet the faculty — I knew it even then — was a hard-shelled group that did not throw its words away. Nor had my mother any close friends among faculty wives; my schoolmates, some of them daughters of professors, had made me conscious of this. Yet questions seemed out of order and I let the matter rest.

Everywhere we went, from first to last, Ernesta and I kept diaries; it was she who started it. We wrote in school notebooks with marbleized covers, Ernesta in the bold backward slant then fashionable among young women, myself in a round, quite childish script. Even at eleven, twelve, thirteen, my efforts were painfully conscientious. I covered pages, struggling to describe the Taj Mahal or a Japanese No play in Tokyo: "The curtain went up and revealed a forest of flowers with some soldiers nosing around for some general." I think in all my marbleized volumes there is not a really original observation. Ernesta was always a good hand at physical description; I tried to keep up with her. She said Aunt Beaux trained her visual perception when she stayed at Gloucester in the summers and that Mamma had it by nature, though Ma's taste was "not impeccable"; she often liked "the wrong things." But Beaux "could sit in a Chestnut Street trolley car for three minutes and afterward describe the passengers so that you listened enthralled." Ernesta called it the painter's eye.

I read Ernesta's diary and she read mine. Perhaps this made me self-conscious. At any rate my lucubrations were plainly directed toward readers; this was no secret document. "Now look at that sentence!" I wrote. "I am going to begin over again, and please excuse the way this page is written." From Cairo to London I tried to reproduce the guides' talk, the talk of casual acquaintances in hotels and trains. Nothing is more difficult and of course I failed miserably. Spelling did not faze me. The school where my brother Jim had played cricket I set down as Eaton. "We remembered Papa's birthday at the last minute and bought him a bottle of saccy." In Paris we climbed the Ifle Tower, and at the Louvre there were "a great many Rubans and I didn't like them because they consisted mostly of a jumble of naked men and women. But I am not good at describing so I will leave the rest to Ernesta. I am always laughed at when I try to describe." It is easy to see why. "The gate of Hadrian is lovely," I wrote; "not exactly lovely but I can't think of a suitable adjective."

Early out, the diary settled on a system for disposing of bothersome factual detail: "We saw the image of Sek-het. It is made of ———— as they all are. . . . We rowed to the temple of Philae, sticking up above the water. All I know is that the temple was built ———— before Christ. . . . We found ourselves steaming through the most beautiful ———— and turning a corner beheld Hong Kong. . . . The Baron Fuchida entertained the Engineers. Lunch was served under a glorious pavilion of ———— put up for

us. . . . This great bronze Buddha is made of five hundred
———— of bronze and so very big that it is impossible to understand its vast size unless one has seen it."

The "one" must have come from Ernesta. Anyhow I beat my
way through the language as best I could. "Mrs. Shields took Ernesta and me to the zoo and left us there while she, her or whatever you say, went on a visit." And in Jerusalem, after a full page
about the weeping wall: "I *must* learn to say things in a small
space. I write too much about 1 thing."

Occasionally I broke down and said what I thought, all in a
jumble: "Sat. Dec. 9. P. & O. Steamer *Moldavia:* Tomorrow we
reach Bombay and leave the *Moldavia* for good, quite a lot of
good, I say. Fred and Percy have left and the red ants are the limit
and the flour has gotten musty and tomorrow we have to pack and
the second officer has proposed to Ernesta. Of course the second
officer doesn't matter except I am sorry for him, poor man. The
Captain took us to the galley yesterday and let us make fudge.
English people don't know about fudge, imagine! We passed one
of the king's ships and it was a beauty, all white and so very
stateley."

Fred and Percy I remember vaguely as admirers of Ernesta's,
though I seem to have put them in one category with the ants and
the second officer — whom I remember not at all. Today's cruise
passengers know nothing of red ants and musty flour. Packing the
trunks was hideous. We traveled, as did everyone, with steamer
rugs, dusters and veils for motoring, "best hats," linen skirts and
blouses which must be pressed, and a degree of paraphernalia unthinkable. Always one big trunk stayed in the steamer hold, a
stifling place; I can recall going down with Mamma and a steward
to find things for the ship's dance.

My mother's fervent Presbyterianism was never more evident than on these European trips. She did not hesitate to use the word "idolatry," and childlike, I took my cue from her: "We went to an old temple in Hong Kong," I wrote, "and there I got an idea of what the 'heathen Chinee' really is. 63 wild wooden gods sat around in a semi-circle against the wall. It seemed horrible that grown men and women prostrated themselves on the ground in worship." The devils depicted over gateways were to my mother proof of "a fearful superstition." Yet outside Shanghai one day I heard her say she wished *she* could paint a devil as lively and wicked as one she saw on a barn wall.

Wherever we were, amid cathedrals or minareted mosques, we searched out on Sundays a mission church or some Protestant stronghold that was not filled with chanting and the tinkle of bells. In Rome my father contrived to get three rosaries blessed by the pope, as presents for Bridget, Mary and Tessie. Papa considered this a *coup* and was jubilant. I think he laid it on a little thick, perhaps to tease Mamma, who sniffed and bridled. She said if Papa had kissed the pope's ring he ought to be *fumigated* and please not to tell her what really happened about those rosaries. Poor Bridget would be made happy, gracious! But Mary McClafferty was surely too intelligent to be taken in by such flummery.

It must have been difficult for my mother to reconcile much that she saw in Europe with her ingrained notions not only of religion but of propriety. The luxuriant pink flesh of the "Rubans" ladies offended. Yet Mamma knew enough about painting to admire in spite of herself. Had not her sister (Aunt Beaux) explained the difficulty of painting "flesh tones"? After hearing the choirboys sing at Antwerp Cathedral, I demanded with some feeling why the Presbyterians in Bethlehem had to have such awful music. Mamma sighed and said we mustn't be uncharitable, and the trouble was not with Presbyterianism but with ignorance. European morals never ceased to distress my mother. At such moments she had a way of drawing herself up, her mouth very prim. Years later, when I wrote about Abigail Adams, attending the Paris ballet in 1784 — her delight and her disapproval — I thought of Mamma and that mouth drawn tight, the little shake of the head that signified one must not condone this kind of behavior. In Italy — I think at a Pompeiian villa — we were shown a small anteroom which our guide explained was a vomitorium, where gentlemen retired during a feast to empty their stomachs so they could go on eating. "Kitty!" my mother said vehemently. "The Romans were bad, *bad.*" When I told Pa, he said maybe Mamma meant the later Romans, a remark which I put down in my diary, totally uncomprehending.

In the Orient my father spent a large part of his time roaming the bazaars, buying presents for the Lehigh trustees. At that time people traveled of necessity with a courier. We had a succession of these, who stayed with us a week or longer. Moustachioed, gesturing, voluble, they wore robes over their trousers, a turban or fez according to nationality, and bore names like Sawi or Mohammed. In my snapshots the couriers are always smiling and showing large white teeth. Papa used to take the reigning courier to the bazaars with him, "so he wouldn't be cheated," he said. Mamma however looked on these heathen with a suspicious eye and said they deceived Papa, that he was too easy on them and ought to require a stricter accounting. Papa said nonsense, in the East you don't ask careful accountings from servants and anyway, cheating was an Oriental perquisite. I think his China boyhood came back to him; he kept referring to the porters as coolies. In Cairo he and the current Mohammed got on wonderfully. Mohammed called him Milord and they used to go off to the bazaars, laughing together like children.

The things they bought for the trustees were invariably large and bulky and terribly difficult to fit into our luggage: a huge sword for Charlie Taylor in a scabbard made of uncured, quite smelly crocodile skin, with the head intact; you thrust the sword between the crocodile's jaws. For Bishop Talbot a brass cobra, very heavy, sitting on its coils in the traditional posture, with the head high and the fangs showing. A fearful African weapon had a three-foot handle and a heavy, spike-studded ball at the end; and there was a spear at least ten feet long, ornamented all over with what looked like sharks' teeth, which stuck out and pricked if you handled it wrong. All the way from Algiers to Bethlehem I carried this object, tied in a bundle with our umbrellas. I don't remember which trustee got the mummied head, but it was wrapped in layers of old Cairo newspapers, and so was the mummied cat. When we arrived in New York and the customs men went through our trunks, they began unwrapping these. Papa said the bundles were "only mummies" and that he had declared them on the customs slip, but the officers did not believe him. All four of us watched while layer after layer of Egyptian newsprint went onto the pier; my father enjoyed every second of it. When the two officials at last held up the mummies there was much joking about who was this one, your Uncle Dudley? To Mamma's distress the customs men threw the mummies back in the trunk all naked as they were, then closed the lid and said that would do for today, they wouldn't go any further. We waved goodby to our steamer friends and left the pier ahead of nearly everybody.

I once heard my mother say that Papa did the most unreasonable things which somehow turned out well.

Going through the Suez Canal at night, Papa watched the banks with his engineer's eye, recalling the Culebra Cut in Panama and the periodic washouts that all but broke the builders' hearts. "We navigated through the Suez Canal by searchlight," he wrote, "keeping up an even progress of about seven miles an hour, even then washing down the banks in places."

At Bombay we went by boat to the Isle of Elephanta, where Papa wanted to see the sacred caves that in some faraway century had been hewn out of solid rock. Once my father got in the caves we could hardly get him out. He measured the biggest one — 130 feet. He wrote home that he had "read up on these rock excavations when writing his book on tunneling thirty years ago."

Papa's reactions to the Orient derived partly I think from his childhood in Macao and partly from reading Kipling, whom he admired. In the *Brown and White* he referred to "our English cousins," who were carrying a "heavy share of the White Man's Burden." The British at close range, he added, don't really like Americans, "though they believe we have a common mission in leading the world for good." Looking back, these pronouncements from one's sire are terrifying, considering what is happening to the "White Man's world." Toward the end of our stay my father's tone changed; he expressed outrage at the way the British treated "the natives" and said when he got home and took up his Thackeray again and Major Bagstock bullied "his unfortunate Indian servants," he would know whereof he read. At Benares we drifted in a little steam launch down the Ganges to where scores of pilgrims stood bathing in the sacred waters. Papa wrote that among them all he "saw no evidence of indecent exposure. The women and the men kept themselves decently covered, the women washing under their saris or veil coverings, and all were courteous to us."

How can one put this down as "quaint"? It was what a man thought and said and felt in his time; whether we laugh or cry we are heirs to it.

The only bone of contention in our traveling Eden was my mother's worry over what she called Papa's extravagance. She fussed about the cost of à la carte dinners until Pa hit on the fiendish device of procuring the menu ahead of time and inking out the prices. Papa told me privately that as a young woman Mamma never had any money and now that she was comfortably off she didn't know what to do with money except to save it. For her part, Mamma said that when she and Aunt Beaux lived in West Philadelphia she used to go all the way to the Market Street Wharf in the horsecar for oranges because they were cheaper purchased off the boat. She tossed her head when she told us, as if the story somehow justified everything. Scarcely any of Mamma's clothes came from the shops; they were made in our sewing room, though she contrived to look very nice. In Bethlehem she had a trunk filled with feathers and bits of velvet and silk, out of which she created hats for herself and for Ernesta and me. She could make the most enchanting children's hats. A generation later I watched her embroider straw flowers around the crown of my daughter's sailor — bright red and green and yellow blossoms, growing straight up on their stalks.

Mamma was an eager sightseer, busy with her Baedeker, and going out prepared like a girl on the way to classes. Her enthusiasm was infectious; she made me feel excitement over a trip to Notre Dame or ten minutes with the Winged Victory. She loved Raphael, Constable, Millet — pictures that did not assault the senses but led one gently along. She also loved Turner. In a London gallery when we came across *The Fighting Téméraire*, Mamma clutched my hand and cried out, "Wouldn't Cecil adore this picture?" I thought at once of the ballad "The Revenge"; *And he said, "Fight on! Fight on!"* Mamma recognized the quotation. "Oh, Kitty!" she said. "Aren't we *lucky* to be standing here?" Over my parents' bed at home hung a large engraving of Millet's *Angelus*, and on the opposite wall, Sir Joshua Reynolds's head of the winged cherub, done from different positions. In the Louvre and the National Gallery Mamma sought these out, and because I had grown up with them I felt they belonged to me, were a part of my life. In spite of Harry's strictures, Mamma loved Greuze. But best of all she liked Velásquez and the Dutch pictures. I began to know Charles I and Philip II at sight and talked easily of the Hapsburg lip. I think the great portraits became for me rather actual people than works of art. Hating Philip because he fought England, when we stood before him I used to make, privately, a bad luck sign I had learned at school — by way of cursing the Armada. But in Holland, Rembrandt's *Night Watch* would not fit into its title. "I am sure," says the diary, "that it must be labelled wrong for there is nothing to do with a night watch about it. It looks to me as if there was a bonfire in the night and all the people came running out of the dark to see it. The picture is marvelous. I can't think of any other word for it." And at The Hague: "Harry's little Velásquez boy is in the gallery here. We call him Harry's boy because Harry likes him so much. After this I think he ought to be called the Drinkers' little boy."

Without doubt I remained deplorably provincial all around the world and back again. This could not be said of Ernesta, who took to Europe like a duck to pond water — a predilection that would last; much of my sister's later life was to be lived abroad. Nor did Ernesta's diary describe the object in terms of anything but itself; no Velásquez could be Harry's boy to her.

My father did not go with us to art galleries or churches; he had other affairs to pursue. In Egypt he went quail shooting with our courier, Sawi, and when he wasn't buying presents for the trustees he busied himself looking up Lehigh graduates and arranging for them to dine with us at our hotel (with the price marks blacked out, of course).

Ernesta never suffered from homesickness, but I did, and so, I think, did my father. He wrote to Lehigh that he longed to see the chestnut trees again and to "hear the boom of the old college bell." As soon as we landed at Hong Kong he rushed to cable the football team, which was due to play their great rival, Lafayette, next day. At the Moravian Seminary where I went to school I belonged to a debating team. Before starting round the world our topic had concerned woman suffrage. "Resolved: that votes for women will benefit society." I had been elected captain of the affirmative side and had done considerable boning up, with the help of Mamma, who, despite a temperament admittedly domestic, showed herself a spirited feminist before the word was current. "There is no reason," she told Ernesta and me, "why girls cannot be as independent as boys" — adding that her sister had earned a living at painting before she was twenty.

I grew so involved with votes for women — still nine years

short of national achievement — that the announcement of a trip around the world came as a blow. I pled to be allowed to stay home and be a boarder at the seminary, but I got nowhere. I was the more gratified therefore at my father's eventual show of sympathy. When our train finally left Bethlehem station, headed west, Pa sat by me. Perhaps I shed a tear, I don't remember. Anyway he laid his hand on mine and said, "Kitty, be comforted. We are traveling counterclockwise. But remember that from this moment and this mile you are on your way home."

I had left school in midterm. Yet the only textbooks we took along were algebra and Latin. Papa said geography was right under our feet, on land and sea, and that English — at school we called it rhetoric — would have to take care of itself. I cannot remember the algebra sessions (I loathed mathematics) but the Latin lessons are clear as if they had been yesterday. I see my father, seated on the upper deck of some P. & O. steamer, leaning against a stanchion, the book in his hand. I am beside him. I hear his voice: *"Gallia est omnis divisa.* . . . Now you take it, Kitty. And read clearly; never mind if you stumble." When he talked about using *w*'s for *v*'s he said we could thank the Germans for it, and though he didn't like Germans they had certain scholarly propensities.

At home in Bethlehem I had hated Caesar and all his works and words. But Papa made the legions live. Under his tutelage they became real as the full-skirted soldiers we saw along Athens' streets, or the bearded Sikhs who stood magnificent, directing traffic in Calcutta and Bombay. When I got back to school I found myself pages ahead of the class. As for not liking Germans, Papa's view of all "foreigners" was parochial in the extreme; today he would be put down as a Wasp of the worst order. You could not argue with him, on that or any subject. Arguing with Pa was like arguing with Ernesta's beauty. Nothing changed, nothing gave way. Ernesta said Papa was a benevolent tyrant; she didn't see how Mamma stood it, and she said it in the lobby of Shepheard's Hotel in Cairo. I remember just where we were standing. She said also that when she married, her husband was going to be someone she could argue with at breakfast, dinner and supper.

In his letters to the *Brown and White,* my father's chauvinism emerged frank and unashamed, though to be just I should add that with him it did not appear as hatred of other nations but rather as pride in his own. At Nara in Japan he was "intensely interested" to find that the supporting columns of a certain ancient temple were being "strengthened and reinforced by the United States Steel Company." In the best Republican party tradition he went on to remark that Japan, "not having been educated to the point of attacking its own prospering industries, and being free from the blight of the political exigencies of a Sherman Act, presents a most favorable contrast with the labor-union burdens of England, and the unnecessary and irrational attacks on great enterprises in the United States."

All over the East — at Yokohama, Shanghai, Hong Kong, Singapore, we were met and fêted by American members of Standard Oil, to whom Papa had letters. From the Bay of Bengal he wrote that "the Standard Oil Company is recognized as a great and efficient agent in the spread of civilization and good business." Today it sounds like caricature. Yet my father harbored no slightest doubt that the two were synonymous — civilization and good business. Theodore Roosevelt toured the East that spring, after his second term as President of the United States. To Papa the trustbuster's name was anathema. At home I had seen a collection of Opper cartoons that showed Teddy grinning and shaking his Big Stick at the "malefactors of great wealth."

"Teddy Roosevelt," says my diary for March 22, 1910, "reaches Luxor this afternoon, and Mamma wants to go to a reception he will give. I wonder if Teddy will be famous some day because of the big busyness row he made. Pa hates him. He knows Aunt Beaux very well and she has visited him in the White House lots of times."

This was inaccurate; Cecilia Beaux stayed at the White House not as a visitor but to paint the President's wife and daughter, Ethel. Anyway we went to the reception, all but Papa. Standing in line to be introduced, I suffered acute apprehension lest Mamma, directly preceding me, stop and say something about Aunt Beaux. My fears were realized. She stopped, and I heard her say clearly, "I am Cecilia Beaux's sister," upon which I turned away my head — and a moment later noted in astonishment that the President was still holding Mamma's hand and the two were talking enthusiastically.

America today occupies so different a world position, and people in general are so much better educated, that it is hard to credit the proofs of American ignorance, half a century ago. My father's first letter to the *Brown and White* contained quite unbelievable anecdotes concerning our fellow passengers on the cruise. Just before the steamer reached Greece, a clergyman at dinner asked what was the use of stopping here — "Nothing to be seen in Athens, is there?" Walking on the Acropolis a man whom Papa described as disconsolate and homesick, "sighed and said, 'The only natural things around here are the grass and dandelions.'" A woman, after wandering (my father wrote) till her feet hurt,

remarked of the Parthenon, "Say, this place is mostly mythologi-
cal, ain't it?" And in Rome, while we were looking at a marble
figure labeled *Matrona Romana,* a woman stepped up and asked if
that was a vestal virgin. Pa said he didn't know.

All this proved useful as text for a little sermon to Lehigh engineers. Let them not concentrate blindly upon their profession, my
father wrote, but take advantage of the art courses in college,
learn what they could of history and literature, "our precious inheritance," so that when they in turn might find themselves in foreign countries, they would appreciate what they saw. He said he
spoke "from the standpoint of a Mining Engineer and as one who
has had to battle with the rough and tumble of practical, hard
engineering work." My father also discussed the lessons we could
learn from Europe and the East about sleep and afternoon siestas
and letting the body rest and renew itself, rather than burning up
our energies "and then dying early, or dropping into a mean and
lean old age, at a time of life which they call a man's prime in
Europe."

This second homily was received by the *Brown and White* edi-
tors with more than a grain of salt; their next issue came right
back at him. "Oh! Where did he of all men," they wrote, "learn to
feel the truths he so well sets forth? Did he contract a touch of
Nirvana when resting perchance beneath the Bo Tree? Dr.
Drinker preaching moderation in work! Saul among the prophets!
Let us hope that our beloved President will himself heed the good
advice he gives us, for he is an asset that Lehigh greatly prizes
and loves."

I had thought that when we reached home, all would be as
when we left and the world the same; one need only take up the

hours and use them as before. Of course I was mistaken. When I walked into the day scholars' room at the seminary my friends gave me cordial greeting. But their interests all were changed; they scarcely remembered the woman suffrage debate and who had won or who lost. I could not talk to them about India and they in turn didn't know how to begin with me. I felt chagrined, uncomfortable. The old proportions were gone and the old balance.

In truth it was not the day scholars' room that had altered but myself. Surprisingly, I recovered standing with my mates simply by using what I had learned. One noontime somebody spilled milk on the floor and I said to leave it there, "for the cobras." Before I knew it I was executing a snake charmer's dance, round and round the milk as I had seen fakirs do in Calcutta with a live cobra. I writhed, pointed, hissed, trilled: I collapsed on the floor in a trance and sprang up again. I was first the fakir and then the cobra and my success was spectacular. The day scholars laughed until they wept.

All that term I repeated the performance, on request.

VIII

Ernesta

I T WAS in Europe I think that I first recognized the quality of Ernesta's beauty. At home people took this for granted; certainly it made no marked impression on my brothers; I never heard them speak of it. But abroad we were among strangers, and moreover we were always together. "Is that beautiful girl your *sister?*" I would be asked, and Mamma said that with her they used a like approach: "Is that beautiful girl your *daughter*, Mrs. Drinker?" Mamma and I used to reply half in pride and half in exasperation; Ernesta said they sounded as if she were something in a zoo. More than once I saw her shrink from the turned heads, the persistent following eyes. In my diary I wrote, "When people in the railroad cars stare at Ernesta it makes her so furious she can hardly stand up. She doesn't seem to realize how pretty she is. When they look at her she says, 'I don't see what they want to look at *me* for, they must think I am a good deal of a curiosity.' I have never seen anybody as goodlooking as she is."

It is not easy to describe Ernesta. I have said she was black-haired, black-browed, with high cheekbones, and that her eyes were large and lustrous. To this day I am not sure of their color, if brown or green. I used to think her eyes changed with the clothes she wore, or that somehow her irises reflected the light, shifting suddenly from bright to shadow. There was no single feature to celebrate, such as a noticeably fine skin, a beguiling mouth; Ernesta's teeth were small and not quite regular. Nor was her figure seductive in the usual sense. She was much too thin; her wide belts and sashes seemed necessary to hold her frame together. She wore brilliant colors as if she were born to them: Chinese red, orange, purple; when her hair was down Ernesta had a gypsy look. All her movements were quick. She had the long, tapered fingers of a Botticelli Venus.

Actually it was the structure of her face that fascinated — the bones beneath, as Aunt Beaux had said, the line of brow and chin. Whichever way my sister turned her head on that long neck there was enchantment. I have seen men catch their breath, looking at Ernesta. And immediately they wanted to talk about it — to tell her or even tell me of their discovery, as if what they saw would vanish if it were not proclaimed.

Of course, at eighteen my sister knew her beauty. How could she help but know it? I think however that she was still a trifle bewildered by it, like a person who had come into a fortune and must learn to handle it, cope with it. The power of beauty is of course spectacular. Our parents must have discussed the emergence of this swan, this unlooked-for phenomenon in their midst, though I think my father tried to sidestep it, put it from him. Much later in life I asked Ernesta if Pa had ever said anything about her looks and she replied that yes, when she was about sixteen he told her, "Nettie, don't ever let me see a mirror catch your eye." For some reason this rather pallid exhortation impressed her.

My mother however met the situation head on. She was a practical woman who wanted things to work. Moreover, her own life had always been lived moderately. And now here was this daughter whose beauty had marched past the comfortable point and in itself threatened to become extreme, unmanageable. It would have been more convenient to possess a merely pretty daughter, who could be dressed in tucks and butterfly hair ribbons and who would respond nicely to small compliments, rather than this raven-haired creature who went about knocking men over like pins in a game and seemed scarcely to notice the havoc. When Ernesta was about twenty-two Mamma told me she had kept count of the men who proposed marriage until it got to fifty, when she gave up. "The whole thing seemed ridiculous," Mamma said.

My mother was proud of Ernesta, no doubt of it. Yet to her Presbyterian soul so much beauty seemed overluxuriant, Romanish, though in the physical sense it showed spare and classic. At any rate it was suspect, on the edge of self-indulgence. "Nettie," Mamma told my sister, "you'd be a very stupid girl if you didn't know you were beautiful. But if you take credit to yourself, you'll be *really* stupid. It's just as if you had been born lucky, with a certain kind of hair and eyes. You had nothing to do with it."

At home there had been followers, of course — friends of my brothers', or young men who sent flowers from Philadelphia. But abroad the pickings were apt to be romantic, or at least different enough to be worth mentioning. On that first trip we traveled by a Clark Cruise; much time was spent aboard ship. "The second officer," said my diary, "proposed to Ernesta today. It happened on the *Moldavia* three weeks ago, too. Mamma says not to feel sorry for him and that he probably falls in love every trip. Yesterday he dropped a folded-up note from the bridge and it landed on my steamer chair. All it said was, 'You are looking very sweet this morning. Do move your chair a little nearer the railing so I can see you.'"

I can reconstruct these swains only from the few lines of the diary; their faces are gone and everything about them: "Last night that man sat with us again at the hotel concert. A Dutchman with a moustache. He picked us up walking in the square. Ernesta has won him over. It took her almost ten minutes." Then there were the two young Englishmen on the ship *Delta*, crossing the China Sea, whose names were Craster and Alabaster, which they pronounced with a broad *a* that I thought screamingly funny. Added to this, both their first names were Geoffrey, which bade fair to convulse me. Crahster and Alabahster followed us everywhere. Ashore the four of us made expeditions on donkeys, on camels or climbed the pyramids with our cameras slung over our shoulders. Ernesta never minded having me along. In fact she welcomed my presence. Perhaps it made things simpler. Ernesta's manner was direct and she had a talent for intimacy — doubly dangerous combined with her beauty. When we got to Avignon, Mr. Austin and Mr. O'Neill appeared, I don't know from where. (In those days first names came only after long friendship and a polite request from the gentleman.) "Mr. O'Neill," said my diary, "is *very* generous. He gave me *two* boxes of candy." I accepted such tribute easily, though in return for what I cannot imagine. It could not, as I have said, have been for keeping out of the way.

Usually the admirers came and went singly, both abroad and at home. My sister never attained to being a "popular girl." No hordes of active young surrounded her. She once told me she couldn't talk to college boys. When the admirers grew too intense, Ernesta banished them in her own way, though she seldom told me about the partings, the final adieux. In Cairo there was the whirlwind business of the young Scotchman, on whom I never actually set eyes but whose behavior charmed me. Shepheard's Hotel, where we were staying, gave a dance one night; I set it down as a "ball." The Scotchman followed Ernesta outside and chased her round the garden. She told me she ran — literally ran. She jumped over bushes, she tore her Liberty scarf on the branch of a tree. When the Scotchman caught up he said at once that he intended to marry her. "Didn't you see me following you around all day? The minute I laid eyes on you I wanted to marry you." He said he was digging for oil on the Red Sea and must leave Cairo next day. His name was Mackenzie and he would one day be the head of his clan. To prove it he pushed up his coat sleeve and slipped off a heavy gold bracelet, which he explained was a family heirloom and a pledge. He tried to give it to Ernesta but she told him no, she didn't want to be engaged, that she was still "a schoolgirl, and going to Miss Ferris's in Paris next winter."

I think when it came to the crux Ernesta was afraid of these suitors, though she certainly invited pursuit and I am sure adored being chased in her dance dress through the gardens of Shepheard's Hotel. But the catching up was something else, and the declaration. To this day I can see my sister under the blowing, tree-hung lanterns, her face on its long neck turned away, her eyes wide and still, waiting for this manly aberration — which she had indubitably encouraged — to be over, blessedly to cease. Years later I inquired what became of Mackenzie; did she hear from him after that night? Ernesta said yes, he wrote for two or three years, and then he vanished. "I don't think," Ernesta said, "I would have enjoyed living in some gloomy Highland castle anyway."

Women as well as men were forever offering handsome presents to Ernesta; it was a condition that lasted all her life. When we were young I considered her refusals quite crazy, and asked if she thought it would be "improper" to take these gifts. She said yes, it would be improper, but the real reason was it wouldn't be *fair*. This silenced me. Anybody raised with four older brothers early learns what is fair and what is not. One's place in the pecking order depends on it, perhaps one's daily existence. There were occasions, however, when Ernesta suffered regrets — for example, over the sultan's bracelet. He happened not to be a first class Rolls-Royce type of sultan, only the ruler of a very small principality in what was then the Aden Protectorate. Lehej, his realm was called. In the diary I spelled it Laheege and referred to its ruler always as "that old Sultan." I hated him because of his black bushy whiskers. Moreover, he accorded me none of the bantering regard I had from the others; no boxes of candy were forthcoming from His Highness.

We met the sultan on board ship, en route from Suez to Marseilles; I still have his photograph. The ship was filled with notables returning from the Durbar. King George V had been crowned in England that year (1911) and then had gone to Delhi to be made King-Emperor. The sultan came aboard at Aden with fifty-three rascally-looking retainers, carrying rifles and wearing scimitars at their belts. His Highness sported a series of beautiful turbans and a gold-handled sword which he said he had bought when he saw the king-emperor wasn't going to give him a present after making obeisance. Before we knew it the sultan offered Ernesta a bracelet. (The captain had introduced him through an interpreter.) Much later, Ernesta said she would be sorry to her dying day that she couldn't take the bracelet and that it had stones in it big as uncooked peas. The sultan invited us — all four of us, of course — to visit him at Lehej. Sir James Bell, governor of Aden, was on board and offered to escort us to Lehej with a regiment of his that he said hadn't enough to do. The sultan promised to give us a royal welcome, which, according to Sir James, meant they would slay many camels at the gate. In the interpreter's absence Sir James told us that Lehej was "a twelfth-century sort of place where they still put troublesome people between boards and saw them apart." Sir James seemed much entertained by the situation; he might have been a little taken with Ernesta himself.

But my father was not entertained. He said positively there would be no visit to Lehej, and one day I heard him ask my mother in her deck chair how long we must be plagued with this kind of nonsense. Couldn't we get Nettie married off? My mother replied that Nettie was only a girl and didn't Papa *enjoy* her triumphs? She added that Ernesta's beauty would last till her nineties, it was in her bones. "And besides," Mamma added, "marriage won't put a stop to anything."

In the end my mother proved exactly and prophetically right. But what she said startled me. What could Mamma mean? To me it went without saying that she herself had never had a suitor except Papa, before or after marriage. My mother was in some ways a very conventional woman, who tolerated no irregular behavior.

Ernesta's Sultan

Yet she had a way of laughing when my father became anxious. "You look after the boys, dear," she would tell him. "Haven't you always said the girls were my province?"

By today's notions I should have been consumed with envy for my beautiful sister, expressed in silent rivalry, asthma, or loud recriminations and the striving for revenge. Rivalry however was out of the question; one might as well have tried to rival the moon. Occasionally the diary broke out: "Oh, if only I was pretty! I would give *anything* to be pretty." And again (at eleven), "I wonder if I will be as gay and popular as Ernesta when I grow up. I don't believe I would like anything better. I know I won't, because I have no rich friends, like she has. Besides, I am so shy that nobody would want to talk to me. I hope I will improve as I get older."

By the time we went round the world I had reached fourteen. The night before our ship landed at Bombay — Christmas Eve — a young ship's officer came up to me at the deck rail and began to talk. "I was so shy," says the diary, "that I told him it was time for me to go to bed, and I went. He said, 'But that is going to bed with the chickens.' Next morning he came to the library where I was returning books. He began picking up magazines. I think he wanted to get up his nerve to speak to me but lost it. I really think he is actually scared of me, it is the most extraordinary thing I ever knew. The only trouble is I can't tell him from the other young officers and so am afraid to speak to the wrong one. I am really so tired of seeing Ernesta having beaux that don't pay any attention to little sister that I would take any-one. Of course it is perfectly natural for Ernesta, who is older, to have beaux and I none where there are no young people, but I do think they might be decent and not regard me as an absolute zero."

The notion that it was perfectly natural for Ernesta to have beaux because she was "older," I am sure came from Mamma, as did the earlier pious hope that I would improve as I grew up. Ever since I can remember, my mother intimated that things got better when one was older. She made me believe this implicitly, letting me know, however, that such betterance did not just happen, one had to make it happen. Mamma was no flatterer, but somehow she conveyed to her youngest the news that though a sister had been born to physical beauty, nature had other endowments to bestow. And that while Ernesta could do nothing about these looks that came to her from heaven, such gifts as I possessed were to be worked over, now in my youth and forever, and that the work could be exciting, joyful, and quite as rewarding as anything my sister (or even my brothers) experienced.

It has taken me half a century to realize it, but I think my mother possessed an inspired eye for the essence, the nature, of each of her six children and that she fostered what she saw. Mamma did not urge. Rather, it was as if she opened a door and said, Now, child, walk through if you wish. Your world is there before you. ("To play the violin is difficult. Do you think you will be up to it?") I could have been destroyed by my sister's beauty; there is no doubt Mamma recognized the danger. She kept us in separate worlds, so that from the first our friends and our ambitions were marked off and did not cross. On the trips abroad I took my violin, though to my parents this must have been a nuisance; a place had to be found where I could practice without annoying the passengers. "The most exciting thing that happened was the ship's concert," says my diary. "Ernesta and I played in it. She was awfully scared but for some reason I was not hardly at all. I sent Harry a program. I played three pieces."

I cannot here pretend that my mother balanced the artistic genius of one daughter against the physical beauty of another. In truth my talent was small. I loved music passionately and could never hear it without leaving the place where I was and moving closer to the instrument. Also I enjoyed the muscular challenge of using hands and wrists, the conquering of various finger positions and bowings as one progressed — indeed, the feel of a fiddle under the chin. My brother Phil once told me I better quit fussing about having a long jaw, because it sure was convenient to hold a violin with. In the diary I set down my practice times: "¾ of an hour before breakfast . . . half an hour before supper . . . an hour on Saturday morning." Compared to the discipline endured by young professionals, let alone *wunderkinder,* this was minimal, almost ridiculous. Much later, in my thirties, I came across an analysis of musical talent, prepared in a laboratory by some earnest researchers. It gave five ingredients: digital dexterity, sense of pitch, musical memory, sense of rhythm, and love of music. There was no possible doubt that the last two comprised all and everything I possessed.

I have sometimes wondered why women do not write more about the condition of being born homely. It is something that colors a woman's life, almost from the moment of consciousness. A woman is supposed to be beautiful. To please men is her métier, her constant occupation, her living. By pleasing men she puts food in her mouth, a roof over her head, it is thus she earns status in her community. Nor can I see that this phenomenon has changed in two thousand years, despite the books on bachelor girls, on the joys of living alone or on the feminine mystique in general. Every girl who lacks beauty knows instinctively that she belongs to an underprivileged group, and that to climb up and out she will have to be cleverer and stronger and more ruthless perhaps than she would choose to be. Various women, notable in their field, have spoken to me about this. (Had they not been eminently successful, the subject could never have been approached.) Agnes De Mille told me the condition made her fiercely ambitious. She was damned if she'd sit down under it — and she didn't. Lack of looks she said was a spur, a goad that never let up. Oddly enough, women who use their talents to the full become handsome in later life; they grow to a special beauty of their own. Perhaps fury gives them stature, makes them hold their heads high; rebellion quickens all their movements and their faculties. Martha Graham informed me that her mother was beautiful — a small woman, she said, and delicately made. Mr. Graham used to carry his wife upstairs to bed every night, "though," said Miss Graham, "she was perfectly healthy." Miss Graham told me her mother used to look at her and sigh because she was not pretty.

Had my mother done this to me I think I would have died — or stabbed Ernesta with a kitchen knife. It helped that Ernesta was not only intelligent but that she remained basically good-natured. She did not enjoy small victories, mean conquests over the people close to her. She had, indeed, a dégagé way of passing over things and through things as if they did not exist. Mamma said Ernesta got this from my father. "Papa and Nettie," she told me, "don't know what's going on around them half the time. It's not selfishness. It's just that they are absorbed in their own affairs."

When somebody said a sharp word, Ernesta seemed not to hear, or at least not to comprehend. This left her defenseless in situ-

Ernesta, by Cecilia Beaux.

ations where most young people would have fought back on the instant. Afterward she would tell me, with a peculiar hesitancy, "Alice said something the other day. She couldn't have meant it." And she would give a brief recital that appalled me. I wanted to shout, "Of course she meant it — the slob — she was jealous!" But something held me back; whatever I said, it remained tentative. I could not talk to my sister on terms of parity where her own business was concerned. We had reached our forties before our ages seemed equalized and I could say what I thought.

What I thought was that even beautiful people have to fight back. I asked Ernesta how a beautiful person could possibly let herself be put upon. I said that if I were beautiful I would be queen of the world and people would listen to me talk and nobody, but nobody, could sass me and Ernesta had better *practice* saying sharp things.

My sister's early ambition to marry a man who would let her argue with him did not materialize. With her first husband I think no woman, beautiful or ugly, could have held her own. But her second husband, a man worldly, subtle, canny, said to me, "People have ideas about your sister. They expect her to be wily and difficult. Actually she's as simple as bread."

After our final European trip, Ernesta vanished to school in Paris, thence to a Philadelphia début and marriage in the Lehigh Chapel to William C. Bullitt, with Bishop Talbot presiding in all his magnificence. After that she moved out of the family life. We met only sporadically; my sister began to seem a dazzling visitor, clad in clothes by Poiret or Worth and wearing jewels which became her vastly. Nobody in the family had jewels; I felt as if she must have borrowed them.

Somewhere between the Paris school and marriage, Ernesta had a term at Radcliffe, studying sociology and economics. I don't know how the powers were persuaded to enroll a girl without degrees or academic credits, except that Felix Frankfurter, then teaching at the Harvard Law School, had something to do with it. He admired Ernesta, and, like various of her men friends, desired to "educate" her. Actually, Ernesta was the only one of the family with a social conscience. At eighteen, one of her visiting Philadelphia beaux had taken her walking through the laborers' part of Bethlehem. Next day she told Papa she was going to build a "milk station," where the steelworkers' babies could get clean milk, and that she planned to ask Charles Schwab, Warren Wilbur and the others for donations. Papa, much agitated, forbade her to approach the Lehigh trustees; he said it would be using his position for her own ends. Ernesta however kept right at it, obtained the money and built her milk station.

All her life, Ernesta flew high. When she was twenty-two she told me that she didn't propose to be bored and she was going to keep out of boring situations. Actually, I think she succeeded, though the escape required at times a skill approaching virtuosity. She lived much abroad; once she sent home a stag's foot mounted on wood; the inscription said Ernesta had won it hunting at Versailles. We had letters from Paris, London, from magnificent country places: "I have the great State Chamber with its carved oak bed and quilted curtains. They found Queen Anne's gin bottle under the platform of my bed a few years ago. Drake's ebony and ivory camp bed is outside my door."

IX

The house on west Spruce Street.
Cecilia Beaux.

S HORTLY before her seventy-first birthday, Cecilia Beaux received a seldom-awarded gold medal from the American Academy of Arts and Letters. By now she possessed enough medals to stock a shop counter, though more were to come, as well as honorary degrees from Yale and the University of Pennsylvania, first prizes in exhibitions American and European. Aunt Cecilia's paintings hung in galleries from San Francisco to Florence, where the Italian government had commissioned a self-portrait for the Uffizi. The list of honors seems unbelievable, now that it is all gone by, as are the letters and tributes of her portrait subjects. "Mademoiselle," said Cardinal Mercier, after the final sitting, "you alone have painted the spirit . . . *vous êtes la seule qui a fait l'âme.*"

The day she got her Academy medal, Aunt Cecilia stumped to the podium on heavy braces; she had broken her hip. The master

133

Cecilia Beaux's self-portrait for the Uffizi Gallery.

of ceremonies — Edwin Blashfield the painter — ignoring the crutches, inquired at the end of his speech whether in the making of an artist there could be a more fortunate background than Miss Beaux's: New England through the mother's side; a father from the South of France. The one brought integrity and discipline; the other, poetry, light, and music. *"Sur le pont d'Avignon,"* chanted Mr. Blashfield genially, *"on y danse, on y danse."*

When my mother and Aunt Cecilia talked about their youth on west Spruce Street, I listened avidly, and as I grew older, used to go to my room and write down what they had said. I wanted to remember, make these people mine — the dauntless grandmother, the valiant young aunts who had been reared in luxury and yet who, when hard times came, went out to earn their share in the household — and who laughed and sang, played the piano, drew and painted and made their own clothes. "It was exciting to go to that house," one of Mamma's friends told me. "People loved it. A plain house, but those aunts were amazing. Beside them other women seemed like stuffed dolls."

The house belonged to my mother's grandmother — Grandma Leavitt. But it was Uncle Will who kept things going and paid the household expenses, that same Uncle Will Biddle who wrote Latin congratulations to my brother Jim at Haverford College. And it was from under this mansard roof that in 1879 my father extracted his bride, Ernesta Beaux, carrying her triumphantly if not very adventuresomely to a snug homestead three blocks farther east. In her eighties, Mamma remarked casually one day that Papa had proposed first to Cecilia, "who refused him, she wouldn't marry anybody" — adding that Cecilia as a young woman was enchanting, she had French roses in her cheeks.

135

When I told my brother Harry (omitting the French roses) he was indignant, and said he didn't believe a word of it. For myself the matter would not rest; my mother's bland unconcern seemed extraordinary, even after half a century. I asked if she had been jealous, with her sister right there in the house, and then almost next door. "Jealous?" Mamma said. "Of course not! Cecilia didn't *want* a husband, she had another life before her. And besides, she adored me and she adored my children when they began to come." My mother paused. "But we used to fight dreadfully when we were girls," she said complacently.

There was no mother or father in that household. My mother's mother had died at thirty-two, after the birth of her second child, Cecilia. The widower, Adolph Beaux, placed his small daughters under the care of his wife's mother — "Grandma Leavitt" — and simply decamped, fled back to France and stayed there for sixteen years. Oddly enough I never heard a complaint about his desertion. Aunt Cecilia said her father was "an idealist," who "couldn't turn over money," and that he had never prospered. At the age of thirty-eight he had come to America to found a silk factory; the Beaux family raised silkworms at Avignon and Nîmes. Inconsolable after his wife's death, he could not bear to hear his child called by her name, Cecilia, — couldn't bear indeed to live longer in this country.

The relatives on Spruce Street must have had compassionate hearts to foster so mild and romantic a legend. The girls grew up with pride in both parents. "Papa never realized," Aunt Cecilia said, "the priceless heritage that we received from him at birth." My mother was more candid. She had been four when her father left, and twenty when he returned. "We didn't love Papa very much," she told me; "he was so foreign. We thought him *peculiar.* He roasted the chickens on a spit over the fire; he said they weren't fit to eat any other way." When I remarked that this didn't seem much of an indictment, Mamma said, Oh well, her father had been very religious in the French Huguenot manner, and that he hated the Roman church, "because of the persecution."

I thought of Protestants drowned in the Seine on Saint Bartholomew's Day, and of my mother's indignation when Papa had Bridget's rosary blessed by the pope. I almost inquired how memories could be so long between centuries, but I did not. Perhaps I smiled, because Mamma exclaimed briskly, "Nonsense!" as if she read my mind. Then she said that she and Cecilia liked to sing hymns from the French Evangelical Church in Philadelphia, where their father had been used to go. The tunes were simple and "unadorned," Mamma added, and she taught Cecilia to carry the alto. There was one hymn they loved best; in her old age my mother used to recite it, with a little ghost of a tune:

> *Du Rocher du Jacob,*
> *Toute l'oeuvre est parfaite.*
> *Ce que sa bouche a dit,*
> *Sa main l'accomplira.*
> *Alleluia, Alleluia.*

Among the family memorabilia is a piece of faded blue notepaper on which is written a notice displayed by Grandpa Beaux at his silk factory:

Considering that God in his mercy has permitted us to unite in this place from week to week, and that his smile is on our labors, I feel that we ought to give him thanks at least once every week; and for this purpose the work will stop every Saturday at half-past five o'clock, beginning today. The exercises which will consist in a prayer will take only a portion of the time allowed, but still those who will think them not agreeable with their feelings will be at liberty to retire.

I have speculated on how many workmen came, and if my grandfather in his broken English led the prayers. All that I learn of him is serious and a little sad. The factory failed, the workmen were dispersed, Grandpa Beaux turned tail and vanished. Perhaps the household felt relief: one less mouth to feed and the chickens roasting neatly in the oven. In truth the medal-disposing Academy speaker must have had things backward. To me at least it seems that Grandpa Beaux gave off an aura of piety, French Protestantism and defeat, rather than poetry, light and gladness. Yet a legend persists, romantic and prideful, that music and talent seeped into our family with the French inheritance, and that all of us have reason to feel grateful to southern France, to the troubadours of Nîmes and to our ancestors who indubitably danced the farandole across the Pont d'Avignon.

I think I enjoyed my mother's tales about west Spruce Street chiefly because the household seemed so full of life and high spirits. I used to wonder at it. Five women, all in-laws of Uncle Will, all dependent on him financially and each in her way talented — why didn't they quarrel, turn bitter, show discontent with their lot? These were the women of New England descent to whom Mr. Blashfield had referred. They came from a long line of people with names like Kent, Ruggles, Dudley — hard-working,

God-fearing citizens who took considerable part in local and even national history. And it was these women whom Uncle Will had rescued after their father's business failed: namely, Emily, whom he married; her sister Eliza; her mother — Grandma Leavitt — and later on, the two all but orphaned nieces, Ernesta and Cecilia Beaux.

Yet in truth the household had more than its share of energy and talent. These ladies were conditioned to work, and they worked. The early history of my Grandmother Beaux reads like a plot from a Brontë novel. She was the eldest of the eight Leavitt children, of whom five were girls, brought up in New York City and remarkably well educated for the time. When their father lost his money, the town house was sold, together with a handsome country place across the Hudson, called Oakland, which the family greatly loved. Very shortly, the sisters saw a newspaper advertisement for a governess to teach French and music to the new owner's children. Cecilia applied, obtained the post, and not a week after leaving Oakland, returned there in the capacity of an upper servant.

When in due time young Cecilia Beaux knew that she must launch out from her uncle's house on west Spruce Street to earn a living, I cannot help thinking it was the maternal example which inspired, rather than the rather sorry romantic from Avignon.

4305 Spruce Street lay unfashionably at the western edge of town, giving onto green fields, woods and a brook. The house was large and solid, full of heavy family pieces which the Beaux sisters polished every month with a lump of beeswax ("not that stuff in a *bottle*," my mother said), and adorned by old silver which the girls cleaned on Saturday mornings. Uncle Will, a retired mining

139

engineer, seems to have been comfortably off, or would have been, had he not undertaken to shelter such an army. Cecilia Beaux has said that after Grandma Leavitt, Uncle Will was the strongest and most beneficent influence in her life. As a child I knew him; he lived until 1910 and died at our house in Bethlehem. He belonged to what in Philadelphia are known as the Quaker Biddles, to distinguish them I suppose from the stylish Biddles. People called him Captain Biddle because of his service in the Civil War; he had been on General McClellan's staff and was proud of his record.

In my youth however I knew none of this, and recall Uncle Will as a handsome old gentleman in tweeds, sporting curly side-whiskers and a heavy watch chain and fob, and who could draw most engaging animals on a slate, always doing surprising things. Elephants sat on tree branches smoking tobacco through their trunks; giraffes danced on roller skates. In an upstairs workshop of his house, Uncle Will carved sailboats, racing ones about three feet long, complete with spars and rigging, and wildly successful on a pond. Uncle Will played the piano, wrote hymns and edited hymnbooks, and he hated grand opera, which he looked on as contrary to all the canons of art — an unnatural exercise, not half so graceful as giraffes on roller skates. One evening he even debated the subject publicly with Henry Krehbiel, the New York critic.

Cecilia Beaux often said that for a painter it is an immense advantage to be reared among musicians. In the evenings, Uncle Will and Aunt Emily played duets on the big square Chickering in the parlor: Hungarian dances, German songs, the great symphonies arranged for four hands. When Uncle Will and his wife went out, his sister-in-law Eliza played alone, sometimes for hours, while the child Cecilia lay face down on the rug and listened. Aunt Eliza was by all odds the best musician in the house, of professional caliber. During her affluent youth in New York she had studied with Otto Dresel, a pupil of Mendelssohn, much sought after as a teacher. Uncle Will's musical provenance was less distinguished. There survives a piece of paper in the form of a bargain made in Uncle Will's seventh year. *Agreement*, it says, between *Wm. F. Biddle and his mother:*

> H. F. Biddle promises to pay her son William on the first day of July 1840 the sum of $3.00 for half an hour's faithful practising on the piano every day for six months beginning on the first day of May.
>
> > H. F. Biddle
> > Wm. F. Biddle

I don't know if the bargain was kept. But concerning the "faithful practising," I do know that in the west Spruce Street house, no one was permitted to sit at the piano and bang or trifle. You played your best or you stayed away from the instrument. My mother in turn would one day require the same from her brood of six. Moreover, the room must be silent during performance; those who wished to talk went elsewhere. It is a little surprising that Uncle Will with his Quaker heritage caught and held the contagion of music. Behind him lay many generations of Philadelphia broadbrims. The original William Biddle of London, one of the proprietors of West Jersey, had been granted 42,000 acres by a Stuart king, after which he turned Quaker and found himself in

141

Newgate Prison, along with other Biddles, named Hester and Thomas. Hester wrote angry pietistic tracts, which I am told are to be found today in the Bodleian Library at Oxford University. Somehow Hester got herself to France and into the palace at Versailles, where, it is said, she "commanded the grand monarch in the name of God to sheathe his destroying sword." The son and namesake of the first William fell heir to his father's acres, emigrated, named his West Jersey plantation Mount Hope and lived there apparently in all enjoyment.

Uncle Will inherited neither Hester's flaming spirit nor the broad acres of his grandsire. Nor did he, after his boyhood, use the plain language, the *thee* and *thou* of his early letters. The household on Spruce Street held, indeed, a striking mixture of worldliness and simplicity. Uncle Will led prayers each morning in the parlor, then went off in his own time for lunch and billiards at the Union League Club, smelling strongly, I am told, of cologne. I do not think God was much bespoken on west Spruce Street, but He made His presence felt. Every afternoon at six, Grandma Leavitt retired to her room with the door shut, and nobody allowed to approach. If asked what she did during that half hour, she only said that she was "being quiet." Somehow this struck the Beaux sisters with awe, and at an early age. On Sundays after church there was a getting of psalms by heart, also Revelations and the Song of Solomon. My mother never forgot the words, and when in her eighties she recited them, her old voice would grow strong, as if animated by the magnificence of the poetry.

I once heard Cecilia Beaux say that the reason young girls today don't pick up French and music and "fine sewing" is because they have no spinster aunts living in the house with them. My

"The best musician in the house." Aunt Eliza Leavitt,
by Cecilia Beaux, circa 1885.

mother remembered Aunt Eliza coming home in the rain after giving music lessons, and sitting down, her long skirts sopping, to hear the Beaux sisters read French. Where work was concerned, the aunts, the uncle, the grandmother were unrelenting. When the girls learned to sew, every stitch must be perfect, "just like every other stitch," my mother said. "Otherwise Aunt Emily made us rip it out. But Aunt Emily was *amusing*," Mamma added. "She made us laugh. There was something contagious about Aunt Emily." In the long, hot Philadelphia summer days, the aunts brought down old handwoven linen sheets from the attic, spread them on the cool parlor floor and set the girls to mending weak places. "We crawled on our knees," my mother said, "and patched them *perfectly*." When I inquired if it hadn't been tedious work, Mamma replied in her emphatic way that of course not, Grandma Leavitt read aloud while they sewed. *The Chronicles of the Schönberg-Cotta Family*, by the redoubtable Mrs. Elizabeth Charles, and Walter Scott's poems and Longfellow's poems. And she read *Pilgrim's Progress;* "Oh! several times," my mother said.

Of this last the girls loved especially the opening sentence; when Grandma brought out the book they would chant it together: "As I walked through the wilderness of this world, I lighted on a certain place where there was a den, and laid me down in that place to sleep; and as I slept I dreamed a dream. . . ." "When Grandma got very old," Mamma added irrelevantly, "she could see as well as anybody. She walked by the hall mirror one day and she waved at it and said, 'I don't know that old woman.' We loved Grandma very much. We would no more have disobeyed her than — Oh my!" Mamma finished, her hands uplifted in default of words.

There is no doubt that of the two sisters, Cecilia was the stormy one. One day she flew at my mother and scratched her. Mamma told me about it. The girls were making the beds and practicing the Shorter Catechism while they did it, one on each side of the bed, question and answer. "Aunt Emily made us learn the Catechism as far as the Ten Commandments," my mother said. "We quarreled every day about the responses. That morning I went downstairs with a great scratch on my cheek. I had to go out to give French lessons to our cousins at 1712 Spruce Street. Oh, I was so ashamed! I wouldn't have admitted for anything that Cecilia did it."

I used to wonder how my mother lived and maintained the peace with such a tiger cat. Mamma never kept a diary, being one of those rare souls whose thoughts are on other people. It seemed natural for her to do things for the persons around her, and make them comfortable. She always ascribed this to bad eyesight. "I couldn't read and do abstract things like that. I couldn't even read piano music very well. So I just did things for other people. I made Cecilia's aprons and bonnets. I made tippets for Grandma and slippers for Uncle Will and I made my own dresses." Mamma settled early for this little rationalization and stuck to it. If asked how she could sew with those bad eyes, she simply shrugged and said sewing didn't require the same kind of concentration.

But Cecilia Beaux kept a diary. She was an artist and her thoughts were on herself. The diary opens on her fourteenth birthday. Somebody destroyed most of it; I have wondered why. The pages that remain are little more than lists of duties performed. The sisters clean the silver, bake a cake; my mother shampoos Cecilia's hair and they read aloud, "out of a book Uncle Will

Grandma Leavitt, by Cecilia Beaux, about 1885.

brought home the other day." Cecilia blacks a pair of her uncle's boots, for which he pays her "5cts. a pair." Occasionally she gives us a scene, vivid and very much of the time: "This morning we walked to town, and when we got to about 19th st. Etta caught her bottom hoop in a scraper, and down she came books muff lunch basket and all. We had to go down a little side street and straiten her out."

Cecilia knew she was a sinner; in that disciplined household she could not help but know it. She was late to meals, she scratched her sister. . . . "Why is it harder," she wrote, "for some people to be good than others, a great deal harder? Some people seem to be good naturally like Etta. . . . Sometimes it seems to me as if I were tied down in a spiritual way to a string of a certain length. I get on very well at first and feel so free and happy, feel as if I was getting better, when suddenly I come to the end of my string and am thrown back to the old place again."

Yet the sisters, early or late, showed no resentment against the discipline, the reserve and self-restraint under which they were reared. Cecilia wrote indeed, that she believed this condition had prepared her for what she was to meet, and that the very spareness of life on west Spruce Street allowed "the delicate fibres of a young consciousness to expand slowly," in their own good time. Perhaps this was mere fantasy, and Cecilia only succeeded in overcoming the drawbacks of her environment. Today such a rearing would be considered stultifying, and, for an artist, positively dangerous. The members of that household painted, drew, sang, played the piano; some of them even made money at it. But they never talked about "art." Years later, Cecilia Beaux was to remark that the term "self-expression" is never heard from the lips of robust talent, and that a student goes to art school to absorb, not to give out. When the master enters to inspect the easels, said Cecilia, "a little wholesome trembling" on the students' part is a good thing.

Surely this attitude, in itself robust, must have been fostered within the house on west Spruce Street.

X

Kate Drinker. Macao to Philadelphia.
The families meet, and Cecilia goes
her way alone.

CECILIA was sixteen when Uncle Will escorted her, one morning, downtown to Catherine Drinker's studio and left her there. The girl had often visited art galleries with her uncle and aunts, had studied the pictures and heard them discussed. But this was the first working studio she had seen. Under home tutelage, Cecilia had shown some aptitude at drawing. The aunts considered she might learn enough to become a "copyist" or illustrator — she herself being well aware that she must earn money. Already, I think, Cecilia had a taste for independence.

Catherine Drinker was a relative of Uncle Will's — he called her Cousin Kate — who made a living by contriving historical and Biblical pictures, for which she did immense and careful research.

I cannot imagine who bought the pictures; they must have been used as illustrations in books. The basement of the Pennsylvania Historical Society harbors a canvas labeled *James Madison,* and signed, "Catherine Drinker, after Gilbert Stuart." It is nicely done and, the original being unavailable for photographing, I used it in a book called *Miracle at Philadelphia.*

Catherine Drinker was my father's older sister, an extraordinary woman whom in her later years I came to know as Aunt Kate. Of powerful intellect, she was small, full of energy, and so homely that my mother, throughout the birth of six children, remained fearful, she told me, that one of them would look like Aunt Kate. Kate Drinker's clothes were all wrong. No matter how styles changed, Kate remained one lap behind. When women wore plain sailor hats, hers had flowers; if their stockings were beige, hers stayed black. Nevertheless, as a spinster in her thirties, she captivated Thomas Janvier, eight years her junior, a talented writer and a fascinator if one ever lived — caught him, married him, and outlived him by some ten years.

At the time I write of, Aunt Kate, still single, maintained a studio on the top of an old house at Fifth and Walnut Streets, close to Independence Hall. Here Cecilia Beaux came and went, a blooming, pink-cheeked girl, with abundant light brown hair, her father's blue eyes, a quick step and a pretty figure. Cousin Kate set her to copying lithographs. Cecilia knew hard work, she had been trained to finish what she began. Yet I cannot think her progress was brilliant; she said afterward she had been dissatisfied with everything that she did. But as Uncle Will saw the situation, a seemly girl, bound to marry before long, was "safe" with Cousin Kate. The gloomy old studio with the dark Chinese furniture and the figure draped currently as "Daniel," offered fewer hazards to

Aunt Kate's Troubadour. Thomas A. Janvier by Cecilia Beaux.

maidenhood than a regular art school. When a young newspaper-
man, Tom Janvier, dropped in from time to time, "handsome as a
troubadour," Cecilia said later, it never occurred to the girl that
he could be Cousin Kate's fiancé. Old women of thirty-odd had
finished long ago with love.

Kate Drinker by this time had lived enough for three women —
by no means however in the erotic sense. Merely, life had offered
experiences beyond the common and she had met them with
spirit. In the winter of 1850 my grandfather, Sandwith Drinker,
had moved his wife and two children to Macao, China, where as a
merchant captain his business was based. The children were Kate
and a brother, Morton; my father was born the following November. I have a painting of Grandpa Drinker's warehouse in Macao,
done at the time, in oils, by a Chinese artist. The big shed is one of
a crescent-shaped row — people called them *factories;* they belonged to foreigners and gave conveniently on the harbor. Sam-
pans ride at anchor in the picture, and at the water's edge a bright
yellow beach is busy with fishermen and what I suppose are merchants. One of these wears a turban; the man conversing with him,
a high-crowned black beaver hat. In the background are mountains and a sky full of fleecy, postcard clouds. With its companion
piece of Hong Kong harbor, I thought the pair very valuable until
a museum director told me that in the 1850s, journeymen artists in
China did such paintings by the yard, for the foreign market.

Sandwith Drinker had been in the Oriental trade since at least
1838, when, as captain of his ship, he kept a diary of a voyage to
India, eloquent with delight at all he saw and heard, though
oddly enough he professed to loathe the ocean. From Delaware
Bay at the start of the trip he writes, "At 6 P.M. discharged our

pistol, made all sail and with a fresh fair wind went off swiftly bounding

> O'er the glad waters of the dark blue sea,
> Our thoughts as boundless and our souls as free.

How I do detest the ocean, a ship, and everything connected with them. The more I see of them the less I like them. . . . Yet could I have my own Sue with me, I would go from one end of the world to the other, without murmuring."

In point of fact the diary, which is long and full, never complains about anything except the filth of various Arabian ship's cooks and crews. Grandpa tells cheerfully of opium wars, of Chinamen officially strangled for smuggling, of a chase by what he calls "a Mandarin boat," when he and his first mate lay in a sampan concealed by tarpaulins. At Anjer Lor the centuries come together when Grandpa remarks that the governor "speaks excellent French, having been one of Napoleon's bodyguards." On board ship Captain Drinker holds daily prayers for the crew, but is vastly irritated by the missionaries he meets, "mostly young men from the interior [of the U.S.] without knowledge of human nature, who have never read anything but missionary journals and who at home would not be able to get charge of a country school."

Fearful things happened aboard ship. I suppose contemporary skippers took such incidents for granted: near mutinies, storms where the crew manned the pumps all night and all day. And there were lighter incidents. A passenger who had sailed with Grandpa wrote how one night the sailors became terrified and panicked, convinced that a ghost stalked the decks; they said they

"How I do detest the Ocean." Captain Sandwith Drinker.

had heard his voice asking the helmsman hollowly, "How do you head?" My grandfather, hearing a commotion, came from his cabin, "in his light silk pajamas," the account says, and proved the ghost to be nothing more than his own voice, speaking through a tube which he had had installed before leaving Philadelphia.

Light silk pajamas? I had thought a mid-century skipper would sport a flannel nightshirt. The stories Aunt Kate and my father used to tell were amazing not only for their content but for the homely, matter-of-fact way in which they were delivered. Grandpa it seems was a Free Mason, unusual with his Quaker background. Once when voyaging in an open boat he was boarded by Chinese pirates. As a desperate chance he made the masonic sign. The pirate captain recognized it and let Grandpa go unharmed, with his crew and his papers, though they took such money as he had with him.

On his return from the 1838 voyage, Grandpa Drinker married his Sue in Philadelphia, though twelve years elapsed before he brought the family to China. I have a letter from a Mrs. Kinsman who sailed from Macao to Manila and back with Grandma and Grandpa on his ship, the *Geneva*. She says, "Mrs. Drinker has her piano on board." Since my grandfather's early letters to his Sue, before marriage, were filled with exhortations for her to practice and to learn new songs, no doubt the piano came on board for his delectation.

The 1850s were the years when Commodore Perry and Consul General Townsend Harris came to negotiate trade agreements with Japan and China. Both gentlemen were friends of my grandparents and stayed at their house in Macao. Papa remembered "Mr. Harris" very well. The consul general became fond of Aunt

Kate as a girl; I have one of his letters to her, and the present of a silver napkin ring. Harris wrote that he missed their rides together on horseback and that he hoped Kate was diligent with her mathematics lessons. A corvette of the Russian navy, *Olivuzza*, was due shortly at Hong Kong; Harris had given the officers — "Captain Korsacoff" among them — letters of introduction to the Drinkers. "Some of them are very good-looking," Harris wrote, "and you know all Russians dance well. Don't let them steal away your heart from me. You do not know how I long to hear from you all."

The commander of the *Olivuzza*, incidentally, an older brother of Rimski-Korsakov, the composer, put in for ship repairs at an island near Macao. Grandpa Drinker wrote to Harris that the officers all enjoyed themselves. "We gave them numerous parties. Kate was particularly pleased with Captain Korsacoff and I think he liked her very much. What a perfect gentleman he is." * Macao was, actually, a sophisticated international society, in spirit as well as mileage a world away from Philadelphia. Grandpa's diary tells of receptions and dinners given by the great Hong merchants, at one of which fifty courses were served, from deer sinews to sharks' fins and birds' nest soup. In our library at Bethlehem there hung, framed in carved ebony, a large engraving of a distinguished looking Chinese gentleman with a narrow grey beard, his figure richly dressed in embroidered satin robes. Papa said this was his godfather, a friend of Grandpa's, "a merchant named Mr. Hukwa," and that when Aunt Kate reached fifteen Mr. Hukwa proposed a marriage with his son. Years later I saw in the Metropolitan Museum the original, in oils, of this engraving, and learned that Mr. Hukwa was one of the most powerful mer-

---

* I am indebted to Oliver Statler's *Shimoda Story* for this letter, also for the item concerning Sandwith Drinker's ships, *Thistle* and *Queen*.

chants in China, and that the fragrant tea which I drank came originally from his plantations.

On my wall today is a portrait of Aunt Kate at sixteen, done in China. Her smooth dark hair is drawn back, her face a pleasant oval, her pretty young shoulders bare. She is not homely at all. I remember telling Papa that Mr. Hukwa's son could have sought farther and fared worse. Pa smiled and said that Mr. Hukwa was a very fine gentleman in his way, and he wished his own sons had manners half as courteous.

The gayety, the dancing and horseback rides were achieved in despite of plots, stratagems and the violence of opium wars. Three ships from the firm of James and Drinker — the *Thistle*, the *Queen*, the *Lilly* — traded with Canton, Hong Kong and Macao. Just before New Year's Day, 1857, the *Thistle* was captured; the Chinese beheaded eleven European passengers. The *Queen* also was to be lost — taken by Chinese passengers on board. In December the Chinese had set fire to the European quarter of Canton, causing much damage and driving away most of the foreign residents. "You never saw such desolation," Grandpa wrote to Harris. That January, Grandpa gave a breakfast for officers from English and French vessels in the harbor. The chief baker in Hong Kong, incited "by the authorities," my father later told us, put arsenic in the dough, aiming to poison certain English troops. Grandpa, all unknowing, served the bread at his breakfast. He found out about the poison, and with a doctor rushed off to each of his guests and saw that an emetic was administered. Unfortunately he neglected to treat himself. "I suffered much," he wrote to Harris; "lost most of my fingernails."

A few weeks later Grandpa Drinker died, whether from the effects of the poison we never knew; Harris heard that it was dysentery. Sandwith Drinker was buried in the English churchyard at Macao. His tomb, erected by friends, can still be seen there.

Grandmother, with Kate, my father (aged eight) and a younger daughter, set sail for home. (The second brother Morton, had previously been sent back to be educated.) The ship was small, about 18,000 tons. At Anjar, India, Grandma laid in a big supply of coconuts for the crew; Papa remembered seeing the fruits piled on deck. He remembered, too, the long, torrid voyage through the China Sea, where they were becalmed for several weeks. He saw the "poisonous sea snakes" wriggle to the surface of the water and lash about. (Were they eels? I never asked.) From time to time a boat was lowered, and seamen towed the vessel away from her accumulated filth. One day the captain harpooned a dolphin and they had fresh meat. But the captain, addicted to his bottle, became crazed with drink and they put him in irons. Aunt Kate, a girl of sixteen, had been taught navigation by her father. Apparently she had learned her lesson well, for she navigated the ship during the greater part of the voyage home, including the perilous journey around the Horn. Aunt Kate told me that one day when she took food to his cabin, the captain, delirious, pulled a knife from under his pillow, jumped out of bed and went for her. When I asked what happened next, Aunt Kate said she told the captain to give her that knife at once and get back to bed, which he did.

To me these stories would have been incredible, had my father and aunt not been the most punctilious of talkers; they never exaggerated or made things up. Aunt Kate in her old age wrote a novel called *Captain Dionysios*, about a sea captain in the time of Herodotus — filled with classical learning and the lore of ancient seamanship, and so excruciatingly dull it proved once for all that she simply could not have invented the tales about Grandpa and the voyage home.

The Drinker family returned from China almost penniless. My father said a partner of grandpa's had cheated him. I don't know the details, but he lost everything. In Baltimore my grandmother opened a school for boarding and day pupils, which did very well. When Grandmother died, Kate took over the establishment, though she was only twenty. But about 1865, somehow or other Kate moved the family from Baltimore to Philadelphia and fixed them in a tiny house on Pine Street — including my father, then fifteen, and his maternal grandmother known as Grandma Shober, a diminutive old lady, very deaf, very dominating and wearing full Quaker dress. (I have her gray silk bonnet in my attic, and a white cambric fichu.) By this time, Kate Drinker had turned to painting, how or why I do not know. I think she simply went at it doggedly, with all her intelligence, and stayed at it until she had commissions and students enough to keep the household going. On both sides of the family the women possessed a determined streak — people like to call it "masculine" — and a passion for independence which would not let them indulge in the vapors or go into fashionable declines when fate turned against them. These ladies evidenced indeed stiffer backbones than their brothers — my father and *his* father being notable exceptions. Yet these also were reared by strong-minded females. Could it be that the excessive masculinity of my four brothers, the competitiveness and athleticism, the shootin' and huntin', were a necessary defiance of the powerful matriarchal influences that stood behind them for three generations?

Cecilia Beaux worked in Cousin Kate's studio for a year, and quite naturally became intimate with the Drinker family, going often to the little house on Pine Street. Next winter found her at art school under the direction of a Dutch painter, a Mr. Van der Whelen. Again, it was Uncle Will who paid the tuition, escorted his niece that first day and left her. As at Kate's studio, a lithograph was laid out for copying and enlarging. From this Cecilia progressed to plaster forms — cubes, blocks, a sphere, and to lessons in perspective, which Van der Whelen taught by drawing, on a blackboard, long lines of lampposts which diminished to the vanishing point. One day a girl student brought to school, wrapped in tissue paper, a complete set of skull bones, perfectly preserved as to edges and contours. The girls copied them in lead pencil; Cecilia never forgot her excitement at the forms, the ivory color, the almost translucent texture.

After two winters, Mr. Van der Whelen, for reasons of his own, retired, giving over his school to Cousin Kate, now Mrs. Janvier — she had married her handsome troubadour. Kate in turn asked Cecilia to take her class at a girls' school, called Miss Sanford's. "My sister looked so young," Mamma told me, "that I made over her hat into a bonnet with strings."

Cecilia had been experimenting, on the side, with lithographic crayon, on paper. Uncle Will, observing these activities, led his niece downtown to a lithographing establishment and they went through it together. (Cecilia once told me that she always felt at her best with Uncle Will.) The owner of the establishment, a Mr. Meyer, invited Cecilia to draw, on one of his stones, a head in black and white, which she did. Next day Mr. Meyer sent a stone out to west Spruce Street, on which Cecilia copied from a photograph the head of a young actress. Mr. Meyer printed it as an advertisement.

By now the Beaux sisters had transformed their third-floor bedroom into a studio of sorts. My mother told me they slept surrounded by plaster casts portraying "all the heathen gods and goddesses." Cecilia began to work on a group of small fossils, which if successful were to be used in a report of the Geological Society. The work was hard, with its backbreaking difficulty of reversing, and Cecilia's solar plexus rebelled. She used to go downstairs at intervals and run round the big cherry tree behind the house. In old age, after her hip was broken, Aunt Cecilia talked to me about that solar plexus. "In every picture I've painted," she said, "there came a time when it was impossible to continue. There was a hill I couldn't climb. It's then, when that pressure bears down on the solar plexus, that you must keep *on!*"

Every morning Grandma Leavitt came upstairs and, while Cecilia worked, read aloud hour after hour in a clear, even voice, without emphasis, first instructing the household that there were to be no interruptions. Cecilia's finished engravings pleased their commissioner, the paleontologist Edward Drinker Cope (a cousin), who forthwith brought to west Spruce Street his most cherished possession, the fossil head of an extinct ass, with teeth like tusks, the whole still embedded in the rock. Professor Cope was a Quaker, tall, dark and taciturn. When Cecilia saw his carriage drive up on visits of inspection, she ran downstairs, "feeling pale," she said. After the ass's head, Professor Cope brought the fossil skull of a small camel, much easier to do, as it did not need reduction. Moreover, being white and clear of the rock, it took the light readily, Cecilia noted.

The young artist was now twenty-one. For her private life, her social life, the records are scanty. "As I stumbled through the rough country of those years," says her autobiography — reminiscent of the *Pilgrim's Progress* — "there were puzzled searchings for the path. It was the time for love, and the little god was constantly about." But the men to whom Cecilia felt drawn were, she confesses, "exceptionally ineligible," those whom she "could never be conquered by." She speaks of "agony and some clear-cut drama in a setting of November days. The terrible standard of what love should be held back the romantic heart."

How could it be otherwise, with a woman artist in the nineteenth century, perhaps in any century? Of course Cecilia could never "be conquered"! What man would have permitted her to go on with her work? She must have known it, sensed it early. Had not even Uncle Will, whom she adored, set his back against the life class at the academy? Thirty years later, in the full tide of success, Cecilia's diary still rebelled when she felt herself emotionally endangered: "J.W. wonderful at the party last night, standing near. I am afraid of him. I feel almost too free and happy among admiring eyes and bending-over heads." "Gay time last night," she writes again. "I cannot *afford* this. J.W. thinks me young. Shall I dare to tell him that I watched Lincoln's funeral train?"

Just when my father came along and proposed to Cecilia, I don't know. But surely the conjunction of two wills so strong, with interests so different, would have been unfortunate, not to say disastrous. Cecilia's "terrible standard of what love should be" may indeed have "held back the romantic heart." Yet Cecilia is more credible when she speaks of the "one rock-bottomed reality" of her young womanhood: the necessity to earn a living and if possible, contribute someday to the family expenses. The thought of becoming "an artist" did not occur. Simply, she seized on such commissions as came her way and executed them. *St. Nicholas* magazine sent her nine dollars for an illustration entitled, *Uncle John's Coat.* (I have their receipt for the amount.) Cecilia did an engraving of two sleepy cats looking over a chair back, just their heads and paws showing. The faithful Mr. Meyer published it, a newspaper gave it half a column. A hundred were sold at once, upon which somebody made off with the stone and put an end to the project. After this a month's lessons in overglaze painting resulted in a rash of orders to do children's heads on china plates. These productions, nearly life-size, caused mothers to weep with joy. Cecilia never saw the children face to face but painted from photographs sent by mail, together with a lock of hair, a ribbon the color of the subject's eyes. Somewhere, Cecilia found a kiln and fired the plates herself — and she never ceased to hate the result. Years later, she may have been remembering that period when she wrote, "Talent is like a fine silk cord. Try to break it and you will cut your fingers first."

Long before the engraved kittens and the china plates, Cecilia would have been a student at the Pennsylvania Academy of Fine Arts, but for Uncle Will's unchanging opposition to the life class, held among what he called a rabble of untidy art students. But he consented to his niece's sharing a private class under the tutelage of William Sartain, who came from New York once a fortnight for the purpose. Cecilia said later that working under Sartain was an adventure that should be written with a pen of fire. Now at last Cecilia *saw* the model. Her world took on a new dimension. She turned a corner into an existence whose demands were great — yet answerable, if the gods willed it, to her own abilities, her hand and heart.

When, in 1879, Harry Drinker married my mother, Cecilia said she watched her sister "float off on the happiest of marriage destinies, without one backward glance." Surprisingly, Grandfather Beaux gave his daughter away in church. At some indeterminate time he had returned from France, though he did not live with the family. The young couple settled in a little house on nearby Irving Street, taking with them Papa's grandmother, the tiny and determined Quaker lady — Grandma Shober. Children commenced coming, my mother's domestic course was launched.

Cecilia had acquired a big, barren studio on the top floor of a house in downtown Chestnut Street, furnished with six kitchen chairs, several leftover easels and an etching press, bought by Uncle Will at an auction. Fired by the room's size and her new, delicious solitude, Cecilia decided to attempt a large composition; other portraits had stopped with the head. She chose as subject my mother, seated with her firstborn, Harry — now three years old — on her lap, his head leaning against her breast, his bare legs dangling. Cecilia saw it as warm in tone, and when the title came to her, she said it came in French, *Les Derniers Jours d'Enfance.*

This painting, as it happened, was to be Cecilia's first real success, determining her immediate future and setting her in the direction that she wished to go. But the initial difficulties were formidable. In the first place, would my mother consent to sit? It meant an hour's trip in the horsecars from Irving Street, a climb of eighty-four steps — and who knew if the venture would succeed? The big empty studio had turned Cecilia's head, said the aunts.

TWO SLEEPY CATS, *by Cecilia Beaux. Dedicated to Aunt Kate.*

And who would look after the new baby, Jamey? Grandma Shober was too deaf and too "delicate." A mother, however, will do anything to have her child's portrait, Cecilia said, "and the same energy and confidence burned in my sister's veins as in mine." Before the first sitting, Cecilia arranged her background. The kitchen chairs would not do. An old steamer chair came down from the storeroom, on which, with the aid of two flat cushions, the model could take her position. The family lent a rug for the floor — "one of their best rugs," Cecilia said — and a small table. My mother wore an old black jersey, for which Cecilia made a black satin sleeve, close-fitted, with lace at the wrist; only one arm was to show. Around the model's knees they draped a Chinese shawl of Grandma Leavitt's, dyed black, and possessing what Cecilia called a "rich, hanging texture." Feeling the need of a strong horizontal mass across the canvas behind the group, Cecilia found a piece of paneling in a carpenter's shop, stained it to look like mahogany and set it up as wainscoting. The high point of interest was to be the group of four hands in the very center of the composition, the boy's fingers showing a little dark on the back of the mother's white hand. "Artists," Cecilia was later to write, "spend their lives inventing ways of doing things."

Somehow the sittings proceeded and the picture took shape. Thomas Anschutz of the Philadelphia Academy saw it, hung it in the big north gallery — and it won the Mary Smith prize. A young woman friend of Cecilia's, planning to return to Paris as an art student, insisted on taking the canvas with her; she said it must be sent to the Salon. Cecilia pronounced this "an insanity." No one in Paris had heard of her; she was nobody's pupil or protégée. But the two women unframed the canvas, rolled it up, and off it went.

It was accepted and well placed on a center wall. Beyond that

Cecilia heard nothing, no word or sign. Months later the canvas returned, bearing the French labels and numbers. Cecilia sat before it in the bare studio, wondering about the scenes it had passed through, and what the master who chose it had said and thought. It was then that she determined to go to Paris herself and study.

New York. Sunday, March 8, 1903

Well, dear ones all at home. I think you would be amused if you could see the crowds staring at the works of your child at Durand-Ruel's. Two thousand catalogues have been used and two thousand more have been ordered for next week. You had better hurry or you will not be able to get in! I asked the woman at the office yesterday if it was so full because it was that hour of day, and she said, "O no, they begin coming at half past eight in the morning." Then she looked at me in a funny way and said, "You don't know, you don't realize what it is."

Your child.

Cecilia was forty-eight when she wrote that letter; she knew that she possessed an international reputation. Yet always there was a new painting in progress, the hazards of which left little time for complacency. The road had been long; Cecilia was thirty-three when she went to Paris as a student. In 1896 the Beaux Arts made her a Sociétaire; each season her paintings at the Salon received glowing notices. "Not one of our women painters in France," wrote Henry Rochefort, the critic, "is of sufficient strength to compare with her." When the *Century Magazine* sent Tom Janvier to interview her, Cecilia wrote him, as an old friend

LES DERNIERS JOURS D'ENFANCE, *by Cecilia Beaux*.

and Cousin Kate's husband, a bantering letter about climbing the ladder upon which she said she had put her foot at sixteen. "Some of the steps have been difficult and dangerously far apart. So that I have even fallen through, but by strength of wrist and some pretty adroit kicking I have managed thus far to swing up onto the next rung."

By 1903 Cecilia had carried off the bronze and gold medals at the Paris and Pan American expositions. She had won the Dodge Prize at the National Academy of Design, the Gold Medal of Honor at the Pennsylvania Academy of Fine Arts. "The main thing about a medal," she said, "is the work that gets it for you." Critics spoke of Miss Beaux's "boldness of execution," the "vitality and nervous force" of her portraits, their "honesty and humanity." Royal Cortissoz wrote of "spontaneity, nervous swing, the self-confidence of her painting and its quite enchanting fluency." Crowds stood before Cecilia Beaux's paintings at exhibitions, in particular her portraits of children, which were said to be "small breathing personalities, with emotional impetus but a cheerful lack of sentimentality, an absence of the degrading prettiness we see in children's portraits."

The china plates and the overglaze had left no scar. Cecilia never became a "fashionable portrait painter"; all her training and philosophy prevented. She painted what she chose and refused whom she chose. She made money enough to maintain a studio apartment in New York and to build a summer cottage and studio in Gloucester, Massachusetts, far out on Eastern Point, where she lived and worked from May to December each year. She remained amused and a little irritated when critics continued to speak of her as a woman portraitist, a woman painter. "They don't write about *men* painters," she said. Zorn, the Swedish artist, had "expressed astonishment on learning that Miss Beaux' portraits were by one of the gentler sex." A critic declared that "Miss Beaux' originality seems to be due to no lack of femininity." Still another inquired how a female could combine such "womanliness of bearing," with the "sanity and strength" of her painting. In 1908, when Cecilia received the degree of LL.D. from the University of Pennsylvania, a poet, reading from the platform, advised her, "Lady, shrink not."

There was no shrinking about it, Cecilia would have said. What you earned you took thankfully, and went on with the job at hand. "Stage-fright this morning over doing Miss Irwin's left hand," says the diary. The family on west Spruce Street refused to be impressed. After Cecilia's return from Paris, when honors — and commissions — began to flow in, Aunt Emily one day got hold of a penny newspaper called the *Item,* and read it aloud hilariously at supper: "The *Item* does not hesitate to declare that Miss Cecilia Beaux is the best female portrait painter in Philadelphia." Certain battles would never be won by a woman, Aunt Emily said, not if she wore on her chest ten medals in a row.

Yet it was this same Aunt Emily who during the early post-Paris period made Cecilia's bed each morning and "did" her room so she could start early for the studio — and who followed her always to the door with her lunch packed neatly in a basket. Cecilia appreciated this care, and the fact that the household had never once asked her to do an errand downtown. In the late afternoons when she returned, dead tired from standing all day at her easel, the aunts demanded neither entertaining conversation nor domestic help, but let Cecilia lie companionably on the sofa while they came and went.

I do not know just when Cecilia left home and went to live in

*Aunt Beaux, after receiving her honorary degree from the
University of Pennsylvania.*

New York. Nor does the rest of her story belong here: the commission, after the First World War, to go abroad and paint Clemenceau, Cardinal Mercier, Admiral Beatty. . . . The exhibition of these portraits in Paris. . . . The breaking of Cecilia's hip in 1924. "Yours to be remembered," she wrote home, "as on a narrow path, with a very small lantern." In 1935 came the triumphant Retrospective Exhibition at the Academy of Arts and Letters.

Fashions change, and the glory has departed. Today the portrait painter is not of interest to private collectors. *Likeness* has become a bad word, nor does anyone wish to look at happy people, "normal" people — ladies in furs, or small girls holding the hand of a nurse in a starched apron. Cecilia Beaux's world has gone, and taken its values with it. Yet there are those, knowledgeable in art, who think she will return, who say that good painting is good painting in any era.

Cecilia's star shone over her own day; indubitably, she made an impression on her times. "The Pennsylvania woman," wrote Lorado Taft after the Carnegie Institute exhibition, "has emancipated her sex; she has shown the potentialities of her kind. Every woman should rejoice that her own artistic horizon has been thus enlarged." Certainly it is a life that is worth scrutiny; Cecilia broke down many barriers. Throughout her career, the influences of youth and upbringing are strikingly evident; the reserve and discipline, the struggle against demands that came with worldly success. "It is well for an artist," she wrote, "if in his work he may be truly lost, cloistered in it, and that his life with it is one of uncompromising probity and patience, an unflinching tenacity of energy and will."

Cecilia Beaux was an attractive woman, vital, witty. "Tall and strikingly handsome," wrote a newspaper interviewer when Cecilia was in her forties, "with a face young and finely chiseled." She found herself sought after by society wherever she went. In her files is a letter from Theodore Roosevelt, written after she had painted Mrs. Roosevelt and Ethel. "My dear Miss Beaux, we have had very few guests in the White House whose presence gave both Mrs. Roosevelt and myself such genuine pleasure as did yours." I remember her ready laugh, the enchanting, caustic stories she told of people who had crossed her path. She knew well the danger, to an artist, of overpraise. "An artist must not be petted," she said. "The painter of portraits naturally falls in with humanity on every side. And it is part of the necessary poise and control of his life that he must not squander this relationship if he would produce works worthy to take their place among the great vital examples of the past." When Cecilia despaired, we know it only from her diary. "Down, down, down," she writes. "Now the middle and the bottom are shaking." And on a summer morning at Gloucester: "Wonderful July day. I wonder what will happen to spoil it." After some disappointment of intimacy, some betrayal of friendship only hinted at, Cecilia writes of a "bad night, little sleep" — then adds, wryly and characteristically, "It is not well to be made of glass if one is a locomotive."

XI

Harry. Full tide. The law and music.

MY BROTHER and I never discussed his career in the law. Not until he had retired from the firm did I come to know the extent of his reputation and why it was that in his eighty-fifth year the American Bar Association gave him their highest award. Actually, he and I never discussed anything, let alone the law. When we played chamber music the program was rather that he told me what to do — how to take the turns in Mozart, which repeats must be made and which (very rarely) it was permissible to skip. Neither my father nor his four sons ever sat down at home to a discussion of their profession, or indeed of politics, philosophy, or even the vagaries of human behavior. They would talk at length of hunting or fishing, which guides were most expert in the woods and whether Bimini was best for tarpon. But if their wives started up a conversation about why Cousin Alice had divorced her husband or what certain New Deal legislation might do to the country, my brothers at once fidgeted or turned the pages of a book. Even my brother Jim, for all his geniality, used to dismiss certain young women from the conversation by saying they were good-looking but they talked too much. As for Papa, he held any exchange intolerable if it reached the discussion stage. I have seen him rise and leave the dinner table when my sister's husband, William Bullitt, began to animadvert on politics or what he thought about the Bolsheviks.

I don't know how this odd family trait originated, perhaps with the Philadelphia ancestors who, while they went willingly to prison for their beliefs, were by the Quaker discipline averse to taking sides in worldly politics, let alone indulging in gossip. Certainly the Drinker reticence rendered communication difficult, and it was small wonder that Ernesta and I made our first marriages with men who would discuss anything at all, and showed marked pleasure in the conversation of women.

When Harry was in his late forties I lived across the road from him in Merion, not ten minutes' drive from Haverford College and the haunts of early youth. My parents had moved from Bethlehem when Papa retired as president of Lehigh; Mamma called Merion "home," a word she had not used in Bethlehem. My two young children and I occupied the third floor of my parents' house, consequent upon a pending divorce from my husband, Ezra Bowen. Harry's house was new, set behind tall hedges. He had built it around a music room that held easily two grand pianos, a Hammond organ, and one hundred and fifty people sitting on folding chairs singing Bach cantatas. The organ, being electric, had a muffled, oversweet sound; Harry always explained he needed it for the brass and woodwind parts when he couldn't get good performers.

All this equipment and the "singing parties," as we called them, had come about through a fortunate accident. A musical guest, Augustus Zanzig, fell ill in the house on his way to make a professional survey of music across the country. For a week he heard Harry practicing piano parts of chamber music, day after day, then complaining angrily because he couldn't play them better. Moreover, it was beginning to dawn on my brother that he would never in a lifetime be able to do justice to the Brahms or Schumann piano quintets, nor indeed to the classical violin-piano sonatas which he so much loved. Sophie had said she was desperate, with Harry pounding away at the piano the minute he came home from the office, then all evening, and up at seven to give the children their music lessons before taking the train to town. She said she believed he was headed for disaster with this everlasting practicing and not attaining; he knew too well how things should sound.

Zanzig, observing the situation, told Harry he could have a much pleasanter time singing in a chorus than trying to play the piano; besides which Sophie could be a part of it. At Zanzig's suggestion some twenty musical friends, mostly string players, came to dinner without their instruments and Zanzig led them while they sang the Brahms *Liebeslieder-Walzer*, also Bach's embellished chorales, with Harry's daughter Cecilia playing obbligatos on the flute.

The evening generated much excitement. Harry was in heaven; the string players said they loved sight-reading the parts and wanted to meet again. Next time forty singers came, then sixty until, over the years, we were one hundred and fifty. It was rumored that ours was the only chorus with enough tenors; young men flocked to us from Haverford College, Princeton and the University of Pennsylvania. No one was invited who could not sight-read; there were no passive listeners and we never gave a concert.

Singing Bach, Harry conducting. Author, with glasses, playing in the orchestra.

We had a string orchestra of eight or ten in which I played, delivering the parts ahead of time and seeing that the players were in the music room at three o'clock on the designated Sunday for rehearsal. Singing began promptly at 5:30 and ended at 9:30, with an hour in the middle for supper. For the first two seasons we were led by guest conductors, friends of Harry's. But Harry grew restless under this regime, ambitious to lead the chorus himself. He took lessons in conducting and began practicing at home with the victrola. Walking through the house one heard Bach's chorales sound from the music room, and passing the door one saw Harry, baton in hand, standing before the record player in the big empty room, going over and over the hard places.

At first Harry's conducting was clumsy, and though he always did his homework and knew the music note for note, he sometimes found it difficult to bring the soprano or tenor sections back in if they got lost. On such occasions the singers, with a mighty effort, found their way back without him, and the next time round they kept the place. One evening Willem Van der Wall came from New York to sing with us; for years he had been harpist under Toscanini. That night we sang a collection Harry had made of all the works where Bach used the choral melody, "Wer nur den lieben Gott lässt walten." We began with the Choral Fantasia from Cantata 93, which no one in the chorus had heard or seen before. After page two there was chaos among the tenors, though they recovered themselves. We sang the music three times, until finally it went so well the altos sprang to their feet at the final chord and bowed to applause. At supper Mr. Van der Wall told Harry he had been skeptical, wondering how a man with little experience in conducting could attempt such music. Now he professed himself astonished. "The sound," he said, "is *good*." He could not attribute

179

it merely to my brother's enthusiasm, though this was contagious. "Mr. Drinker, you are the only choral conductor I ever heard who allows the music to go from Bach to the singers without getting in the way."

Harry's philosophy behind all this was, quite simply, the joy of reading great music and getting to know it. To enjoy reading *Hamlet*, he used to say, must a person be a professional actor? As the years passed we did indeed come to know the Bach cantatas, two hundred and seventeen of them, also his *Saint Matthew Passion* and the *Mass in B Minor*. We sang Brahms' *Requiem* and Mozart's and Verdi's, Beethoven's *Missa Solemnis*, and Honegger's *King David*. We sang oratorios and motets, madrigals, magnificats both ancient and modern. One summer at the Staatsbibliothek in Berlin, Harry came upon the choral works of Bach's four sons, as well as of six of his cousins. These he transcribed into modern clefs and wrote out the orchestra parts on the steamer coming home. For thirty winters we sang, ranging through the literature, and to our surprise the occasions grew famous. When I went off lecturing in Kansas, Oregon, California, I used to be asked if I were related to the Mr. Drinker back East who had the singing parties.

There was nothing haphazard about our programs — no "request numbers"; Harry had it all timed to a minute. Every Saturday during winter, two young choral conductors — professionals — arrived, and with Harry searched out choral works that would be feasible and interesting to sing — not overly difficult sight-reading for our chorus. On Sundays when we met, Harry planted in each section of the singers a professional soprano or two, a tenor, a bass. (For some reason the altos managed by themselves.) Harry put so much work into all this that Sophie might

have been baffled anew except that she saw its indubitable success, and moreover she developed her own chorus of women,
which met in the music room on Wednesday mornings. They
called themselves the Montgomery Singers; Margarethe Dessoff
traveled from New York to conduct. As Sophie came to know
choral music, she grew indignant — enraged is a better word —
because the great church music was sung by men and boys when
much of it really belonged to women. The *Magnificat*, for instance. How, Sophie asked furiously, could Mary's joyful words
be pronounced before the altar by little boys in surplices? It was
an insult to the female sex, a travesty of their function and their
innate genius. Sophie not only developed a chorus to sing women's
music but she wrote a book, called *Music and Women*, which took
her six years, was translated into German and published here and
abroad.

So much music went on in Harry and Sophie's house that
people used to ask my brother how he found time to be a lawyer.
Harry always replied that he spent eighty hours a week on the law
and twenty hours on music. "Sophie and I don't play golf or
cards," he said. "And we don't go to the theater or accept dinner
invitations if we can help it. That gives us plenty of time for
everything we want to do." It was after the singing parties were
instituted that Harry's firm changed its name from Dickson Beitler and McCouch to Drinker Biddle and Reath, with Harry as
senior partner. Remote though I was from the profession of law,
one could not live close to Harry's household without knowing that
for him the law came before home, children and country. Just
where it stood in relation to music I was to find out later, by
Harry's own confession. He did not talk about his legal cases, yet

we knew them by name; they were in the air and often enough in the newspapers: *United States v. Morgan and Company, United States v. General Foods, United Mine Workers v. Coronado Coal Company, Cold Metal Process v. Carnegie Illinois Steel.* The Sugar Institute cases in the 1930s, when the price of sugar dropped from twenty-two cents a pound to seven cents, and eight hundred Pennsylvania grocers refused to fulfill their contracts. Four hundred of these cases came to Harry's firm. Harry was retained by the Edward G. Budd Manufacturing Company, makers of locomotives and railroad cars, through a tangle of quarrels between the American Federation of Labor and an independent union. Some of these lawsuits were argued for years — seven years or twelve — making their way from the lower courts to the appellate court, reaching at the end the Supreme Court in Washington, with Harry standing up to argue in striped pants and a cutaway, talking without notes. I never saw this performance, but my sister Ernesta did; she said Harry was smooth as silk and afterward she thought she must have dreamed it.

Harry's colleagues told me he did not win his cases on showmanship; he was not an actor. They said his strength lay in his briefs; he searched out analogy and comparison that would make the judges comprehend. I thought of Harry's bad eyesight in youth, the rigorous training of his memory at law school. How was it that people with weak eyes became skilled at reading and boys with crippled legs learned to run like Glen Cunningham? Even after Harry got to be senior member of the firm, he wrote his briefs himself, then called on his partners for review. But my brother was not interested in the philosophy of law. When he read legal history it was in connection with a case in progress. Holdsworth, Maitland, or Berle and Means on the modern corporation, offered illustrations for his current brief. "You have to be *clear*," Harry told me. "There's no excuse not to be clear. Can't let the English language down, Katz. It's a wonderful language."

What my brother really loved were the legal puzzles, the contests, the chance to use his wits. I think he liked a good fight, too, and he did not mind being hated. (A young lawyer once told me that lawyers get used to being hated, it's part of the game.) Among Harry's papers is a letter to Sophie, written late at night in the railroad station on the way to Utica, New York. A lawyer named Moore had pirated an edition of Harry's book on the Interstate Commerce Act; Harry was thirty. Quite plainly he smelled battle from afar, and, like the war-horse among the trumpets, his spirit answered, *Ha, ha!*

Tuesday, 11:15 p.m. [1910]

The red sparks are flying out of my aura like a freight train on a steep grade. I can surely fix Dewitt Moore. I never could imagine such nerve. He had copied whole paragraphs verbatim. We leave on the 11:53 tonight and get to Jersey City at 1:35. Take a 2 o'clock train to Utica and get there for breakfast. I have been on the high jump all day preparing the injunction bill and it is all finished in high style. Here I go to the train. Good-night, my darling Sophie.

Some thirty-five years later, convinced — and with less cause — that some one had plagiarized *Yankee from Olympus,* I telephoned Harry for advice. "You should be complimented!" Harry said. "It shows people read the book." He asked if the man had copied my mistakes, and when I said no, Harry said that was how he had won *his* plagiarism case. Then he remarked that plagiarism suits were hell to win, and ended the exchange by asking in his strong, hearty voice if I knew the story of Chanticleer. Before I could reply, he said, "Chanticleer got up on a dunghill and crowed. And the sun rose! Katz, let the thing rest." I took his advice and afterward was glad of it.

There was another time when I called on my brother for legal aid, and that occurred in connection with my divorce. Corporation law firms hate to handle divorces, they are apt to say they don't take that kind of business. But Harry put my divorce through the court at Norristown; I was so inept at presenting the evidence that without my brother things might not have gone forward at all. In judges' chambers when I was supposed to recount all the horrors, I floundered and stumbled. Harry said that in the next — and final — hearing I simply must speak up, and what was wrong with me anyhow, shying back like that and upsetting all the evidence we had laid out? On the morning in question I woke with my voice gone, though I had never had bronchitis in my life before. Speechless, I crossed the road and climbed into Harry's car. "Well!" he said. "No voice, eh? Bully for our side, Katz! When we get there you just *sit*. I'll do the talking."

During the years when I was writing *Yankee from Olympus,* people kept asking if my brother had steered me into legal biography. "He must be a great help to you," they said. (Up till then I had written about musicians.) The fact is that beyond Harry's saying thank God Katz you've finished writing about Tchaikovsky — what kind of a composer was that compared to Mozart? — we did not talk about Justice Holmes at all, though Harry knew him and called on him whenever he went to Washington to argue a case in the Supreme Court. It was not in the cards for me to quote

Holmes as saying that artists and poets shrank from the law as from an alien world.

But I thought about it. What was this "corporation law" that consumed those eighty hours, and where did the fascination lie? In the library of Harry's house a card table sat by the bay window. On weekends and every evening it was weighted with law business, long sheets of typed paper backed with light blue; heavy books of case references, and always the big yellow foolscap pad covered with Harry's bold scrawl in pencil. One Saturday, passing through the room, I asked Harry what he was doing; he said writing a corporate mortgage for Drexel and Company in the refinancing of the New Jersey Public Service Company. Perhaps I made a face, for Harry was instantly on the defensive. "But I've thought of a new form!" he cried. "I'm cutting down and simplifying. Want to hear a sample? . . . The Company will pay or discharge or cause to be paid or discharged . . . I deleted five words in that first clause alone. Its fun!" Harry cried out. "I'm having a good time!"

And indeed, as he spoke, his face was as the face of one going to Jerusalem. A picture flashed through my mind: Harry at the piano long ago, writing the word *energetico* on the music, where *appassionato* had been. Was this what Harry wanted from life, and had it been this my brother Cecil had meant when he said Harry was headed for safety, and what business had that big black bozo being *safe?* Harry's hair was pepper and salt, now, but his color was high, his dark eyes piercing, and he still had the look of a pirate. I went home across the street and told my mother about the corporate mortgage, remarking that her firstborn liked to engage his mind in the most appalling matters. "With Harry I think its *muscular*," Mamma said serenely.

But it troubled me. Was Harry then content to spend three-quarters of his life on oddments and quiddities, and could a man nourish his spirit on *dust?* Edmund Burke had said that law sharpens the mind by narrowing it. If we had been a family that teased and "kidded," I could have challenged my brother. But we were not accustomed to that kind of bantering communication. Such kidding as occurred came from the top down, not from youngest daughter to eldest son. Once only, I let go. We were driving to town for a concert of the Philadelphia Orchestra; I sat in front between Harry and a young lawyer from the firm. That morning I had happened upon Dr. Holmes's challenge to his son, when Wendell decided to make law his career. "A lawyer can't be a great man," the Doctor had said, and he quoted an English barrister: "If you can eat sawdust without butter, young fellow, you'll be a success in the law."

Harry and his young partner were talking across me, something about the Revenue Commission and a half-million-dollar depreciation on the hexylresorcinol patent. By the time we reached the parkway I could stand it no longer. "Sawdust without butter!" I said. "How can you bear it, day in and day out?"

Harry all but stopped the car plunk in front of the museum steps. "Sawdust?" he said indignantly. "But I like the law better than playing the piano! Now this morning, for instance, Ed Howe and I started writing a brief at a quarter past nine, and by three o'clock we had thirty pages written. Thirty pages of the most beautiful . . ."

"About what?" I asked.

"About income tax on transferred securities," Harry said. "The most beautiful — well, it wasn't a *novel*. But for sheer art, let me tell you . . . every point fitting so nicely, so perfectly, one after the other for thirty pages, bang bang bang bang. . . ."

I had my answer, and it so impressed me that when we got home I set it down word for word in a little notebook I kept, though at the time I had no intention of writing about Harry Drinker. Justice Holmes had said that for him the rule of joy and the law of duty seemed all one. Plainly, it was so with my brother, who threw himself into legal work the way he hurled himself into chopping wood out by the garage on Saturdays and Sundays. The bigger the tree stump, the happier Harry looked. The telephone company delivered discarded poles, the Merion Township Commission dead trees — one time an oak stump as big as the hull of our old yawl, the *Gee Whiz*, that sat in the backyard by the vegetable garden. "Ha!" Harry would cry, his face flushed, sweat showing at the neck of his old grey jersey. "See this log? It'll be firewood in four sessions. . . . Don't you believe me?"

He had a way of asking if I didn't believe him. On occasion he even asked Sophie. Sometimes the formula altered: "You want to bet, Katz?" I just laughed; I would as soon have made a wager with the sun: Would it set tonight, would it rise tomorrow? Yet concerning the business of corporation law I think Harry in youth had had his doubts. After *Yankee from Olympus* was published I saw a letter from Justice Holmes, dated 1909, evidently in answer to one from Harry which had announced he was sending the Justice his book on the Interstate Commerce Act. Harry's letter must have expressed doubts about some phase of his career, for Holmes wrote back, "I am moved by what you say. To keep one's ideals is a hard task. I remember saying at the Tavern Club that 'common sense' generally means taking the lower view. Business is apt to be cynical and one cannot prove the superiority of what one thinks the best any more than one can prove that the taste of beer is good. You have to fall back on the ultimate dogma of your personality. . . . I think it is a good augury that you have tackled a hard headed practical thing at the start. The bogus ideal delights in generalities and in shirking the detail. I send you all my good wishes and thank you for remembering me."

Justice Holmes said that business was cynical; elsewhere he had declared that the test of truth was to get itself accepted in the marketplace. Here were no absolutes, no ideological seekings and searchings for a better world. My brother's life in the law was concerned indeed with business, big business, its moves and tactics against restraint from above and below — from government or from labor. To play this game a man has to like power, be drawn to power and revere it. Harry Drinker believed in power as the saints believed in compassion. With all his healthy being he responded to competition and despised the weak. My father too had had pride in American "enterprise," though he cared little for moneymaking and in his mid-fifties had retired forever from the business world. I thought of the letter from Japan to the Lehigh *Brown and White*, deploring "the blight of the Sherman Act and the unnecessary and irrational attacks on great enterprise in the United States." My father had lived in the very heyday and high day of unrestricted American enterprise; Harry followed close after. Both men were Republicans, right through to the backbone. When Franklin D. Roosevelt came up for election the second time, Harry was nearly made ill by it. I remember election morning of 1936, and Harry stopping as usual at our house to say good morning to Mamma before taking the train to town. He stood in the doorway of the dining room where I sat at breakfast with my children, his usually ruddy face white, his hat pushed to the back of his head. He looked shaken — to us a sight as bewildering as if the roof had blown off and we lay exposed to the weather. He asked if I were going to the polls, he knew I was a Democrat. Then he said, without smiling, "Will you bite the hand that feeds you?"

In point of fact nobody was feeding me; by that time I had become self-supporting. But to my brother the New Deal legislation, both present and pending, was anathema, a holding back of "progress," and counter to the American dream as interpreted by Calvin Coolidge. I have been told that during the 1930s, Harry was one of three lawyers — the others were John W. Davis and George Wharton Pepper — known for arguing against New Deal legislation in the Supreme Court. Like Papa, Harry remained quite passionately antiunion — when unions got in the way. He was convinced that neither labor nor the federal government should be allowed to impede American enterprise. Business took the risk, investing capital; let businessmen rise or fall according to their abilities, and not be halted and estopped from above or below. Harry's cases often concerned strikes and bargains between workers and employers; his law firm was known for it. Harry won many such cases for management, especially on appeal, after the lower courts had decided adversely. But the lawsuit he considered most important of his career, and the one he worked on longest, Harry lost, hands down, after twelve years of litigation. *United Mine Workers v. Coronado Coal Company* became a leading case in the history of labor legislation.

The circumstances were wildly dramatic. In the hills of western Arkansas, Harry's client, Franklin Bache of Philadelphia, owned bituminous mines which were set in deeply unionized country, whose workers lived in towns called Prairie Creek, Frogtown, Mammoth Vein. Bache decided to run his mines open shop, thus outbidding his competitors, who at once called on the United Mine Workers of America to protect them against Bache's low-priced product. The U.M.W. demanded a closed shop; when Bache refused, mine owners became involved all the way from Colorado to West Virginia. Bache dismissed his union men, made them vacate their company houses and proceeded to recruit non-union workers, strangers from out of town. The abandoned mines had become flooded. Bache brought in Burns guards, set posts and wire around the pits. Local No. 21 had guns shipped in and stormed the mine, burning the tipple to the ground, killing two nonunion men and destroying the plant by dynamite and fire. Over the ruined mine a flag flew. It said, "This is a union man's country."

Mr. Bache retained Harry Drinker to sue the United Mine Workers for triple damages under the Sherman Anti-Trust Act. The number of times this case came into court in twelve years is bewildering to the layman. There were proceedings for injunction and contempt, a demurrer overruled, a nonsuit and two trials resulting in hung juries. The first decisive hearing, held at Saint Paul, Minnesota, consumed six weeks and resulted in a triumphant verdict for Bache of $200,000, which, when trebled and costs added, amounted to $825,000. This judgment was confirmed by the Circuit Court of Appeals, upon which the U.M.W. appealed to the Supreme Court. The case reached Washington in 1921 — nine years after the strikes and the riots took place. Counsel for the miners was, surprisingly, none other than ex-Chief Justice Charles Evans Hughes, who by reputation had hitherto been as owner-oriented as Harry Drinker, John W. Davis or George Wharton Pepper.

The Supreme Court's decision went against Bache, the judges holding that sufficient evidence of the U.M.W.'s involvement had not been produced; it appeared rather that the local union, District 21, had been wholly responsible. Also the Court was not convinced the strike had been a "conspiracy aimed at restraint of commerce," and therefore suable under the Anti-Trust Act. Concluding his delivered judgment, Chief Justice Taft remarked that the case had been prepared by counsel for the plaintiff (Harry) "with rare assiduity and ability," and that "circumstances were such as to awaken regret" that the decision must stand as it did. The Court remanded the case to the district court for further proceedings — which meant that Harry must return to Arkansas and begin over again. He did so, and three years later, in 1924, reappeared before the Supreme Court with new evidence as to the United Mine Worker's involvement. Ex-Justice Hughes had meanwhile retired from the defense.

Supreme Court decisions are not made public at the time of trial; the judges must first convene, discuss, and assign one of their members to write the decision. The usual interim occurred, therefore, while both sides waited. One day, Harry happened to be watching the ticker tape at a client's office in Philadelphia and saw it spell out, UNITED MINE WORKERS HELD LIABLE FOR DAMAGES IN THE CORONADO COAL CASE. Jubilant, he ran to telephone Mr. Bache, then hurried back for details, arriving just in time for the announcement: CORRECTION. MINE WORKERS WIN DECISION IN CORONADO COAL CASE.

Harry always said this was the hardest blow of his career. The reason for the ticker tape confusion was that the judges had declared the circuit court's original decision in favor of Bache to be "affirmed in part and reversed in part," which turned out to mean that the United Mine Workers were not liable for damages, but the local union, District 21, was liable. This was in part a victory for Harry: unincorporated labor unions had not hitherto been considered liable. Mr. Bache took small comfort, however, the local union being poor, with no money for damages. The Supreme Court again remanded the case for a new trial in the lower courts. But Mr. Bache had lost heart. He was described as bankrupt; Harry's fee for twelve years' work was $5000.

The Coronado story is indicative of what a corporation lawyer may encounter in the course of business. (Incidentally, I was heart and soul on labor's side.) Now that time has passed, it is easy to see that throughout the case, Mr. Bache and Harry had been running counter to current history. Already in the 1920s a prolabor momentum was under way. Companies had grown immensely powerful, the pendulum swung to the left. Unions fought and lost, fought and gained an inch, up through the days of New Deal legislation and the "Roosevelt Court." Not until the 1940s did it become apparent that the unions possessed too much independence rather than too little, and there crept into case law a certain skepticism.

Considering my brother's deep-dyed conservatism and persistent championship of property rights, his stand during the anti-Communist hysteria of the 1950s was surprising. Philadelphia had its share of court trials concerned with men and women suspected of Communist leanings; newspapers and television gave them extended coverage. At first the suspects had much difficulty securing competent lawyers to defend them. The Bar Association called on the six or seven best-known city firms to lend experienced men for the purpose. The big firms dragged their feet and temporized. It was Harry, I am told, who broke the logjam by announcing that Drinker Biddle and Reath would furnish an experienced trial lawyer whether anybody else did or not.

My brother despised the word "liberal," and looked on American Communists as a scruffy lot. But from the constitutional angle he believed every suspect entitled to his day in court; he intended when possible to see that they got it. The firm lent for the defense one of their brightest young men, Henry Sawyer — red-haired, fiery and most definitely a liberal. Sawyer appeared in *United States v. Kuzma et al.; United States v. Schempt* — a total indeed of nineteen cases. Two of these reached the Supreme Court and won national attention: *United States v. Knowles* concerned the Quaker librarian at Plymouth Meeting who refused to acknowledge the power of the Senate Internal Security Subcommittee to inquire into her past political associates. Mrs. Knowles had been sentenced to a year in prison; the Supreme Court reversed the decision. In the other case, *United States v. Deutch*, a graduate student at the University of Pennsylvania, subpoenaed before the House Un-American Activities Committee, refused to name his political associates and was given nine months in jail. Here Sawyer based his defense not on the traditional fifth amendment but on the first, and won by a five to four vote of the justices.

Sawyer I think enjoyed his part. Not only did he despise Senator Joseph McCarthy but he liked a good fight in court and was rather pleased when he discovered that certain interested parties outside the firm were endeavoring to have him fired. One day Sawyer happened to come down in the office elevator with a senior partner, Charles Biddle, who was if possible an even more convinced conservative than my brother. Mr. Biddle said the partners were proud of the work Sawyer was doing; the firm wanted to stand back of him. "But my God, Henry!" Mr. Biddle finished. "What if you keep on winning?" It was Sawyer who told me of the morning a powerful client from the industrial world telephoned Harry to say that he had seen by the papers the firm was defending Commies in the courts; in consequence he considered taking his business somewhere else. Harry told the client his partners were lawyers and would choose their cases as they saw fit, the client could take his business where he liked. It is pertinent also that at the height of the McCarthy scare, Harry delivered the Gaspar Bacon lectures at Boston University, entitled, "Some Observations on the Freedoms of the First Amendment." The series began with colonial days and came down to Jehovah's Witnesses and the Bible-reading cases of the current decade — an orderly, scholarly presentation, in no way impassioned and indeed much like a legal brief, yet in its own way surprising.

In his fifty-third year, my brother had a letter from the University of Pennsylvania, announcing that they wished to grant him an honorary degree: Doctor of Music. By this time Harry had become a public figure in the city and beyond, being on more boards than one could count, from the Saving Fund Society and the Child Guidance Clinic to Haverford College and the University of Pennsylvania, the Juilliard School of Music in New York, the Westminster Choir College at Princeton, vice-president of the Pennsylvania Academy of Fine Arts, also a term as president of the Wilderness Club, and Philadelphia's Franklin Institute. Harry took the university's letter to his law partners, asking if he had

better refuse the degree. Would it be bad for the firm to have its
senior member made a doctor of *music?* The partners laughed and
said they thought they could live it down.

Harry did not win this doctorate, or others to come, by any
prowess in playing the piano. But with the singing parties — now
well established — he had become deeply involved in projects of
scholarship and musicology, such as the translation into English of
Bach's choral texts, and the consequent development of what
came to be known as the Drinker Choral Library. He had decided
that in singing German or Russian texts, English performers
missed a large part of the emotional reaction they were entitled
to. Bach's cantatas, for instance, depend much on the meaning of
the words — the drama of great Bible stories, the poetry of the
Psalmist, of Isaiah or Ecclesiastes. Each musical syllable has a
literary as well as a musical justification: Bach's texts prove it.
With a German scholar at his elbow, Harry arranged it so that
every English syllable was printed under the corresponding note;
he invented a way of typing it out. Over the printed German text,
between the lines of music, he pasted gummed strips on which
were written English words. Harry delivered these pages to Kal-
mus, the New York publisher, who reproduced by photolithogra-
phy cheap multiple copies for use by choruses. Harry wrote out
directions, entitled "Suggestions for Reproducing Multiple Copies
of Non-Copyright Choral Works," and beginning,

Use the greatest care to space the English words so that the
middle of each syllable comes exactly under its appropriate
note. In translation, syllables of many letters such as "strength"
should be avoided. They will not go in. . . . The carriage of
the typewriter can be held back with the left hand so as to

place the letters closer together than the normal spacing. . . .
When all the English words have been typewritten in, cut out,
with scissors, the four chorus parts, with words, and paste
them, evenly, four systems to a page, on the white paper,
bringing the entire music and text within the space of 9½ by 6¼
inches. . . . Before pasting, figure out how many pages the
matter will cover and allow for sufficient space at the beginning for the title, any history or explanation of the work, the
indication of omitted numbers, and designation of the instrument used in the original. Use black ink and Grippit paper
cement.

Employing this system, which my brother confidently expected
would be adopted by countless students as eager as himself, Harry
translated and saw to the publication of 159 Bach cantatas, 389
chorales, the Saint John and Saint Matthew Passions, the Christmas
Oratorio, all the vocal works of Brahms and numerous vocal compositions of Mozart, Schumann, Wolf, Medtner, Moussorgsky,
Schubert, Beethoven and Schütz. The editions were made available in multiple copies to the many hundred members of the Association of American Choruses.

Harry took great joy in this work. The musical typewriter, the
Grippit cement, the scissors and the piles of choral music sat on a
card table in the dining room, adjoining the library. On finishing a
page or a section, Harry would move through the door to the library card table which held his legal problems — the corporate
mortgages or the lawsuit currently at issue. I used to wonder if he
had a timetable, so as not to exceed, in the dining room, the
twenty percent of life that had been allocated to music. Harry's

system of translation proved a real boon to singers; for instance, instead of strangling over the German "sch," they sang an English syllable with a vowel. Whenever indicated, Harry used Biblical texts and verses. Bruno Walter adopted Harry's translation when he performed Bach's Saint Matthew Passion with the New York Philharmonic and the Westminster College choir. During preparation for the concert the two men carried on a correspondence by mail, ending with Walter's apology for having queried certain of Harry's translated syllables in relation to slurred notes.

July 17, 1942

Dear Dr. Drinker,

Let me tell you that I never in my long life had found such deep understanding for Bach's art, such "being at home" in this world combined with the most astonishing linguistic wealth and resourcefulness. My diversions on the enclosed sheet now seem to me very presumptuous and I certainly would not have dared to write them, if I should not have done it before I got the declaration of your philosophy on the problems of translation. . . .

Subsequently, Harry went into a veritable vortex, a dance, a passionate rite of public explanation concerning the importance of singing great music in one's native tongue. Speeches and articles poured out: "Amateurs and Music," "The Place of Music in our Colleges," "On Translating Vocal Texts." Characteristic was an article in the *Musical Quarterly* entitled "Bach's Use of Recitativo Secco," expressing Harry's purism, or what at home he called "not fooling around with Bach."

197

Translators of Bach's choral works have apparently felt at liberty to substitute, especially in the Recitatives, a single English syllable for two in the German, necessitating the use of slurs not in the original. They seek to justify this on several theories; the most plausible applies only to passages in the text quoted directly from the Lutheran Bible. . . . The more one studies Bach, the greater becomes one's reverence for what he has done, and the stronger the conviction that he intended exactly what he wrote and that not a note or musical phrase should be changed except for cogent reasons, one of which is certainly not the convenience of the translator.

The article goes on to present seven classes of slurs: "the appoggiature; the do-sol vocal cadence; slurs in preparation for a cadence; slurs in preparation for an arioso; slurs to give emphasis to striking words, phrases or ideas; exclamations or short isolated phrases; the mordent on the seventh." All these Harry illustrated. Had he been writing a legal brief he could not have produced more telling examples to bring the judges round.

As time went on, when a musical problem did not present itself, my brother invented one, such as compiling a thematic index to the Bach chorales, so that on hearing a chorale, a person could, after a measure or two, identify the cantata from which it came. The system was based on whether a particular chorale begins on a strong or weak beat, whether the second note goes up or down and by what interval. (Harry later printed the index at the back of his edition of the chorales.) One day while he was working on it I happened to be in the room. A friend telephoned to say that a Bach chorale was running through his head and he couldn't place it. Harry said, "You say it goes do-mi-re-do twice, in minor?" He turned the pages of the index. "That's the melody *Wir Christenleut*," he said into the telephone. "It's number 35 in the Christmas Oratorio and it appears in three cantatas — numbers 40, 110, and 142."

Harry put down the telephone and gave his great laugh of triumph. "Ha!" he said. "How's that for system, Katz!" — and went back to work.

During these years of the singing parties, Harry and I did not stop playing violin-piano sonatas; for him a built-in fiddler across the street was something made to order. At first, like any young woman whose home has been broken up, I existed in a state of chronic exhaustion; moreover, the program called for writing books all morning and in the afternoon following small children around the backyard. But that anybody should be too tired to make music never entered my brother's head; he had always some urgent reason why we should play. At such times it seemed to me I actually staggered, going down the steps to the music room and crossing to the piano. After two sonatas Harry would look up. "You tired?" he would ask. I always shook my head; it was not possible to tell Harry Drinker one was tired. "Me neither," he would say, and place a third sonata on the violin stand.

Against these onslaughts and enthusiasms Harry's household had its own defenses, though Sophie seemed immune, and could subdue my brother with three sharp words. It was hard to get Harry's attention. "*Shout* at him!" Sophie would tell me. "Make him listen!" Concerning music the daughters were amenable, played and sang easily enough, as if they had been born singing.

Of the two sons, one repudiated music early; the other, who was talented and played the cello, ended by refusing all music except jazz, and took to going up and down to his room on a rope ladder, eschewing the staircase. It was Sophie who coped with such emergencies. If matters grew really threatening my brother simply went to pieces, showed genuine anguish and remorse or even took sick. When matters quieted down, he arranged to take the entire family on an elaborate fishing or bird-spotting trip somewhere — up the Peace River in northwestern Canada or down to the Florida coast.

When the last of the four children married, Harry met me at his front door the day after the wedding. He looked haggard, quite wild. "How are we going to *live*," he said, "in this big house with nobody in it but Sophie and me?" A week later he stopped at our dining room as I was alone at breakfast; he had been upstairs with Mamma, who persisted in being sorry for him because all his young had "fled the nest." "I can't seem to make Ma realize," Harry said, frowning, "what fun Sophie and I are having, living alone like this." He said he never before had the music room to himself; somebody was always wanting to play the piano or sight-read a duet. Now he could come down at seven in the morning and have a whole hour to himself before breakfast.

Harry's absorption with his own interests aroused antagonism beyond the family circle as well as within. Friends used to say indignantly that they had passed my brother on Chestnut Street and he cut them dead. When I spoke to Harry about it he merely looked vague. "What do they care if I speak to them or not?" he said. With the chorus he could be equally brusque. He had a bias against professional soloists, particularly singers, who, he said, cared more for their divine epiglottis than for the music, and held high notes beyond the beat, to show off. One Sunday evening at intermission I found a soprano being sick in the upstairs bathroom. I told Harry and he said pay no attention, the girl wanted to sing a solo and he had informed her there were no solos in the chorus. "She ought to know *that*." Harry stepped onto the little platform where he stood to conduct, between the orchestra and singers. "Katz," he said, "if those darn fiddlers of yours have to tune, get them together and do it now, quick, while people are eating. I don't want an A-natural sounding just before we start on the A-flat chorus."

Harry had a short way with celebrities, though he was pleased when they wanted to sing with us. The Trapp family singers came one evening, a round dozen of them in costume. John Erskine the novelist came, and Olin Downes of the *New York Times:* Vilhjalmur Stefansson the explorer: instrumentalists such as Arthur Schnabel, Olga Samaroff, Ernest Hutcheson, Ralph Kirkpatrick; Kincaid and Tabuteau from the Philadelphia Orchestra, Aronoff and Orlando Cole of the Curtis Quartet. Also composers and conductors: Nicholas Medtner, Vaughan Williams, Randall Thompson, William Schumann, Sir Robert Mayer. Harry never introduced these guests to the chorus; I think he did not want anything to distract from the music. One Sunday we sang Vaughan Williams's *Benedicite* and his *Mass in G.* Afterward at supper a Haverford College student exclaimed at the remarkable sight-reading of the singer who had shared his music and hadn't missed a note. "That was Dr. Williams," Harry said. I remember also the evening Ruth Draper the monologuist, who was staying in the house, made a late entrance to the music room, sweeping in, splendid in red velvet. Halfway up the aisle she paused and looked at my brother with charming hesitancy. I am sure she expected to be introduced to the chorus. Harry's baton was already raised to begin. He lowered it. "What's wrong?" he demanded. "Somebody got your place? You an alto? . . . All right, sit *there*." And he pointed with his baton.

XII

Aunt Cecilia refuses to die

I T WAS AUTUMN of 1938 when Aunt Cecilia came to visit us for the last time. There were already seven in the Merion house, and even without Cecilia Beaux the place was too small, though the spare bedroom and sitting room remained always empty and we managed to fit in somehow: my parents, my two children, Bridget, our cook for some thirty years, she who had left her money on the automobile fender — and Mary McClafferty, now gray-haired and of imposing appearance, whose brother drove the fast freight between the Mauch Chunk mining district and the coast.

Our house was plain enough, with a flat grass plot in front, from which my brother Harry's high hedge and chimneys could be seen across the road. Behind lay a sloping lawn; my parents called these the front and back yards and they persisted in planting saplings from Papa's pet arboretum at Lehigh, until so many half-grown trees made it hard to find a patch of sun to dry the clothes.

My mother at the time was seventy-eight, two years older than her sister, whose age nobody ever mentioned. And indeed Aunt Cecilia looked a handsome sixty, even with her heavy steel brace and crutch; it is to be remembered that she had broken her hip at seventy. My brother Cecil, now a physiology professor at Harvard, had told me the brace was her own fault. "Beaux," as he called her, refused to have a steel pin put in to hold the cracked places — a new operation then and she feared it, being, like many persons of extraordinarily good health, timid about illness — the only fact of life, I might add, concerning which Aunt Cecilia showed timidity.

Since the days on west Spruce Street, Cecilia Beaux had come a long way; the "adroit kicking," which by her own confession had swung her up the ladder, ended by toughening more than the leg muscles. "Work is a struggle to conquer something," she wrote. Cecilia's eyes, once cerulean like Grandpa Beaux's, had darkened to a steel-blue; their glance could cut. In her eighth decade she wore a red hat tilted over one eye, furs up close around her chin, and beautifully made tweed suits. I admired her brilliance, her wit, and most of all the indomitable spirit by which she had achieved her present state of eminence. Being a "woman artist" in my aunt's time carried a stigma, something to be battled and overcome.

Cecilia had won the battle. But I cannot say I loved her. It has been remarked that all genius has in it something monstrous, and in truth Aunt Cecilia possessed a self-absorption which at the same time attracted and repelled, bringing to mind Nietzsche's remark about "the artist's egotism, which shines like brass and will not be denied." I remembered an incident at Cecilia's household in Gloucester, when my sister Ernesta fell on the stairs one morning and broke an arm. She told me it never occurred to her to call Aunt Cecilia, who was down the hill in the studio with a sitter. Ernesta had been well trained; *nobody* interrupted those working hours. My sister telephoned a doctor and was at the hospital by noon when Cecilia returned to the house — nor did Ernesta resent the incident. Caring for the sick or the heedless was not Cecilia's business. That lay elsewhere. We all knew this and respected it.

With me, Aunt Cecilia had never permitted an intimacy or scarcely a friendship. Yet her courage and steadfastness of purpose had been before me always. By the time of that final visit, having published three books and launched myself on a fourth, I knew something of the passion that informs the artist's life, the risks Cecilia had taken, the things she must have denied herself. Over the years she and I had developed a sparring relationship. Harry told me she was jealous of me — palpable nonsense and I told him so but he stuck to it. "You're coming up, Katz," he said. "She sees it." This made me acutely uncomfortable. I could not but notice that when Cecilia told a witty story she looked at me warily and looked away. If she forgot and addressed herself to me she was apt afterward to say something faintly disagreeable, calculated no doubt to put me down. In the mornings when I disappeared upstairs with my typewriter Aunt Cecilia showed restlessness and made veiled remarks about certain daughters who lived at home and devoted themselves wholly to their aging parents, plainly, a reference to west Spruce Street in Grandma Leavitt's advanced age, when the Beaux sisters took care of her.

I had trouble keeping a straight face. "You old Tartar!" I

wanted to shout. "You know very well it was the other way round. Don't pull my leg, Auntie; you and I are too much alike for cozening."

None of these encounters, however, detracted from the magnetism, indeed the inspiration, of Aunt Cecilia's presence. Her strength flowed out; her vision of the world and of beauty held contagion. My debt to her was great; also her obvious affection for my mother touched me. The Merion visits were annual; I had been through them before and looked with some apprehension upon this one — not for my own sake but for my parents and the household. The Beaux sisters, superficially alike in temperament in that they were quick to show amusement or irritation, wrote affectionate brief letters while they were apart, saying they longed to see each other. I think they meant it, but I think also the feeling was compounded more of what had happened in the remote past than of what they saw as they faced each other, when a series of small explosions resulted, like the setting off of those old-fashioned firecrackers that came in packs on a single fuse and popped off one by one. My father accepted these visitations as he accepted old age or a stormy day — something to be endured without complaint. The Cecilia of 1938 was indubitably remote from the girl he had proposed to; Papa retreated to his study and let commotion rage. During my childhood a significant conversation had taken place in the spare bedroom at Bethlehem, with Aunt Cecilia standing before the oval pier glass arranging her evening dress, and my mother watching. At the time I set it all down in my diary, with angry expletives because Aunt Cecilia, accepting Mamma's compliments on her figure, had remarked that of course, Etta, you can't expect to keep your figure after having six children. "And two miscarriages," my mother added. She always included these as if they counted with the other trophies. "But Etta," my aunt continued, "you chose the better part in life. Think of Harry and six children! Every woman in the world can envy you Harry and those four sons."

It fascinated me to hear my father so called; my mother usually addressed him as Father, or Papa. "No, no, sister," my mother replied. "*You* chose the better part. Imagine staying in the White House and painting the President's wife! Oh, my life has been humdrum, compared with it. Think of living in Paris, and all the fine people you know!"

When my mother spoke of fine people she did not refer to character. It was a phrase she clung to even in old age. I used to wonder at it, seeing by that time my mother had herself traveled over most of the habitable globe, lived well enough at home and could meet whom she chose in society or out of it. Her shyness before the fashionable world distressed me a little; as a child I had felt offended that she should humble herself with Aunt Cecilia. To this particular conversation there was no ending, nor did it ever become resolved, but from time to time the discussion repeated itself. There could be no doubt of Mamma's pride in her celebrated sister. Yet she gave indication of dreading the annual visits; I think Aunt Cecilia still made her feel shy. When she came from New York Cecilia always brought her maid, Anna Murphy, a red-haired woman whom her mistress bullied and cajoled and who had lived with her some forty years. I often wanted to ask Anna why she stayed on and put up with such treatment, but of course I never did. We used to hear laughter from the kitchen in the late mornings when Anna sat having tea with Bridget and

Mary — explosive screams of Irish mirth. I knew perfectly well
that Anna was telling stories about her employer. No doubt she
recruited her spirit that way, getting ready for the twice-daily ordeal of doing my aunt's hair — twenty minutes of controlled strife
so intense one marveled the two of them survived it. Mamma said
Cecilia couldn't do her own hair because she had rheumatism in
her arms and it hurt to lift them. Nobody believed this for a minute, but it was not to be gainsaid.

The day of that last, fateful arrival dawned cold and windy.
Behind the house my father's young maples flamed; on the side
porch, dry leaves blew and gathered in corners by the rail. It was
my aunt's custom to arrive about teatime, in an old bright blue
Packard touring car, driven from New York by an admirer. Cecilia
and the admirer occupied the front, which was enclosed in rain-
proof curtains with windows set in. Anna Murphy sat in back,
carrying a folded steamer rug and a French clock in a leather
case. The steamer rug was "something to throw over you," but
why they traveled with the clock I never understood. The exact
mate of it stood on Mamma's bedroom mantel and struck the
hours; every summer she carried it to Beach Haven. Concerning
the admirer, my aunt had possessed these willing followers ever
since I could remember — ten or twenty years her junior as the
case might be. Most of them were noticeably good-looking; my
aunt did not like to be with ill-favored people. Long ago I had
heard her tell my debutante sister, Ernesta, that when a woman
reached a certain age she might expect well-mannered young men
would send roses and take her to Sunday concerts at Carnegie
Hall.

My aunt's penchant for good-looking people was, as I earlier intimated, a trifle hard on the rest of us. I never saw her do it to a man, but when introduced to a woman she stared, squinting a little, her head and body drawn back. I knew that sooner or later we would hear the familiar comment about bones. Never mind the complexion. It was the set of the eyes that mattered and the proportion of brow to cheek, the way the head grew out of the neck and upper shoulders. When my brother Phil became engaged he took his fiancée to call on Aunt Cecilia. Sue was a shy young woman from Providence, Rhode Island, fair-haired and blue-eyed, with a pretty complexion and a tendency to plumpness. For this *visite de cérémonie* she had dressed carefully. "Take off your hat," my aunt commanded at once, as my sister-in-law entered the house. "Now, lift your hair from your ears . . . so!" Cecilia took Sue's head in her fingers, turned it, and told her it was the distance between the ears and the top of the head that counted. "That's where one can tell if there is room for brains."

When my sister-in-law got home she took a ruler and measured her head, though, having nothing to compare it with, the figures gave no comfort. The part about brains did not bother her; Sue knew her own intelligence. What irked was my aunt's assumption that in this case intelligence alone needed measuring. Plainly, Cecilia saw no other qualities.

To my mother, these tricks and manners of her sister seemed in no way peculiar. Cecilia was a painter and that accounted for everything, even exteme ruthlessness toward the female young. My mother never spoke of her sister as an artist; like the household on west Spruce Street, our Merion family had scarcely heard the words, "artistic temperament." Being a painter meant hard

209

work; being a good painter, even harder work — a fact which admitted no indulgence of disposition or character.

It was a Monday of October, 1938, when we looked for the blue Packard containing Cecilia Beaux, the admirer, Anna Murphy, the steamer rug and the clock. As my mother permitted no housework on Sundays, the elaborate preparations of Friday and Saturday must now be supervised for flaws and the final touches set. From breakfast on, the rooms were noisy with carpet sweepers and the shifting of furniture. If my mother had expected President Roosevelt himself she could not have made more fuss. Chairs blocked the upstairs hall; the red satin comforter made its appearance, smelling of camphor, also the best silver tea set and a golden oak commode from the attic, the spare bathroom being "too far for Cecilia at night."

In midmorning the chaise longue was dragged out of my room for Aunt Cecilia's use, and one of the Chinese sofas substituted, carried all the way from the first floor. My mother had two of these sofas and prized them greatly. Grandpa Drinker had brought them from Macao in the 1840s, together with carved picture frames, mirrors, chests with double doors and two magnificent Lowestoft urns which sat on top of a bookcase in the library. The sofas were teakwood, with flat low arms and cane seats, impossible to sit on for more than ten minutes; the backs had an inset elaborately carved, depicting a fight between a knight and a dragon. Since childhood I had thought the sofas marvelous and had been shocked when my sister Ernesta said she hated them and Chinese import furniture was hideous and she wished Mamma would take them out of the living room and put them upstairs somewhere. I think my mother let herself be shaken by these strictures; she had great respect for Ernesta's taste. One of the sofas, at least, always vanished upstairs when Aunt Cecilia came.

About noon on that October day I went downstairs, looking for a quiet place to work and carrying my typewriter, a portable, with me. I passed Mary McClafferty in the hall helping my mother straighten a heavy picture on the wall. I stopped to help and suggested to Mamma that at this rate she would be worn out before Aunt Cecilia got here. She looked vaguely at me, flicked the frame with her duster and told Mary sharply to tilt the picture farther to the right. I was headed for the maids' sitting room, a quiet place behind the kitchen, giving on the back yard. But when I got there I found my father sitting by the window in an old Morris chair, reading *Captain Fracasse*, a book to which he often turned in times of stress. It was a picaresque novel by Gautier, published in an English translation. When my father saw me he smiled, raising both hands in a gesture of resignation, said not to go away, my typing wouldn't disturb him, and did I think Mamma would survive Cecilia's visit, this time. Pans of dough were rising on the windowsill; Bridget the cook came to look at them. At her suggestion I carried my typewriter up the back stairs to the maids' bathroom and worked there until lunchtime. But I worried about Mary. How much harassment would that Irish temperament stand? During my aunt's visits Mary made life possible for all of us. The household understood that Miss Beaux must not be annoyed by the sound of crying or quarreling children.When a fight started, upstairs or down, Mary materialized faster than a fireman at a fire. "Look quick!" she would say, her voice cheerful above the tumult. "There's a big bird climbin' up the rain spout!" Everyone rushed to the window, grievances forgotten. No bird could be seen, but for some reason nobody felt cheated. "Maybe it was an eagle," my son would say, peering up at Mary. "An eagle sure enough," Mary would reply confidently. "Musta slid down before we got to it. Or like it was a big gray owl."

My mother usually had her tea about four o'clock in her bedroom, on a little round table by the fireplace. But this afternoon I found her downstairs, seated on the living room sofa in a tea gown, the fire laid but not lighted, the silver service doing us all credit. My father sat having his tea; this time he was reading *Barnaby Rudge,* though my mother, in her excitement at the impending arrival, kept up a running conversation with anyone who would listen. My son, seated by her, for some reason had been given his tea in a bowl. As I entered the room he looked up. "Grandma says," he announced, "she wishes there were more adverbs in this family."

"Well!" my mother said, with intense emphasis. "When I was young, people didn't say 'Go slow' and they didn't say 'Eat quick.' I don't think they should say it now."

My mother gave me tea; her hand was shaking and I saw that her own cup had not been used. It was late, nearly five, I said. Hadn't she better have a cup before Aunt Cecilia got here? My mother shook her head vigorously. When the doorbell rang she didn't want to have anything in her hand. She wanted to be the first one in the hallway to greet her sister.

"You mean you want to get there quick, Grandma," my son said fiendishly. My father looked up; he never permitted impudence from the young. But when Mamma laughed he looked down again and turned the page. I said I would sit by the window and watch for the car, and rose to take up my station. At this moment the front door burst open, there was commotion in the hall and my aunt's voice, high and filled with pleasure, called out, "Etta, Etta, Harry, here we are! Oh, *here* we are!"

My aunt had not been with us a week when she fell ill. I cannot remember the actual onset of her illness, if it came at once or by degrees. She lay in the brass bed by the spare room wall, facing the door, so that when we passed we could see her, propped on pillows, her eyes closed, her face quite gray. Fred Sharpless said she had lobar pneumonia. It was a day before penicillin, and no questioning the seriousness of the disease. The word hospital did not pass our lips. A day nurse and a night nurse arrived in white dresses, carrying suitcases, and at once the household changed tone, revolving around the sickroom. Every morning I did the marketing and the drugstore errands. The day nurse, Miss Mercer, a North of Ireland Protestant, seemed to us altogether competent and kind. Yet the kitchen hated her with a malignancy unparalleled, and I believe balked and impeded her to the best of their ability. The night nurse, Mrs. O'Hara, a good Roman, was a complete idiot and got on perfectly backstairs. One morning I found a pudding pan, filled with water, under the bed; Mrs. O'Hara said she had put it there to draw the patient's sweat. When I told my aunt's maid, Anna Murphy, she nodded approvingly and said she knowed the minute she laid eyes on Mrs. O'Hara that the woman had mother wit about her.

It was my first experience with what seemed mortal illness in the house; I never ceased to be surprised at the way my parents reacted. My mother promptly caught cold and went to bed. My brother Jim came to see her, with his customary offering, a tight bunch of violets ornamented with a paper lace doily. I can't imagine where he found these; they had long since gone out of style.

Jim lived across the Schuylkill, now, in Jenkintown with his wife and children. He was in his early fifties and had grown handsomer with age. He wore a moustache, dark brown; his brown hair was clipped *en brosse* and he affected bright bow ties that matched the handkerchief in his breast pocket. Jim had a sporty look — the only one of my brothers who cared for dress. He was thin and broad-shouldered and on weekends rowed a single scull from the Barge Club on the Schuylkill; in younger days Jim had been keen for racing.

He kissed my mother, then walked agitatedly up and down the room. "Now, Ma," he said. "Don't worry too much about Beaux. We don't want you to worry." My mother lifted her shoulders under her long-sleeved white nightgown. "To tell the truth, children," she said, "I don't think I'm as worried as I ought to be." The candor of this was startling, nobody made a reply.

My aunt's illness did not run a straight course; she would be better one day and worse the next. Dr. Sharpless, our family physician, had been at Haverford College with Harry and Jim; he was Harry's classmate and we called him Fred. One afternoon Fred came out of the sickroom shaking his head. He said he would go home now, but be back later. Then he walked downstairs to my father's study and spoke to him. When Fred had gone Papa went to the dining room and poured himself a stiff drink of whiskey, took it to the study and sat down in his deep chair by the light. He called me to him. "Well," he said slowly, "I guess Cecilia's time has come." He picked up a book and opened it, then asked if I had read *Captain Fracasse;* he thought it the best book ever written. Did I remember the place where the captain engaged Agostino in a duel on the highroad? If I had a moment, he'd like to read it to me. I could hear my children's voices upstairs and knew that I was wanted, but I closed the hall door and sat down by the desk. "The Captain had quietly drawn his sword," my father's voice began, "and attacked the bandit furiously. Agostino skillfully parried his thrusts. . . ."

I have the book now, a handsome edition in green boards, two volumes, with my father's signature on the flyleaf. I am not at all sure Papa really looked on *Captain Fracasse* as the best book ever written, but I know it served him well. I knew also, that afternoon while he was reading, that if Fred had come in and told my father his own time had come — not Aunt Cecilia's — Papa would have received the news as easily.

My mother recovered from her cold, my children went back and forth to school as usual, but a hush had fallen over the house. On our third floor we did not run the water for baths because the pipes banged. My children tiptoed to bed, their room being directly over my aunt's, and the second-floor landing stayed dark because light shone in the patient's face when the sickroom door opened. My son spent his time in the back kitchen with Mary Mc-Clafferty, listening to football games on the radio. These he eagerly discussed at breakfast, bringing up names like Whizzer White and Bulldog Turner. My mother said a trifle crossly one morning that they were all border ruffians, at which my son, his eyes wide with indignation, put down his spoon and turned red in the face. Mary, passing behind him with a plate of toast, laid a hand on his shoulder and said something about keeping quiet now, with the poor lady upstairs dyin'. This being a word we had all avoided, the boy was shocked into silence.

My daughter seized the moment to put a riddle to my father. "Grandpa," she said, "what is the longest word in the Bible?"

"Metempsychosis?" my father said, smiling. I remarked that I had never heard the word. "What!" my mother said. "You a literary person, and you don't know the doctrine of metempsychosis?"

When my mother called someone a literary person she did not always mean it as a compliment. Since youth she had been surrounded by "literary persons," notably Aunt Kate, who had lived out her old age in my parents' house. I let the remark pass, this time, and asked about metempsychosis. Was it a doctrine?

"A doctrine or a delusion," my mother said at once, and told me to go get the dictionary, the big one.

My daughter said the big dictionary was in Aunt Cecilia's sitting room, and we let the subject drop.

During these weeks and days it seemed as if all subjects were thus at half-mast, everything stopped in midstream. The household was not gloomy, but when we laughed we caught ourselves; if the children fell or hurt themselves they threw their hands over their mouths, their eyes turned toward the sickroom. At the height of my aunt's illness, one incident bade fair to progress into a real row. My son belonged to a sixty-pound football team at school, a fact in which he took inordinate pride. Every night he carried his football helmet to bed and put his feet in it; he said it kept his toes warm. My mother liked to come upstairs and say good night; the first time she saw this performance she cried out indignantly. That muddy helmet must come out of the bed! Ezzy scrambled from under the covers, clutched the helmet to his chest and began to jump up and down furiously on the mattress; in another moment he would be yelling. Aunt Cecilia's bed lay, as I have said, directly underneath. My mother turned and fled — a retreat which astonished everybody. But we all knew the subject would come up again, Aunt Cecilia or no Aunt Cecilia. I underestimated, however, my mother's talent for strategy. Next evening she reappeared with an odd-looking garment in her hands, made of calico, maroon and white, my son's school colors. "I have made a nightgown for your helmet," she told him. To my surprise the boy accepted it, with the proviso that we were not to tell Jackie, next door.

My aunt, by now, was actually beyond disturbance. She did not know us, and a child's cry, if it reached her, would have come from very far away. I remember thinking that if I were that old woman, so fearfully alone in the brass bed by the wall, a child's cry would come to me like salvation, the touch and remembrance of earth. Outside the house, leaves scattered; November winds rattled the glass doors to the living room. Each day before lunch my mother walked briefly up and down the side porch, a scarf around her head. It rested her, she said; at noon she took an old cushion and sat on the porch steps in the sun. And though, indoors, she always had work at hand, sewing or knitting, in the open air she was quiet. "When I have been sitting in the sun for an hour," she told me, "I feel as if I had accomplished something."

In the mornings after breakfast, my mother would call softly from her bedroom as I went up the stairs, and ask me to stop. Before I could sit down she would begin to talk about the household on west Spruce Street, sixty, seventy years ago, when she and Aunt Cecilia were young. It was as if remembering would hold back death, I thought. The bedroom walls were thick with photographs, paintings, daguerreotypes: Uncle Will with sidewhiskers, leaning on a table; Aunt Emily in white stock and silk shirtwaist, looking benign; Grandma Leavitt knitting in her rocking chair, an ivied wall behind her. Grandpa Beaux standing eas-

217

ily, fingers at his watch chain. My father at forty seated by a desk, his chin in his hand, looking intellectual. Harry at twenty-two, resplendent in City Troop uniform; Phil in sailor suit and round hat, holding a baseball bat. Myself playing the violin at eighteen; Cecil at all ages, his ears sticking out.

I went up and downstairs from the sickroom, doing what I could. My aunt's maid, Anna Murphy, was no good at all, she seemed seized with paralysis and could think of nothing but to dust the furniture, which the nurses would not permit. At Fred Sharpless's insistence my mother did not cross the threshold. But she used to stand in the doorway, looking at the bed and the room. Once, when we thought Aunt Cecilia unconscious, her eyes opened and she saw her sister. To our astonishment she raised both hands from the cover, palms up, then let them drop; my mother answered in kind. The mutual gesture needed no words, but when my mother went back to her room she wept a little, the only time I saw her in tears during her sister's illness.

My brother Harry was very close to Aunt Cecilia; the two had a quick understanding. Like Cecil, Harry called her Beaux, and she adored him. Every afternoon on his way from Merion Station, Harry stopped at our house, after his custom. I am sure that Aunt Cecilia's illness depressed him more than it did any of us. When he came he went straight upstairs and saw the nurse, asked what the doctor had said today, then came down and stood in the doorway of the living room with his brown felt hat in his hands, looking troubled and waiting for us to say something.

I was uneasy at his agitation. It seemed to me that a man who knew so much about everything must surely know about death, too, and dying. Sophie had said it would be a calamity if Beaux recovered. Pneumonia often left people with weak hearts, and wouldn't it be simple hell for everybody? She said Beaux had been difficult enough before her illness.

This was entirely true, though none of us would have voiced it. My sister-in-law believed in euthanasia and the lethal cup; she said that when she got old and ill she was going to take a pill and have it over with. We had grown so used to the notion that Aunt Cecilia would die that I was the more surprised, one afternoon, when Harry came down from the sickroom, stood as usual in the doorway and announced that he did not think Beaux was about to die at all. If she had held out this long she could hold out another ten years.

"You know about my automobile license numbers?" he went on immediately, addressing himself to me. I wondered at this irrelevancy but said yes, I knew about them. Harry had been counting license plate numbers for nobody knew how long, trying to get an unbroken series from one to a thousand. He did it mostly in town, walking along Chestnut Street, to and from the Pennsylvania Station to his law office, mornings and afternoons. "Well," he said now, looking at me and frowning, "I always knew that when I reached a thousand, something terrible would happen in the family." He had been at it for two years, he said. Ten days ago he had reached 999. He knew the Wanamaker delivery wagon had a thousand on it, one of his partners had told him. That was its number, one thousand. Next day was Tuesday. "I walked three blocks out of my way," Harry continued, "so as not to see it. Wednesday, too. Thursday I saw it. That's more than a week ago, and nothing's happened."

My brother turned on his heel and without another word walked out of the house. "He's crazy," my father said, mildly. "Harry has ability, no doubt of it, but he's crazy. What is he talk-

ing about, with these automobile numbers? He didn't say good
night to you, Etta." My father turned to me. "It's an odd thing," he
said, "but none of my sons has any manners."

Mamma could not endure to hear her children criticized. I
waited for her outburst but it did not come. "The automobile
numbers are just a game," she said. "Papa, haven't you ever played
games? If you haven't, it's time you began." She put down her
knitting. "But if Harry doesn't think Cecilia is going to die, then I
believe I won't think so either."

Aunt Cecilia did not die. She lifted her head one morning, said
she was hungry and asked where they had put her crutch. For
some time she stayed upstairs. The pudding pan vanished from
beneath the bed, the nurses departed, and Anna Murphy, recalled
from the back kitchen, took over. Swathed in shawls my aunt sat
up in bed, her head wrapped coquettishly in a yellow chiffon
scarf, with a scalawag bow over one eye. At her insistence the
room was kept at eighty-odd by means of two electric stoves. How
we lived through that time of convalescence I do not know. Aunt
Cecilia, who in pain and danger had been stoical, showed herself
querulous now and demanding beyond reason. Soup was too thick
or too thin, her tea too strong, milk tasted of garlic, and with three
maids in the kitchen, wasn't it possible, Etta (my aunt said), to
have something on the lunch tray beside this same faded doily?

My mother trembled with rage, demanded to see the doily, and
when it was not forthcoming, left the room. Somehow the days
passed and my aunt, fully recovered, prepared for her return trip
to New York in the blue Packard. I did not know that I should
never see her again, though she had six years of active life before
her and would outlive my mother. Two things stand clearly in my

mind: the moment when Aunt Cecilia, pausing in the hallway the morning of her departure, laid her hand on my arm and remarked, "This household is quite a burden for those thin shoulders of yours." Had she crowned me with laurel I could not have been more astonished. In all my life it was the first word she had given me of encouragement or affection. And the final tableau of the two sisters, sitting on the Chinese sofa in our living room, the tea things in front of them, my mother bolt upright, Aunt Cecilia with one hand on her crutch and their voices chanting in unison. They were reciting the Shorter Catechism, as they had learned it for Aunt Emily in their youth. My mother put the queries and together they said the answers, their voices bright with pleasure at the mutual feat of memory, and my aunt, when she forgot a phrase, giggling like a girl at my mother's prompting:

"What is the chief end of man?"
"Man's end is to glorify God, and to enjoy him forever."
"What is the preface to the ten commandments?"
"The preface to the ten commandments is in these words: I am the LORD thy God, which have brought thee out of the land of Egypt, out of the house of bondage. . . ."

XIII

Philip, Cecil and Katherine

A MONG the five: Harry, Jim, Cecil, Ernesta, and Philip —
the only one that in youth I met on terms of equality
was Phil, three years my senior, a hearty, noisy boy
with blue eyes, a fair complexion, wavy brown hair, and feet so
big we thought he would never grow up to them. I remember Phil
at Bethlehem, yelling happily among a troop of friends called
Bummy or Eddie or Mickey, with footballs or catchers' mitts in
their hands. At twelve, Phil went away to school in New England,
then to Princeton, so that afterward I saw him only briefly, during
the holidays or at Beach Haven in summer. But I know that our
early association consisted of my badgering Phil and his friends to
let me play with them — just maybe run after balls in the out-
field? — and being told all right, but if the ball comes your way
for God's sake *throw* it and don't fumble round. As Phil grew into
his late teens, his friends inevitably fell in love with Ernesta.
Everybody became used to it, so that when, one day, I showed off

a box of candy and said Bummy gave it to me, Phil stopped dead in his tracks and said incredulously, "Bummy gave you that? What *for?*"

Physically Phil and Cecil bore a strong family resemblance, with the Drinker long jaw and high cheekbones. Phil however was not wiry and quick-moving and stiff-haired like Cecil but much taller, a good six feet two, with big shoulders and a rangy look about him. Also, from youth onward Phil showed himself amenable, biddable; when he shouted at me it didn't mean a thing and I would shout back. Mamma used to say her fourth son's good nature made people take advantage of him; she told Bridget in the kitchen to stop sending Philly to the store at Beach Haven every time she needed bread or eggs.

As for Cecil, he was a year old, in 1888, when his brother Jim, aged six, managed a brief note to Cecilia Beaux in Paris: "Dearest Aunty, When we say Nononono to baby he says Ahaaaa very loud, the bad thing. Kisses from Jamie." It was a prophecy; all his life if people said Nononono, Cecil spurned them; he could never be gainsaid. In the end we were to see him conquered and defeated by his own nature, utterly routed and put down. Yet no matter what befell in those tragic latter days, Cecil remained the strongest influence in my life; I have been astonished at hearing a like acknowledgment from at least half a dozen men, once his students, now moving in exalted research circles of medicine, physiology or surgery. Cecil was the star by which my compass swung, the hero whom I worshipped from the unbridgeable distance of his ten years' seniority. The tales of heroism that Cecil read aloud in the billiard room at Bethlehem in some indefinable way showed me that dedication to work, with all the risks of complete immersion, could be a goal in itself, for girls as well as men. To keep the faith meant using oneself to capacity; anything less was pusillanimous, a betrayal.

Cecil and Phil spent their working lives as research professors, first in the Harvard Medical School, then in the closely affiliated School of Public Health — a graduate college for physicians and those in allied professions. The brothers became equally distinguished in their fields, even though, as I later learned, they looked on life from very different angles. Cecil liked his days to be planned ahead, organized. For him this added to the excitement; you divided up the hours and then followed through, racing with yourself, with time — as it were with destiny.

Phil on the other hand banged along, enjoying life as it came; in college he was known as the noisiest man on campus. When Phil took the train for Princeton as an entering freshman, Cecil saw him off from Bethlehem and gave him a talk about "how to get ahead at college." "But I didn't *want* to get ahead," Phil told me, long afterward. "I just wanted the fellows to like me." After Princeton, Phil discussed with his father a possible career, saying he thought of becoming a mining engineer, the way Pa had started out. Papa said that was fine, if a man didn't mind living all over the habitable globe, in Peru, Chile, Montana or wherever the mines were. Why didn't Phil choose chemical engineering? Then he could raise a family and stay in one place. So Phil enrolled at Lehigh and took a graduate degree in chemical engineering, just in time to put on a uniform, attend training camp and go overseas with the army. Cecil, already teaching physiology at Harvard, remained exempt in both world wars. At twenty-three he had suffered a ruptured appendix and subsequent operations for adhesions. Four long, purple scars ran down his stomach; in medical school he used to be asked to display them in the showers. One of his close friends, Dr. Stanley Cobb the neurologist, told me that was how he first met Cecil; Cobb saw those scars in the shower room and couldn't believe it. "I have," Cecil wrote in his diary, "an abdominal wall that would scare any medical examiner to Jericho."

During that first illness, Cecil had lain in a second-floor bedroom of Curlew Cottage, waiting for the train to take him from Beach Haven to Philadelphia, no ambulance being available. The marvel was he lived through it, those being the days before antibiotics. Early in the morning after the initial attack, Harry led Ernesta and me into the tiny living room, pointed to the sofa and told us to kneel in front of it. I was thirteen. When Ernesta hesitated, Harry put his hands on her shoulders and pushed her down, then knelt by me. "Now, PRAY!" he said.

Four years later, Cecil was graduated from medical school, and I sat with Mamma in the auditorium at the University of Pennsylvania. Out of four prizes announced by the president, Cecil received three; he had led his class through the entire course, with an average of 99, never before achieved at the school. Even Harry had not equaled this record. Yet to me it did not seem out of the way; I had long ago envisioned this world's prizes as part of Cecil's destiny. On the train going home to Bethlehem I said so. Mamma shook her head and replied that prizes are well enough, but sooner or later Cecil had better let go; there was such a thing as being stretched to the breaking point. I set it down in my diary with the remark that Ma was just being silly.

Cecil was barely thirty when he found himself assistant professor and acting head of the department of physiology at the Har-

Cecil, aged forty, in Dr. Krogh's laboratory at Copenhagen.

vard Medical School. There was little doubt about his having "stretched himself." Cecil had been married for eight years. His wife, Katherine, a brilliant woman, herself a physician, worked by his side in the laboratory. The two had met in the spring of 1908. By August they were engaged, though the prospect of marriage remained far off, Cecil being a first-year medical student and Katherine Rotan a junior at Bryn Mawr College. In those days it was unthinkable for a man to marry until he could "support a wife." With Cecil living in West Philadelphia, Katherine on the Bryn Mawr campus, scarcely an automobile on the roads, and telephones used only for emergency — fixed to the wall in some public place — the lovers communicated by keeping diaries. Every night the two set down their thoughts and what the day had brought forth, addressing one another as if they were writing letters. On Sundays they met and exchanged books.

I don't see how two young people could have been harderworking, or more passionately in love. Cecil was twenty-one; Katherine, nineteen — a Texas girl, from Waco, very definitely among President M. Carey Thomas's "new women," entertaining no doubts about her chosen career of medicine, though fully aware this would have to be accomplished against parental disapproval on both sides. To the very altar steps my mother remained sure Katherine would "give up this notion of being a woman doctor." After all, she was a handsome girl, with a good figure, warm brown eyes, a ready laugh, a pleasant outgoing manner — and frivolous enough to love buying hats. What did such a young woman need with a "career"? Cecil aided and abetted his fiancée's ambitions, protesting that he could truly admire this kind of woman. Up to 1908 he had courted a variety of girls, but when he met Katherine, Cecil said vehemently that this one was altogether different. "The real thing, Katz! A worker. None of this 'coming out' nonsense for her."

"Oh, Kath!" Cecil wrote in the diary. "I think there is nothing like being in love for happiness. Sometimes I long for the careless days at College [Haverford] and then suddenly I think, Why you fool they weren't anything. You didn't know what life meant at all."

"Oh, Cecil, Cecil," Katherine replied, "sometimes it seems almost as if I shall be completely carried away by my love for you. Every time I see you it seems greater, and always when I'm with you I have the most blissful feeling of being taken care of. We college women may be learned and independent and all that, but first of all we're women, Goodnight, sweetheart."

Katherine Rotan Drinker became my friend and remained so for nearly fifty years; first and last, I have never known a woman to be so much in love. Cecil reciprocated with equal fervor. Moreover he *liked* Katherine, the two were wonderfully companionable. Indeed it would be hard to say, in those early days, which of the two was the more ardent or the more believing. As for Katherine's feeling that she was "being taken care of," it is an illusion that comes easily to women in love. Cecil possessed a lightning sympathy and perception of one's feelings — a most intoxicating experience, coming from the opposite sex. "First of all we're women," is a dangerous doctrine; it implies a coy acceptance of captivity. Cecil knew how to build up a person; in his company one felt at one's best and better. But Cecil could also destroy. He was a people-eater, devouring those he loved — and in the end, Katherine let it happen. I used to wonder why this woman, who at col-

Phil

lege never had a day's illness, rejoicing over her sound body and her athletic prowess — why in middle age she suffered from "back trouble," dizziness, disturbance of the inner ear and a host of physical ills. Month after month she lay in bed, uncomplaining, yet giving way at times to storms of weeping. The year before she died, Katherine told me she had reached sixty before it occurred to her that Cecil was not always right.

The early diaries, however, hold no hint of such matters; they are eager, hopeful. Cecil gives evidence of that joy in work which his students were later to find so contagious.

January 19, 1909:

"I went out early and bought a beef heart I ordered on Saturday. At the School we dissected it thoroughly. I've never really seen one inside before. Its the first organ we've had. The wonder of it, Kath, has sent me walking on air all day. Have you ever attempted to make something and seen some one else's work that was absolutely so perfect and beautiful it filled you with the greatest admiration and respect? Today I've seen something beyond all making of men and it's made me feel past anything of man's mere handiwork."

Katherine, January 20:

"The mice were fine. We chloroformed them and cut them open. We simply must do a dog at Easter, dear. Goodnight, K."

Cecil, January 22:

"Success in the quizzes is going to come from going slow and keeping cool. It's quite a sporting proposition. Yet, 'from the unhappy desire of becoming great, Good Lord deliver me' — is not for me to say any more. Its the part of me that's gone because of you, Kath. And it's the part Ma used to fear."

Actually the "unhappy desire" was not gone. Katherine could no more have exorcised that devil than she could have caused her lover to grow a third hand. Cecil's ambition was insatiable; and the demands he put upon others were to be matched and over-matched by his demands upon himself. Yet how he enjoyed the game, as he called it! "Piersol examined us today on both arm and leg. We fairly ate it alive. It was good fun. I was almost sorry when he said, 'Get out.'"

January 26, 1909:

"The game's all played, Kath, with the first half year of anatomy. I couldn't tell you, dear, if I wanted, what my mark is. I knew it all, but I was terribly hurried. My, I have enjoyed it, Kath! What an almighty lot of work we'll do if we get loose together!"

And they did work well together; Cecil's joyful prophecy was to be fulfilled. By February 2, Cecil had his anatomy marks. "I got 95," he wrote. His fellow students approached him in the halls and asked his help about a coming chemistry quiz: "They inquired humbly and I could not understand it at all. O Kath but it's queer to be up front in this kind of a game. I've never felt it before. You must jump on me hard when Saturday comes, and remind me al-ways to be careful or I shall go to pieces from being too much pleased. I grinned inwardly and happily all day. Where O where are the high ideals of learning for its own sake, you say. Be lenient, Kath, for this is my first offense. I've never before had a chance for such a feeling."

Whenever the two scored a personal triumph — Cecil's high marks, Katherine's election as president of her class — they deluded themselves into thinking "success" might induce their families to let them marry. "We're not doing badly for a hopelessly ruined engaged pair," Cecil wrote on one such occasion. "Let's keep it up, it's fun." Katherine visited her married sister in New York — Mrs. Frederick Peterson, wife of the neurologist. "Cecil dear," Katherine wrote, "what do you suppose Sister told me this afternoon? She said it wasn't often that a Texas girl had the opportunity I had of marrying into an old and distinguished family!!!! Coming round well, I guess. It was your father who did it, too. She thinks he's all to the good."

Very occasionally there was a holiday visit to Bethlehem. "At last it's come!" Cecil writes. "We're to have more time than we've had since Easter, two whole days and three nights." For modern lovers, two whole days and three nights would mean just that. For this pair it signified two whole days and parting at the foot of the stairs every evening. The amount of chaperonage these strong and passionate young people accepted, today seems incredible. One Christmas they planned to spend with the Rotans in Texas, which meant two days and nights on the train; they were ecstatic at the prospect. In the end Mrs. Rotan arranged to have a maiden aunt accompany them: "Daddy says we can't possibly be on that train by ourselves," Katherine wrote.

Cecil went again and again to his father and to Harry, trying to persuade them. "I see a way out of it," he wrote in the diary, "but it would mean trifling with many high things. I am in great doubt about what is honorable and proper for us to do."

233

Honorable and proper? Today the very words are outmoded. We wonder why the young couple did not openly rebel, and we ask if all this sexual frustration was not bad for them. "Oh Kath, Kath!" Cecil wrote. "Tonight I think I'll go to sleep just saying your name over and over. Oh Kath I love you. . . . Dr. Gwynne says I am too thin. He makes me eat raw eggs, an appalling dose. I say, 'Katherine!' shut my eyes and swallow one."

In June of 1910, Bryn Mawr College held its commencement as usual. The Sunday rotogravure section showed President Taft, shaking hands with M. Carey Thomas, and below them, "Katherine Livingston Rotan, President of the Senior Class," looking serious in cap and gown. Suddenly, the families capitulated; the marriage could take place in September. "The weight of years has lifted," wrote Cecil. "Today seems to have made the world over for me. My, what a lot of happy plans there are; my head fairly sings with them. Beaux has given us five hundred dollars. It means a good deal. She wants us to spend it on our work. Harry is engaged to Sophie Hutchinson and is so full of it he explodes at every step."

On the seventh of September, after an engagement lasting twenty-five interminable months, Cecil and Katherine were married at her parents' summer cottage near Gloucester, Massachusetts. The two made what they thought were final entries in the diary. "Now we are settled in our apartment near the School," Cecil wrote; "both of us studying medicine and more truly happy and contented than we have been in our lives. It passes all the dreams."

"Oh my husband, my husband, my husband!" wrote Katherine. "If only all the days of my life be as happy as these, while I am a bride."

After his graduation from medical school and residency at the Peter Bent Brigham Hospital in Boston, Cecil worked for a year with Dr. A. Newton Richards in his laboratory at the University of Pennsylvania, then with Dr. William H. Howell at Johns Hopkins. At twenty-nine, he was invited by the celebrated Dr. Walter B. Cannon to teach physiology at Harvard. This was 1916, and most of Europe at war. A few months after Cecil's arrival, Dr. Cannon left the Harvard Medical School, called to the European war theater to do research on shock from wounds. With two assistants, Cecil carried the full load of the department until Cannon's return two years later. Meanwhile the nearby Harvard School of Public Health got ready to open its doors, being engaged, among other matters, in developing methods for appraising the healthfulness or harmfulness of working conditions in mines and factories — a program that marked the beginnings of industrial hygiene in the United States. While physicians could diagnose a sick laborer, the initial preventive work needed engineers to devise machines for measuring dust in the atmosphere, or for making quantitative analyses of poisonous fumes encountered in certain factories.

Nowadays we have biochemists, biopsychologists and bioengineers. But such syntheses have taken half a century to develop. In 1916, Harvard research physiologists regarded the engineering sciences somewhat as philosophers of the sixteenth century looked on barber-surgeons — useful creatures but hardly to be included in the guild of scholars. When Cecil proposed the appointment of his brother Philip, he stepped across traditional academic lines.

Cecil and Phil, seven years apart in age, had seen little of each other during their lives until Phil, after graduating from Lehigh, happened to be employed as an erecting engineer for a factory near Boston. The brothers, meeting often, discussed the matter of harmful dust and fumes; Cecil asked if Phil would be interested in doing research on these problems. Phil said he would. In December, 1920, Cecil followed through with a telegram:

EXPECT YOU JANUARY 15 $250 A MONTH AND TITLE INSTRUCTOR IN APPLIED PHYSIOLOGY HARVARD MEDICAL SCHOOL DEPARTMENT OF APPLIED MEDICINE GOOD BUSINESS CECIL

By now, Dr. Cannon had returned from the war and resumed his place at the Harvard Medical School. The School of Public Health, ready for separate identity, moved to its own building, with Cecil as professor of applied physiology and assistant dean, under Dr. David L. Edsall. Phil, the only staff member who did not hold a medical degree, came in with the rather odd title of Instructor in Ventilation and Illumination. Cecil, upstairs in his laboratory, had some six years' headstart in the work. To Phil, aged twenty-six, Dean Edsall gave a free hand to design his own laboratory on the ground floor of the new building, choose his problems for experiment and put together the needed apparatus.

The brothers operated together yet independently, each in his field and workshop.

XIV

The Iron Lung. "Industrial Dust."

I N THE AUTUMN of 1926, Cecil and Katherine sailed off for a year's sabbatical in Copenhagen. They were to work in the laboratory of Dr. August Krogh, Nobel Laureate, celebrated for his researches on the capillary system. While they were away, Philip happened on something that would place him conspicuously — and to him surprisingly — in the limelight. He stood one morning in the laboratory, watching a colleague, Louis Agassiz Shaw, work on a device (originated by Cecil) to measure the breathing of an animal. A cat, anesthetized, lay in a metal box with its head outside, a rubber collar around its neck. Attached to the box was a U-shaped tube called a manometer, half filled with water. When the cat exhaled, the water rose in the tube, showing how much air had been displaced by the movement of the cat's chest. When the cat inhaled, the water went down. It occurred to Phil that if the animal were given curare sufficient to paralyze his breathing muscles, it might be possible to provide artificial

breathing by pumping air in and out of the box. With the cat prepared, Phil used a Luer syringe as a pump, connecting it to the
box by a hose. He pumped air into the box and the cat's chest
depressed; he withdrew the air — thus lifting the pressure — and
the cat's chest rose. "We found," Phil said, "that we could keep
paralyzed animals alive for hours."

Some time previously, the Consolidated Gas Company of New
York had financed a commission at the Rockefeller Institute, to
study methods of prolonged artificial respiration — an endow-
ment no less beneficial because its motivation was practical. (Gas
companies find themselves sued by people in whose houses gas
has escaped from a leaking pipe, or by families of those unfortunate persons who attempt suicide by sticking their heads into gas
ovens.) Phil had been appointed a member of this Rockefeller
commission. Up to now resuscitation had been achieved by pulmotor or by manual manipulation, methods exhausting to victim
and rescuers, impossible to continue for long at a time.

As soon as Phil and Louis Shaw were satisfied with their work,
Phil went to New York and explained the experiment to Consolidated Gas, adding that he thought the method might keep a
man alive as well as a cat. He would like to try, if the company
chose to provide funds. Consolidated Gas gave him about $500.
Phil took the money home and begain by asking a tinsmith to
make a box big enough for a man. A closet at the school contained
a number of secondhand vacuum cleaners, discarded by a company in New York state that manufactured industrial fans. With
two of these cleaner motors and a generous amount of adhesive
tape, Phil made a pump and hooked it to the box; he devised a
hand-operated valve that could blow air in and then suck out.

The principal difficulty now seemed to lie in the rubber collar

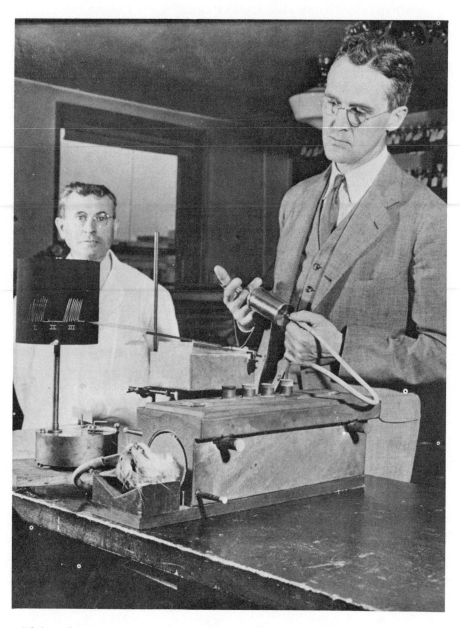

Phil working on the respirator, 1928. Louis Freni, laboratory diener, is at left.

around the subject's neck, which must be tight enough to insure a vacuum in the box, yet not tight enough to shut off circulation. Phil wrote to Cecil in Copenhagen, describing the experiment, and Cecil replied in no uncertain terms that Phil was wasting his time: the collar, if tight enough to maintain an adequate vacuum, would interfere with blood flow to the subject's brain. Dr. Krogh agreed, said Cecil.

All this activity — trial and error — consumed many months; indeed, it would be two years before the machine was perfected. To fit the rubber collar in place, Phil made a copper cone that went over the subject's head like a hat. Then he soaped the outside of the cone and shoved the rubber collar over it. When the collar reached the bottom of the cone, it snapped shut around the subject's neck. Phil then went out and borrowed from a local garage a mechanic's creeper. He lay down and was pushed into the box. His head stuck outside, resting on two big seat cushions placed on the laboratory floor.

At that first trial, when the rubber collar snapped shut around Phil's neck, he thought briefly of what Cecil and the great Krogh had said — but only briefly, being preoccupied with procedure. The pumps whined, pure oxygen entered Phil's lungs via something called a Benedict metabolism apparatus, which measured his oxygen consumption. The test was run for about fifteen minutes. When Louis Shaw stopped the machine, Phil's visible chest motion ceased for seven minutes, until CO_2 in the blood returned to the point where a breath was called for. "At that moment," says Phil's report, "I resumed regular breathing and we terminated the experiment."

The second man in the respirator was Luigi Freni, the laboratory *diener*, known and loved by a generation of Harvard researchers. (See photograph page 239.) Harvey Cushing, the brain surgeon, a professor at the Medical School, showed immediate interest in the respirator and was present when a third subject, young Professor Hatch, climbed in for testing.

It should be said also that while Phil was working on the respirator, Dr. Kenneth D. Blackfan, physician-in-chief at nearby Children's Hospital, came over to ask if something could be done for the hospital's prematurely born babies. Blackfan felt sure that atmospheric conditions had much to do with the survival of these "preemies." The body temperature of babies *in utero* rises or falls with the mother's temperature. Preemies cannot regulate their own bodies to the normal 98–99 degrees and so tend to die unless the environment is regulated for them. Phil suggested building a special air-conditioned room, helped to raise money and persuaded various gas and electric companies to give fans, blowers and insulating material. Under the direction of Phil's young associate, Constantin P. Yaglou, the room was built and the babies placed in it. During the night, if the room's temperature fell half a degree, the nurses called Phil by telephone and he rushed over to make adjustments.

On his way through the wards, Phil saw children dying of suffocation, induced by polio; he could not forget the small blue faces, the terrible gasping for air. The respirator had not been designed specifically for infantile paralysis. Yet when the machine was perfected, the first patient happened to be a little girl from Children's Hospital, suffering from severe polio and expected to be in respiratory difficulty very shortly. Phil had the machine moved into the ward near the child's bed so she could see it and get used to the loud whine of the motor. Early next Sunday morning the hospital called Phil. By the time he reached the child she was in the machine, unconscious, but the staff had been afraid to turn on the power. Phil started the pump, and in less than a minute saw the child regain consciousness. She asked for ice cream. Phil said he stood there and cried.

This was in 1929. So far, only one respirator existed, belonging to Harvard, costing $2000 to build and containing a cot on which the patient lay. The second person to go in was a Harvard senior named Barret Hoyt, brought to the Peter Bent Brigham Hospital with polio. Young Hoyt was choking badly, his face swollen and blue. After a few minutes in the respirator, he too, spoke. "I breathe," he said. Machines could not be made fast enough. Phil procured boxes from a local casket company, sealed them, had a hole cut, through which the doctors put the patients in after motorcycle escorts had rushed them to the hospital.

Newspapers seized on the stories of stricken victims, told how this was not a pulmotor but "a new robot for artificial breathing." Officially it became the Drinker Respirator, sometimes the Drinker Lung. A newsman called it the iron lung and the name took hold; Germany had it as *die Eiserne Lunge*. In 1930, Phil took a machine to England for demonstration. J. S. Haldane showed great interest, having himself done much work on breathing and ventilation. (He knew Cecil and had been in his laboratory.) Lord Haldane was a great man for testing out apparatus on himself; one day he had inhaled a mixture of carbon monoxide for seventy-one and a half minutes, having his blood and vision tested at intervals, and only ceasing on the verge of unconsciousness. Now he announced he'd like to go into the iron lung. Phil said they pulled and pushed but "the old gentleman was arthritic and they couldn't get his shoulders through."

Newspaper cartoonists swooped on the respirator as a vehicle for satire, showed it resuscitating the currency in 1933 or bringing to life some moribund politician who had been defeated at the polls. Pathé News had "talking pictures" of the respirator at all Keith Theatres. A woman stuck her head in a gas oven and the machine saved her. (Consolidated Gas was reaping its reward.) Dr. Wallace Fenn, professor of physiology at Rochester University, asked friends at Harvard to tell Phil, "We put a woman into his 'damned tank,' as he called it, and she recovered sufficiently to be committed to the insane asylum. Another victory for the Drinker Respirator." In San Francisco a man lay in the hospital's only machine. When a woman victim arrived, the man asked to be taken out and the woman put in his place. The entire country discussed the right and wrong of the situation.

It is hard to remember — since Jonas Salk and Sabine and their vaccines — the terror and despair felt by the nation in the polio epidemics of the 1930s. It was natural for the respirator to receive nationwide, indeed, worldwide publicity. The *Peiping and Tienstsin Times* described it, as did the Paris *L'Illustration*. At the Chicago World's Fair the iron lung drew crowds to the Hall of Science. In his daily comic strip, Dick Tracy rushed a child to the machine. The Mutual Savings Bank of Boston asked Phil to act in a film they were showing. Phil refused; the bank showed it anyway. "Say, Doctor," the script reads; "maybe you've got something there, at that! I don't know what earthly use it will be, but let's try it!" Medals were handed to Phil on platforms; schoolchildren wrote compositions about the iron lung and sent them to Phil. (They still do.) Phil's face looked out from magazine articles and news columns, with captions that read, "Thousands owe him their lives"; or, "Champion of the handicapped, the half-shy professor, a rangy engineer. . . ."

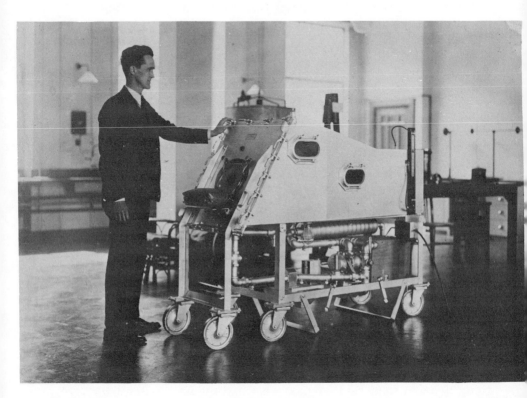

Phil with the iron lung, 1931.

Phil grew very tired of being described as "young, tall, handsome and modest, without a trace of Boston's Back Bay in him." Moreover, scientists are not supposed to be notorious. One day, when a reporter asked the usual question, How tall are you? "Hell!" Phil replied. "Just say I'm a short fat man with wet hands." As time passed, Phil began to look on what he called "all this fuss about the respirator" as out of focus. He said that in forty years' work at the School of Public Health the "damn machine was only one thing, and it just happened. If I'd been a physiologist instead of an engineer it wouldn't have happened. I'd have thought it impossible." Lecturing at Harrogate, England, in 1953, Phil found himself on the platform with Jonas Salk — one of the pleasantest incidents of his career, he said afterward. Phil told Salk — and the audience — how good it felt to meet the man who had done so much to control polio, while his own machine, the iron lung, "couldn't prevent the cases. It could only treat them."

Meanwhile, at the School of Public Health, work with the dusts and fumes continued — done as a rule in teams of two or more members. The results appeared in the professional journals: "Photometric methods of studying and estimating suspensions of dusts, fumes and smokes" . . . "Vapors and Their Routine Measurements" . . . "The Dust Filtering Efficiency of the Human Nose" . . . "Air Pollution and the Public Health." Today all this is a familiar field, but when Cecil and Phil started out, it was pioneer work. Machines designed for respiratory studies in the School of Public Health were, I am told, far ahead of their time. Only now are we beginning to use, on humans, certain of the basic apparatus that Cecil and Phil devised for use on animals. Reading of Phil's experiments with the rock dust disease of the lungs called silicosis, there came to mind how difficult things are at their births and beginnings. Was it King Charles I who showed disgust because "the learned doctors of England spend their time measuring the air"? A large part of Phil Drinker's life was spent measuring the contents of air; eventually he traveled from one end of the country to the other, examining factories, mines, shipyards, to determine how much harmful matter the workers breathed. "I was always very curious," Phil said, "to know what percentage of dust or smoke or fume a man would retain when he breathed a known concentration in air. We made experiments in my lab and carried them out in considerable detail; one, using a dust calcium carbonate which is harmless, and another using magnesium oxide fume made by burning a magnesium ribbon. Known concentrations could be maintained in our dust cabinet. The subject would sit outside and breathe through a valve arrangement and then exhale out through an electrostatic precipitator which would catch and measure the dust exhaled. At the same time through another porthole, we would be measuring the concentration of dust that he breathed."

As a result of this experimentation, what the laboratory called "permissible dosages" could be formulated, for men working an eight-hour day in mines and factories. Since then a table of such dosages has been drawn up, including every dust and fume likely to be encountered by workers. In government laboratories this chart is annually revised. "We weren't trying," Phil said, "to eliminate dust or fumes entirely, or to shut down plants with too much toxic dust, but merely to reduce it to a concentration that we knew was safe."

Phil went into the coal mines of Pennsylvania and Virginia, the zinc mines of northern New York, the lead mines of southeastern

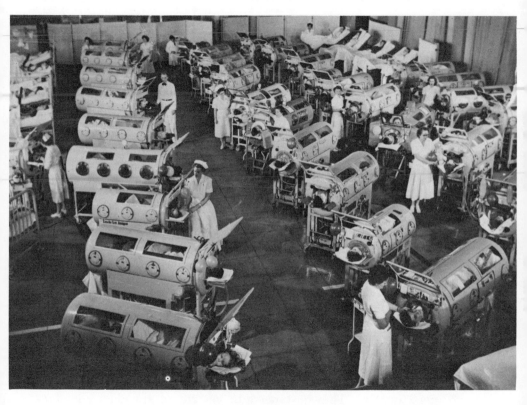

*Iron lungs in a San Francisco hospital during the polio epidemic
of the early 1950s.*

Missouri. When the school did autopsies, looking for the disease called black lung, they did it to devise masks or methods of protection — "never to find a cure," Phil said; "that was Cecil's business." I once heard Phil declare that New York City is the biggest mining center in the world. He went under Manhattan Island, exploring the Holland Tunnel early and late to see what the engineers were doing about dust control. Miners don't like to wear masks and they don't like the wet drilling that eliminates dust. Phil had to convince the men — and their labor leaders — that he didn't want to shut down mines and factories, or see workers forfeit their bonuses when hazardous jobs were made less hazardous. "At first they wouldn't believe me," Phil said. In one shipyard, men were welding lead-painted structures; Phil told them they should take certain precautions against lead poisoning. "Look, Professor," one of them replied; "we'll weld *anything* if the pay's right."

Factory owners too were suspicious, fearful of being forced to spend money for improvements. On the other hand they feared lawsuits brought by injured workers. Phil has told of laborers who left the factory apparently in perfect health, then fell off their bicycles or dropped on the sidewalk from the effects of manganese poisoning. But why couldn't the plant doctors determine these matters? — owners said. In the New Jersey Zinc Company, when Phil and his colleague entered the big shed, dust was so thick the two men lost each other. "Hell!" Phil said. "These plants don't need doctors. They just need to get rid of the dust." Factory owners liked Phil's practical, abrupt approach; they began to say they trusted him.

On the school staff was the brilliant Dr. Alice Hamilton — sister of the Greek scholar Edith Hamilton — the first woman professor at Harvard and a pioneer in the field of industrial medicine. Together Phil and Dr. Hamilton made their tours. Management did not take kindly to female advice. "Get that lady doc out of here," they told Phil — but in the end they respected Dr. Hamilton and even welcomed her. It was Dr. Alice, Phil said, who first told him that he would find labor his worst opponent, and that what labor leaders wanted was to see workers compensated for industrial diseases. During the 1930s there flourished what was known as the "silicosis racket." Workers and certain lawyers brought suits for lung disease which often enough proved to be neither factory-caused nor silicosis. Phil used to be asked to testify in court, sometimes for one side, sometimes the other. He dreaded it. Standing in the witness box — large, blunt, candid, Phil gave his replies. Afterward he told us those law fellows could twist a man's words inside out. "They know how to make a fool of you in two minutes flat."

Phil became a world authority on industrial dust. He and a colleague, Theodore Hatch, produced a book with that unpromising title which is, I am told, a classic on the subject. The field broadened. With fellow scientists Phil helped to form a society for discussion — informal, without dues or officers, but much valued by members; they called it the Konicide Club — Greek for "kill the dust." During World War II, the U. S. Navy asked Phil if the school would work out a national health education program for shipyard laborers. Could a course be established for Navy doctors and engineers? The federal government planned to take into the yards about a million and a half workers, many of whom would be green men, employed in dangerous jobs such as gas and electric welding. The School of Public Health knew all there was to know about electric welding and cutting, about the injuries to the eyes called flash burn, about metal poisoning and metal fume fever. Phil and his colleagues set up a crash course, where a year's work could be done in three months. No sooner were one set of Navy officers and doctors trained than another set rolled in. Even today, Phil remembers that he has never been so tired in his life.

After three or four dozen of these men had received training, Phil was invited to be chief consultant to the Navy and Maritime Commission. The job implied a continuous survey of shipyards all over the country — East Coast, West Coast — then reporting back to Washington what needed to be done. Phil asked for the necessary personnel, but the Navy refused, saying the men were needed for combat duty. Somebody in the Medical Corps asked Phil if he knew anyone in the Navy. When he replied that yes, he'd been to college with Secretary Forrestal, they said for God's sake what's holding you back? Go and see Forrestal and tell him what you want.

My brother Cecil, with his native arrogance, would have pulled strings long before, at the outset. Phil, however, had an inborn simplicity that never ceased to surprise the men with whom he dealt. An appointment was arranged. "Forrestal seemed his old self, a darn good fellow," Phil said afterward. When Phil asked for a staff of eight officers — two doctors and six engineers — Forrestal said it made sense to him, but he didn't like to decide the matter for himself. "So he rang a bell," Phil said afterward, "and Admiral Nimitz came in with all his regalia. Forrestal said, 'Chester, this is an old friend of mine, Phil Drinker, from school.'" Then Forrestal asked Phil to repeat what he had said earlier. He complied, and Nimitz said all right, and would Professor Drinker please make out a list of the officers he wanted, and send it on. Phil pulled the list from his pocket, ready and typed. "They both laughed to beat the band," Phil said; "and I got the officers and kept them throughout the war."

The Maritime Commission's domain and territory comprised the entire coastline of the United States, also the Great Lakes and on down the Mississippi, every place where the government built ships — even Pittsburgh, whence the vessels were floated south by river and out through New Orleans. When Phil, at home near Boston, received a telephone call to go to Portland, he would ask, "which Portland?" — and tell his wife and children, as nearly as he could, when he would be back.

Phil's laboratory developed a device for quick sampling of the air in shipyards. A manual of safe practice was produced, suggesting the location of new hospitals, giving specifications in ventilation and indicating how many nurses and doctors would be needed for every thousand employees — questions that would ordinarily take considerable time to work out. The school did it in a week — and did it correctly. Phil's inspectors had a routine by which they examined a new ship in early stages of construction — about one deck deep. His men would go into these "double bottoms," as they were called, crawl all the way through and come out the other end. Often enough, Phil went with them. "It got to be common knowledge round the yards," he said, "that our inspectors really knew their stuff."

Some years earlier, Cecil had suggested to the Remington Rand Corporation that the School of Public Health could do better work if it had a good-sized tank that would take pressure up to four atmospheres. Mr. Rand had heard of a doctor out west who had a big steel ball into which he put patients at normal atmospheric pressures, claiming miraculous cures. Mr. Rand asked Cecil and Phil, "Could your laboratory do anything with such a tank?"

Phil said they sure could and never mind the miracles. If Mr. Rand would let them fix it with changing air pressures — rising and falling — it wouldn't cost much more.

"So now," Phil said, later, "we had this pressure tank, in a sort of cabin attached to the school. When the Second World War came, they wanted work done on high altitude masks, which we were beautifully equipped to do." This was before the use of pressurized cabins; altitude masks were very important. Phil and Cecil and their colleagues — notably Leslie Silverman — experimented with various types of "face pieces," as they called them. Staff members from the Carnegie Institution joined in, along with three army officers experienced in respiratory apparatus. Between them they evolved the L-12 oxygen mask, also the A-9 and A-10, which proved greatly valuable in high altitude bombing. Phil and his colleagues next studied breathing requirements for a protective gas mask; in four years not only was a mask perfected, but a new device for measuring air speed into the lungs. Reports which went to the Office of Scientific Research and Development still serve as basic design criteria for gas mask equipment, also for clinical studies of breathing in asthma and other pulmonary diseases. One of Phil's colleagues told me you never knew what would happen, working with Phil. "Dangerous business," he said. "There you'd be with the wind in your face at a simulated three miles a minute. Or inhaling dust out of a box. Or two hundred feet under water in that tank, breathing helium and nitrogen. . . ."

In 1939, the submarine *Squalus* sank off Portsmouth, New Hampshire, with all its crew. Navy divers took down emergency breathing masks and the crew got out alive. But after the incident, the Navy sent one of its divers to the School of Public Health, together with a doctor who had been a student of Phil's. The two

Navy men worked with Phil for some time, ultimately perfecting a breathing apparatus, "whereby," Phil said, "they had the right mixture of helium and nitrogen." The Navy never forgot this, Phil added. "We had been warm friends before, and after this we were even warmer."

XV

Cecil.

"The hardest living asks its price."

Diary, at 22

I DON'T KNOW when it was that Cecil began to drink, though it must have been early; at twenty-one the diary says, "It seems impossible to be sociable without drinking something. I can't do this and so I'm in a sort of position of isolation that at times is uncomfortable." About my brother's alcoholism, three things appear strange almost to the point of fantasy: (a) so few people seemed aware of it until disaster came; (b) the colossal amount of work Cecil got through in spite of liquor; (c) the fact that his wife, Katherine, remained loyal, loving and enduring toward what had become an erring, quarrelsome and fiendishly difficult husband.

At the School of Public Health, Cecil acted as assistant dean from 1923, and as dean from 1935 to 1942. During this latter pe-

Cecil aboard the TAUTOG, *1937*

riod Cecil made more enemies than he could likely count. He was then drinking heavily; they say he used to walk about the school carrying a bottle of Coca Cola, laced with alcohol from the lab. Once he rolled all the way down the steps from the second floor. Luigi Freni, the lab *diener,* picked him up and hustled him home, with nobody the wiser.

In his cups, Cecil became paranoid, imagined that his colleagues were making plots and preparing slights for his humiliation. Against these threats Cecil invented counterplots. In certain academic medical circles, Cecil busied himself with elaborate forms of infighting, concerning who was to be appointed professor of physiology or who would succeed him as dean of the School of Public Health. Cecil had long believed the school should be amalgamated with the Harvard Medical School; he said separate organizations wasted money, and the two would be more effective as one. President Conant did not agree. Rockefeller money, which largely supported the School of Public Health, would not be forthcoming, Conant said, if the Rockefellers saw it simply pouring into the vast maw that was Harvard proper. The battles about this grew more intense; Cecil took to speaking of Conant as the Emperor. One day, in 1942, Cecil came to faculty meeting drunk. The minute he was sober he sent his resignation as dean; Conant accepted it without comment. Five years later, after various blatant and almost insane incidents, Cecil saw that the end had come, and resigned his professorship of physiology.

I did not know my brother in those days. He had separated himself from the family and would have no communication with us, though toward the last he and I were to be friends again. Biography, however, cannot surmount large gaps of years, where the subject is lost, wandering in a void. I went therefore to Cecil's former associates, his colleagues and students, asking about his scientific research in the latter years and before, and how he managed to turn out so much work. What was the quality of his production, why did people at the school shield him for so long? And wouldn't it perhaps have been better if they hadn't?

The doctors protested, surprising me by their vehemence; even Cecil's old enemies defended him. "What does the drinking matter?" they said. "Cecil inspired a whole generation of lab workers!" And they told me to forget about the drinking, forget the trouble and the infighting. The men who talked to me are now deans of medical colleges, university professors of surgery or medicine, distinguished in their field. And they were at pains to let me know that Cecil was an artist in the lab; they shouted as if I were an unbeliever who must be convinced. Did I know, for instance, that Cecil blew his own glass cannulas, tiny enough to be threaded through the lymph vessels? And had I any idea of what a difficult process *that* was? "Just to follow him around the lab was an inspiration. Only three men in my life," said Herrman Blumgart, now emeritus professor of medicine at Harvard, "could pick up instruments and use them as Cecil did. One was Harvey Cushing, the brain surgeon."

Sure, Cecil was a hellcat. Sure, he made trouble. But in the lab he could raise questions, and then design experiments to answer them. Nor must it be overlooked that Cecil and his wife, Katherine, had much to do with launching the *Journal of Industrial Hygiene*. Previously, no vehicle had existed for publication of work in applied physiology. "Your brother Cecil was a giant in his field," they said. "Forget the drinking. Skip it!"

Yet no one can write truthfully about Cecil and omit the drinking. It was part of him, chemically, emotionally, spiritually. Who can explain self-destruction? "But when he was cruel," one colleague protested, "it came only in his madness." Again, however, this "madness" must have been part of Cecil, intrinsic to his nature from the first. The intensity we had felt and feared in Cecil's youth, in middle age became overmastering. Yet the quality remained attractive, a powerful ingredient in the magnetism that men spoke of as "so commanding." The Indian sign lay on my brother. He would listen to no one, take no advice, no comfort anywhere. (*When we say Nononono to baby he says Ahaaaa very loud, the bad thing.*) Alcoholics Anonymous? That was for fools and simpletons who groveled on their knees. "God is not interested," Cecil said.

Looking back, it seems extraordinary that Cecil had reached fifty before I so much as knew he drank. I first learned about it at Beach Haven in the summer of 1937, during Papa's last illness. Cecil came down from Boston to act as physician and in general direct procedure. Always, when family illness came, we consulted Cecil, who knew doctors everywhere and could advise as to specialists and hospitals. Papa's affliction, at eighty-seven, was nothing more than old age. His heart had been bothering him and he stayed in bed, cheerful enough but very weak. The household consisted of my parents, the maids, a trained nurse, Cecil and myself. Cecil was quite desperately fond of Pa; on the day of his arrival, when he came out of the sickroom I saw him put his hands over his face with the old shuddering gesture I knew so well.

Two weeks went by before Papa died. And during those fourteen days I think my brother scarcely drew a sober breath. He kept the bottle in his room and we never saw him drink. His voice was controlled, but passing through the house he staggered and put a hand to the wall. At night when I went down the hall to the bathroom I heard him pounding about his room and swearing. If Mamma, at eighty-five, noticed, she never gave a sign. She sat in her room, withdrawn, quite silent; the sound of the sea came through her open windows. Eventually the nurse told me I simply must speak to Dr. Drinker; he was upsetting the household and she couldn't stand it another day; she was "not accustomed to such behavior from physicians." I walked into the small white-washed front bedroom where Cecil slept. In my forty years I had never given voice to criticism against my brother; indeed, such criticism had not arisen. Up to then I had had little experience with drinking people. I don't remember my actual words, that morning, but I know they were awkward and took the form of a question: "Cecil, what is wrong with you, do you *have* to be drunk?"

What I do remember is that Cecil, sitting by the window, did not look at me but kept his eyes on the floor. "I wouldn't be this way, Katz," he said, "if I wasn't so weak."

I stood stock-still. Cecil, weak, and acknowledging it? There are things in life that scarcely bear remembering. After Pa died his body lay for a night and a day in a coffin downstairs, between the dining room and the double doors to the screened porch. When Mr. Cranmer, the local undertaker, came to take charge, Cecil insulted him, almost shoved him down the porch steps, shouted that by God he wouldn't have embalming fluids put into Pa; Pa would have hated it and anyway it didn't work; he knew all about it and you fellows are all buzzards and crooks. Then Cecil rushed inside and collapsed on the creaky hall sofa with his hands over his face. "I can't stand it," he said, through his fingers. "Christ! I loved him. I just can't stand it."

Cecil went through life — I know it now — entirely conscious of his alcoholism, yet never, it would seem, ready for what might have proved painful inquiry into its underlying causes. The diary is filled with entries concerning liquor: "Why I have liked alcohol I don't know," he wrote on his fortieth birthday. "For I have never failed to realize what was happening to me. Undoubtedly the reason for my not doing more striking work during the last ten years has been alcohol. Many reasons have combined in making me turn to it. It is my aim to take no more hard liquor. Beer and wine but nothing else. I have tried this before but always failed. . . . I am using alcohol again which never does me any good but which I seem to want badly in the times when I am tired. . . . I am at the strong waters again. It is a strange business. About five in the afternoon I want alcohol. If I can get through dinner the desire goes away and does not recur until late afternoon of the next day. . . . Home at 4:30 and at 5:30 for some reason I can't fathom exactly, mostly I guess from a vague desire to get away from my surroundings, I went downstairs and had three glasses of aquavit. . . . Worked further on my paper this morning and in the afternoon loafed. Three aquavits, 1 beer and 2 bottles of stout. I seem to be able to last about one day. Tonight had the devil going hard and took 2 scotch, 4 aquavit, 2 stouts, 1 beer and 1 mint. I can't tell why I do this. I had felt good all day beforehand."

The amounts consumed do not seem very great; I have known men to drink more and carry it off. It is my guess that Cecil possessed a light tolerance and got drunk quickly. According to the diary he was invariably sick the following day.

Dr. Eugene M. Landis, the physiologist, told me that during Cecil's working life, he served the School of Public Health with his left hand, directing its policies as dean and experimenting in applied physiology with Phil and the rest of the staff. The right hand was occupied with pure physiology — Cecil's primary love — done at the Harvard Medical School and resulting in the publication in 1941 of his big book, *The Lymphatics, Lymph and Lymphoid Tissue*, written with J. M. Yoffey and still a standard reference. Cecil's monographs on the subject are found in four volumes, under the title *Lymph Papers*.

Altogether, Cecil put out two hundred and fifty scientific monographs, a few of them written alone, others with Katherine or various co-workers.* Bound and dated year by year, the articles sit before me on their shelf in seventeen volumes; they cover the period from 1912 to 1950 — six years before Cecil's death. They range over a surprising variety of subjects, from "Effect of Extracts of Sheeps' Thyroid and of Pathological Human Thyroid Upon the Fatigue Curve of Voluntary Muscle," "Factors of Coagulation in Primary Pernicious Anemia," "Clinical Physiology of the Kidney," to "The Economic Aspects of Industrial Medicine" and "Physiology of Whales" — this last, concerned with a breathing apparatus which permits rapid dives and subsequent rising without incurring "the bends." Now and then Cecil took an excursion into medical biography, such as an article on "John Halle, Anatomiste, Chirurgien, Modernist, 1530–1600," and a discursive piece, "Dr. Smollett," about Tobias Smollett's career as a physician. After quoting Peregrine Pickle's adventures at Bath, Cecil wanders quite delightfully into Jane Austen's descriptions of the town, also Sam Weller's "friendly swarry" therein, "consisting of a boiled leg of mutton with the usual trimmings." Cecil's book, *Not So Long Ago*, tells of medicine and doctors in eighteenth-

* See Acknowledgments.

century Philadelphia. Culled from Great-great-grandmother Elizabeth Drinker's diary, it is filled with most appalling incidents. Dr. Benjamin Rush comes three days in succession to bleed Great-great-grandfather Henry Drinker and takes "more than 14 ounces." The cat falls down the privy. A horse steps on a child's foot; when the skin breaks, Grandmother dresses it tenderly with "a Cataplasm of Cow-dung."

Paging over Cecil's collected papers, I confess to pleasure. These are not dry, abstruse technical articles. Cecil once told me that a man who really understands his subject can explain it to anybody. I am not sure I agree. But certainly, here is writing that interests the layman. Cecil's lifelong affinity with literature comes through; he cannot resist references to Dickens, Kipling, or the Bible stories Mamma had read to us on Sunday afternoons long ago. Cecil's book *Carbon Monoxide Asphyxia,* published in 1938, had a section on artificial respiration, which opens with the prophet Elisha, reviving by mouth-to-mouth breathing the young son of the Shunammite: "And he lay upon the child, and put his mouth upon his mouth, and his eyes upon his eyes, and his hands upon his hands; and he stretched himself upon the child, and the flesh of the child waxed warm. And the child sneezed seven times. And he called the Shunammite. And he said, Take up thy son. Then she went in, and fell at his feet, and bowed herself to the ground, and took up her son, and went out."

Published lectures make easier reading for the layman, of course, than basic textbooks or scientific monographs. The talker is more at ease, touches on his experience with life. The Lane Lectures, given at Leland Stanford in 1941, comprise Cecil's best-known series. Lecture III has a paragraph that embodies one of my brother's cardinal principles: Let the researcher not be overwhelmed by his apparatus. Cecil had first learned this lesson from Dr. Krogh in Copenhagen, having been enormously impressed with the simplicity of Dr. Krogh's establishment. This laboratory, famous throughout the scientific world for its owner's work on the capillary system, consisted of a long room below Krogh's living quarters, and boasted for equipment two tables, a sink with one spigot and a Bunsen burner on which to boil water. (Cecil once told me he had never seen work more skillfully done.) In the Lane Lectures, telling of his own experiments at Harvard, cannulating lymph from the thighs of dogs, Cecil remarks how, "as time passed, the ingenuity and mechanical perfection of the apparatus slowly took entire charge. . . . As is the case with so many experiments which ought to work, but do not, it required many months to consign the increasingly complicated apparatus devised for this effort to a secluded region in the basement and then to start anew. The experiment devised next depended upon mechanical arrangements which were extremely simple. The results were . . . quite satisfactory." And Cecil goes on to describe them.

One feels the speaker's own pleasure in his subject; Cecil was having a good time. At the outset, describing the evolution of the mammalian circulatory system, he reminds his audience of the invertebrates: the sea cucumber, the lobster; the toadfish, who, "like the Fat Boy in Pickwick, if he could speak would say, 'I likes eating.' " Cecil's references to the laboratory have the ease of long experience. "When," he remarks, "one is familiar with the viscous, creamy lymph which may be collected from the lacteals of a dog after a meal of fat . . ." More than once, in the past, I had heard Cecil say that physiologists are mistaken who describe the dead tissue seen in the dissecting room, and therefrom draw deductions. "Function must be seen in the living animal." In the Lane

Lectures, Cecil does not contain his delight at the wonder of such function. Under a microscope the capillaries of the lungs are "an astonishing sight." And Cecil quotes Malpighi, founder of microscopic anatomy, "who broke his text with the words, '*Magnum certum opus oculi video!*' I see with my eyes certain great things."

Cecil's diary comes to mind, and his overpowering excitement as a medical student when first he saw a heart dissected: "The wonder of it has sent me walking on air all day — something beyond all making of men." In the Lane Lectures, Cecil goes on to remark upon William Harvey's misfortune because, throughout his studies on blood circulation, he "never saw the marvel of the capillary system in the living animal. What might have happened, had Leonardo da Vinci turned from studying those many foul corpses to the living animal!"

In my youth, Cecil had told me, in one way or another, that ideas were cheap unless implemented. "You have to work things out, Katz. That's the fun of it." The final Lane Lecture remarks that "new things, new views are of little use until they come to use through some one who describes them reasonably well, and who, if his vision goes farther than the intellectual horizon of the day, adds to his experimental achievement the import of his addition to man's welfare." Cecil uses insulin as an example. A few years before its discovery by Banting and Best, several persons had perhaps secured the same substance in the laboratory, but failed to realize the meaning of what they found. Medicine tempts us too often, Cecil concludes, into thinking, like Kipling's monkey folk, the Bandar-Log:

> . . . *we sit in a branchy row,*
> *Thinking of beautiful things we know;*

Dreaming of deeds that we mean to do,
All complete, in a minute or two —
Something noble and grand and good,
Won by merely wishing we could. . . .

Long ago, Cecil had read to me that song of the Bandar-Log. I
knew it by heart. The year before he died, Cecil spoke to me of
Harry's book, *Legal Ethics*, then newly published, and asked what
I thought of it. I replied, rather cautiously, that it would be useful
to the legal profession; it was a good textbook. Cecil sat in a
wheelchair, smoking his pipe, the book in his hand. He shook his
head. "Dry subjects needn't be dry," he said. "Harry ought to do
better than a textbook."

Cecil delivered the Lane Lectures in 1941; in 1942 he resigned
his deanship. I heard later that the news hit the school "like a
bombshell." There were protests; people couldn't believe that
Cecil Drinker was finished. He entered the newly established psy-
chiatric clinic at the McLean Hospital near Boston and stayed for
three months' treatment, during which time he refused all communication with his family except Katherine. Harry went up there
once or twice, but Cecil would not see him. We heard that, characteristically, Cecil refused to admit his sickness, got involved
with the administration of the McLean Hospital and raised money
for a research laboratory. The next thing we knew, Cecil was making a speech at the dedication of the new laboratory. He emerged
from the hospital unregenerate, and not long afterward became a
patient again, this time at the Payne Whitney Clinic in New
York. I wrote asking if I might come to see him. "Not till I get out

The TAUTOG *in Buzzards Bay*

of here," Cecil replied. His pride would not let me see him in his humiliation.

After 1947, when Cecil resigned his professorship of physiology, he seemed to go quite mad. Once he was picked up, drunk, by the Falmouth police and spent a night in the town jail. The local Portuguese fishermen were his friends; they used to sit on the dock, exchanging stories; Cecil acted as physician for them and their families. He terrified Katherine by going out alone on his ketch, the *Tautog*, carrying his big fishing rods and God knows how much whiskey. He would stay all night, somewhere far out on the bay, and come home next day with his phlebitic legs terribly bruised from falling down the hatchway. I used to think sometimes that Katherine took all this harder than Cecil. She told one of their colleagues she had hoped that when Cecil retired, "We would come into a lovely twilight of our lives together. But we have crashed." And she wept as she said it.

Drunk or sober, until the last few years of his life, Cecil continued to write scientific articles, and even appeared on college platforms as lecturer. His Harvard friends drove down to Falmouth to see him. Their old dinner society, the Exchange Club, met in Falmouth several times; Cecil was delighted. His colleague from medical intern days, Dr. Stanley Cobb, looked after Cecil, gave him Atabrine against his drinking. Cecil took it dutifully for about a year, Dr. Cobb told me. Then one day he swallowed the medicine and drank anyway and nearly died. After that he developed angina and phlebitis; Katherine took care of him. With invalidism the drinking ceased as if it had never been. A year before Cecil's death, the Exchange Club — all of them research physicians — commissioned Cecil's portrait to be painted by Pezzati. It hangs in the Bowditch Library at the Harvard Medical School, on the wall next to Dr. Cannon. Cecil came to the unveiling in a wheelchair and heard his old friends praise him.

Perhaps it is presumption to look at a life in its entirety and pronounce it either happy or sad. Yet my brother Harry's life was happy; anyone could see it. With a kind of furious joy Harry charged ahead with his projects, his music, the law. Philip, hard-working, healthy as a bear cub, rejoiced in the name given by his colleagues: "Mr. Industrial Hygiene." At seventy Phil whistled to his dogs and walked out with a hatchet to trim his woods as if the day were June and six in the morning. As for Jim, he is surely the best balanced of all six siblings, though the condition was not easily won. A second brother, caught between the upper and nether millstones that were Harry and Cecil, Jim occupied what must at times have been a mean position. Yet through the years, Jim seemed to accept his brothers' furious activity easily enough. I am inclined to think he looked on his brothers and sisters as more than a little crazy. After one particularly feverish rash of family medals and honorary degrees, he wrote to Philip, "It's a good thing I'm here to help bring the family reputation down to normal."

The last time I saw Cecil, he appeared surprisingly fit, his white hair thick, his color good, his blue eyes deep in his head but with the same bright look of inquiry. The three of us sat in the sun at Falmouth, watching the gulls wheel, the bay below the meadow and the boats passing. The gentle side of Cecil's nature had returned; I felt it with a pang of sorrow as well as relief. Cecil, not fighting, was no longer Cecil.

Katherine and Cecil died in the spring of 1956, within a few weeks of each other, at the Pocasset Hospital — Cecil of heart-

Phil at seventy-five. Photograph by his granddaughter Susan Funkhauser.

lung complications, Kath of leukemia. Katherine had known of her disease for two years, but had said nothing. She told me she felt no pain and had no "symptoms" until almost the end, when, I afterwards learned, she quite literally bled to death. I could not help thinking — and with all my love for my brother I think it still — that Katherine's bloodletting began years ago, the day she met and fell in love with Cecil.

When Cecil heard that she was dead he stopped eating, left the trays untouched by his bed, nor would he submit to artificial feeding. Harry went to him; on his return he told me, "Katz, Cecil starved himself to death. I *saw* it!" But even as he said it I knew, and shall always know, that if those two were given a chance of living their lives again together — hard work, tragedy and all — they would say yes without a backward glance.

XVI

Green Alley. The measure of our
days. Farewell to Harry.

"ALL MY LIFE," Sophie said, "I have had a bad temper. I used it to get my way. When I was forty-six, I decided to change all that."

It was after her hysterectomy this happened, Sophie added. In her late fifties Sophie referred to the hysterectomy as the Greeks may have referred to Thermopylae: things occurred before or after it. Sophie said she had never begun to *think* until her hysterectomy, no one knew quite why. None of the family noticed a change, but to Sophie it was as if the waves of her being began to move and she became herself. When she made the remark about temper Sophie was weeding her little rock garden at Gloucester, where, since Aunt Cecilia Beaux's death, we spent our summers in three households. My sister Ernesta and her second husband, Sam Barlow, had the "big house"; Harry and Sophie the studio; myself a one-room beach cottage, converted from an abandoned bath-house.

There were four acres on Beaux's place. Green Alley, she had called it, because of the path that ran through the little green wood to her front door. She had built the house and studio in 1905 and paid for it with money she earned by her portrait painting. When she died she left the place to Harry; she said he was the only person in the family who could afford to keep it up and pay the taxes. For some time Green Alley lay vacant. Then I ventured to spend a summer alone in Beaux's house, this being some years before the bathhouse conversion. My husband, McKean Downs, was with the U. S. Navy in the Pacific, my daughter at Radcliffe summer school, my son of sixteen a camp counselor in Maine. Harry and Sophie were in Canada, where they usually spent Harry's vacation. They were not interested in Green Alley, though pleased to have the house occupied; Harry said they planned to sell it when Beaux's estate was finally settled. I propped up a sagging gas stove with logs from the toolhouse, cleared the papers from Beaux's upstairs desk, replaced her books on a nearby shelf with certain volumes of American history, put a new ribbon in my typewriter, stocked groceries and set up housekeeping.

I did not know this house. In youth it had been Ernesta who in summer visited Aunt Cecilia and served as painter's model in the studio down the hill. Cecilia Beaux, as I have said, had scarcely been my friend. Yet now I slept in her narrow, four-posted French bed, in a room giving on an upper terrace — and felt as if the house were mine and I had created it. Phil's wife, Sue, had warned against this move. She said I'd be lonely out there on Eastern Point with the lighthouse beam flashing at night and the foghorn blowing. She said that when she and Phil had visited

Beaux the foghorn made her feel creepy, coming up out of nowhere. To me however the sound was comforting, booming away
like a cello C string, *basso continuo* in an old, familiar music.

Everything about this house suited: Beaux's little private writing room that adjoined her bedroom; the rocky path on the upper
terrace which one could follow from bed to studio, unseen by the
household. Beaux had so contrived it that her current subject —
her sitters, she called these — could sleep in the small front guest
suite, and go downstairs for breakfast while Beaux occupied her
writing room undisturbed. Or she could slip down to the studio
early and work till ten o'clock, when the sitter would be sum-
moned to pose. Outdoors was fragrant with bayberry and wild
clethra in season. Clematis and rosa rugosa grew over the big gray
boulders; downhill beyond scrub pine and catbrier was the bay.
Gulls cried; at dawn each day the Gloucester codfish fleet went
out. Beaux's house was neither large nor elaborate. But it held a
foreign air; to the west the bay and the far shoreline were seen
through arches in a manner not native to New England. Alcoves
sheltered from the prevailing winds; one could sit outdoors in any
weather. Every arrangement, every step taken showed a house
built by an artist for her professional use and consequent rest and
recruitment of spirit. Before the sun went down on my second day
of occupancy, I knew that no one in the artist category — painter,
writer, musician — could live in Green Alley without recognition:
This is my place. Here I can do my work in peace, to the best of
my ability.

After a while I sat down and wrote as much to Harry in Canada. The letter must have been wordy, a veritable outburst. I said
one could feel Aunt Cecilia everywhere, her presence in every
room. The house hadn't a comfortable chair to sit on but it was

heaven, and though Beaux may not have liked me much, I knew in my bones that if she saw me settled here and my work moving forward, she would give me welcome. And that if the current manuscript, a biography of John Adams, ever managed to make sizable money, maybe Harry would sell Green Alley to me? Harry wrote back in three lines that the fishing at Tourilli wasn't good this year, something had happened to the trout, and if Green Alley was all that wonderful he wouldn't dream of selling, so keep your shirt on Katz and maybe we'll live there some day.

Sure enough, the 1950s saw us ensconced — and not at my expense, though John Adams had done very well. At first Sophie had hesitated; she didn't want to occupy Beaux's house. She said her children and grandchildren would descend on her in hordes and overrun us. By now Sophie was writing her third book; the hysterectomy had indeed served her well. (I once heard Harry say that operation had been Sophie's Ph. D. diploma.) For himself Harry did not care what house they lived in; he would simply have ignored the young as he did at home. The Barlows — Ernesta and Sam — had sold their house at Èze on the Riviera; in the Second World War the Germans had occupied it. The Barlows decided to live in Beaux's house: they suggested that Harry and Sophie put in a kitchen at the south end of the studio where canvases and frames were stored. A steep staircase led from this area to a small bedroom with casement windows opening on the bay, and there was a bath.

The studio kitchen appeared on schedule, and the three households settled into their domains. Sophie and Harry got their own breakfast and lunch in the studio, as did I in my beach house. All day we pursued our several businesses, and in the evening met at the Barlows' for dinner. The communal cook slept over the kitchen. Before two summers were gone every chair in the living room was comfortable; the windows had heavy curtains we could draw against the cold of late August nights, the fireplace burned wood without smoking. Ernesta achieved all this with a minimum of fuss. She said she found the curtain material in Beaux's attic. She found also an open, pillared cabinet to hang on my wall for bed linen; Sam said it was a Provençal bread box. For years, things emerged from that attic: stained old mirrors in French frames, India shawls, delightful washbasins and chamber pots of Chinese export ware — most of which must have come down from the aunts on west Spruce Street.

Ernesta and Sam, in short, transformed Beaux's house, yet managed to retain its spirit. They polished the brass and waxed the furniture and the square red bricks on the hall floor. Living alone that first year, I had scarcely noticed the discomforts: for instance, no window screens downstairs. Ernesta said Beaux thought screens spoiled the view and anyway mosquitoes didn't bite her. Beaux *liked* the slippery black horsehair sofa in the living room and the stiff-backed wooden settle by the hearth. Evidently she tolerated no compromise with feeble spines.

Below the terrace, on the bay side, Sam planted his garden. Lilies bloomed all summer, yellow and white and fireman's red; Sam put in mallow and loosestrife, black-eyed daisies and nicotiana. We seldom saw Harry and Sophie before lunchtime. They spent the mornings at their desks — Harry's, a broad deal table in an alcove. His papers in their brown manila folders spilled over to the floor, the windowsills, everywhere. Sophie sat at a small neat desk below the east window. The studio was fifty feet long, the hammer beam ceiling at least as high. Through a tall, arched window came the painter's merciless north light. The big stone fireplace with the bronze cone over it was Italian; Piatt Andrew down the road had given it to Beaux. Two enormous French armoires filled the far corners. Harry hung Beaux's working palette on the wall, the colors still bright. A shabby Mason and Hamlin piano stood by the east wall and had been there half a century. For no reason it stayed fairly well in tune and the hammers worked, despite the fog and the everlasting damp.

If I ran over to the studio on some morning errand for the postman, I would enter and leave without speaking. Sophie and Harry shunned conversation before lunch. They had always been able to work in the room together; a mutual discipline restrained talk to a minimum. In the afternoons Harry did chores around the place, cut away dead limbs, cleaned the beach of rubbish that came in with the tide, raked the heavy seaweed to burn when it dried, sawed driftwood for the fireplace. Between the raspberry patch and the beach he built a stone wall; one summer he hauled great slabs to make a causeway from the grass to the water's edge. Harry took pride in this causeway and liked to show it to visitors, but that same September a hurricane came and swept the heavy slabs away as if they had been oyster shells. Harry asked ruefully if I remembered the beast that came out of the sea in Kipling's *Just So Stories* and gobbled all the stores that Suleiman-bin-Daoud had heaped up so proudly.

It was perhaps our tenth summer at Green Alley when one afternoon I looked out my window and saw a boy of high-school age raking the seawood. I realized suddenly that it had been quite a while since I had seen Harry working on the beach, or heard his saw over by the big rocks. It could not — no, it could not be that my brother was getting old — was an old man and couldn't do what he had always done and wanted to do? Even as I asked the question, I knew the answer. The realization of old age in those near us comes always as a shock, or so I had heard. But I had not believed it, there had been no reason to believe it. It was at Green Alley the summer before his eightieth birthday, that Harry announced they had decided to give up the singing parties. He and Sophie together told me, sitting at their lunch table in the studio kitchen. We don't want the music to go downhill, Harry said. We want people to remember it in top form. Harry and I cried when he said it, and for once Sophie did not demur; she looked out the window and made no sign. At the final singing party that spring I had seen Harry falter, standing on his podium; I had thought for an instant that he would fall.

When we got home in September, Harry and Sophie sent out announcements that the singing was done. Over the years, more than three thousand people had signed the singers' book that lay open by the piano on Sunday nights. All these people received the announcement. At once, letters began to pour in, not by the dozens but by the hundreds. People wrote in plain terms, telling what the music had done for them over the years. They said singing Bach's cantatas was more than hearing them sung; singing made you part of the music. A young man wrote that the music had changed his life; a woman said she had been about to go down for the third time when one Sunday we sang Cantata 93, *Whoso will suffer God to guide him* — and she went away whole. In the letters, people wrote out remembered musical phrases or quoted certain words: *How lovely is thy dwelling place, O Lord of hosts.*

A year or two later, Haverford College held a concert in Harry's honor. The boys sang his favorite choral melodies; our old friend Randall Thompson came down from Harvard to make a speech.

Harry received it all very quietly; afterward he seemed bewildered. Seeing him silent, almost humbled, was something to rend the heart. I wanted him to roar out, show his old impatience: "They took the *Omnes generationes* too slowly, Katz. Doesn't anybody ever learn *anything*?"

I would not have believed that in his old age my brother would be gentle, hesitant. Fred Sharpless — still our family doctor — said his condition was due to arteriosclerosis. But when I asked Sophie if Harry had had a stroke her lips grew tight and she did not answer; in the ensuing months, I didn't repeat the question. Harry's constitution was strong; he held doggedly to his thread of life, though he grew very thin, his legs would not hold him and his high color was gone. He sat in the big armchair in their bedroom at Merion, a shawl over his knees. His hands looked startlingly delicate, the skin transparent. Several times a week I drove from Bryn Mawr to see him. When I came in, Harry lifted my hand and kissed it, an honor he had never before accorded me — remarking that my! it was nice of me to come and see him this way. I told him I liked to come, it was fun to sit and talk; he never used to have time to talk. Harry looked up. "I *used* to be an interesting man," he said, with a half smile.

Always before, the gap between our ages — those sixteen years — had been for me a disadvantage, an impossible hill up which I struggled, knowing I could not attain. Now suddenly the years put me in first place, giving me strength and my brother weakness. I did not like it, and as time went on the reversal threatened me with panic. I still wrote books, still played string quartets on Thursday nights. Yet to what end? The question was absurd, I had never asked it before; I am not sure I actually asked it then. Yet under me the footing slipped. I was aware that my brothers had spurred themselves — and me — to competition. But was it, then, this rivalry that had urged me on so passionately, all these years? I could not think it. Surely, the books I wrote, the music I played had been their own spur and their own reward! Yet even more surely I knew that with Harry's fading some bright bitter taste had gone from the air, some pungent, acrid nourishment was lacking. I hated being sorry for Harry, it was unsuitable altogether. My brother should rise up against this thing, with his old brutality! He had never let himself be put upon. Why did he permit it now, and what was God *doing*?

Job in the Bible had sat among the ashes and cursed God in his heart. Yet in the end Job came round, he surrendered. *Do not go gentle into that good night.* But Dylan Thomas was young when he wrote it; he had not learned Job's courage. Surely, a lifetime is needed for this awful preparation? "Thou shalt come to thy grave in a full age, like as a shock of corn cometh in in his season." The ancient phrases came back. That was how Pa had died, easily, like ripe fruit loosed from the tree — and Justice Holmes and John Adams and Sir Edward Coke that I wrote about. When my parents were in their eighties I had lived in their house, watched them as the days passed, and set down in a notebook things they said and did. Was that why I chose as biographical subjects, men who lived to a great age? Readers often ask why I picked these men to write about. I am sure, now, that I chose them largely because of the way their lives were rounded out, the way they met their deaths.

Seeing my brother sink slowly, month after month, I thought of my parents. Papa, like Harry, had grown gentle with age. "There is a veil between me and reality," Pa told me one day. When he walked, Papa had wobbled badly. I tried to dissuade him from crossing Merion Road to Harry's by himself, against the traffic; he would be killed. Pa only said, "Well then, I'll find out what's on the other side." Mamma on her part showed none of this noble resignation. She rubbed at her rheumatic knee, muttering angrily, crying out at the twinges. She climbed on chairs to arrange the curtains and then screamed for someone to come and help her down. When my brother Jim told her she ought to stay in bed for breakfast, thus conserving her strength, Ma rolled her handkerchief in a ball and threw it at him. For some sixty years her feud with Sophie had been clothed in decent concealment. Now she let fly, making sharp comments after Sophie left the room. When we demurred, Ma stretched out her hand, palm upward. "The devil sits *here*, in my right hand," she said triumphantly. Mamma liked also to announce that when she said something, she wanted the household to accept it as right. "What I say is *correct*" — which meant the household must do as she wished.

In her eighty-eighth year, Mamma had a heart attack, serious but seemingly not painful. Fred Sharpless came and sat by the bed in the old cherry rocker. Ma raised herself — which she was not supposed to do — and peered at Fred. "I had a miscarriage in that chair," she said in a loud voice. "It was between Ernesta and Philly." Fred started a little, I saw it, and Mamma, groggy with sedation, pushed at the covers and said crossly, "Fred, you are a good man, like your father. But I wish you were more *amusing.*"

Mamma died that same year. And she did not go peacefully at all but raged indeed, clutching my hand with a grasp that hurt, drawing her breath in long, painful gasps, with lapses of consciousness and then the fearful return. Cheyne-Stokes breathing, Fred called it. Ma's eyes were terrified, they looked black instead of chestnut and deep in her head, and she fought every inch of the way down. During Harry's last year of life I remembered these things. In his strong middle age Harry had been afraid of death, afraid beyond reason, a neurotic fear, though at the time I did not know it. Sophie protected him fiercely. She herself professed to look on death as rather a nuisance. Just before Mamma's last illness she and Harry had gone to Canada for the autumn fishing. Sophie told me that if Ma got sick not to telegraph, what would be the use, Harry badly needed a holiday. When Pa died, Harry was not in Beach Haven, just Cecil, Jim, Phil, and I. Not until long afterward did I discover that Sophie's messages and wires were simply made-up excuses; Harry was afraid to come.

Strangely, this fear left Harry as his own death approached; at any rate he seemed oblivious. Sophie would not have a trained nurse in the house. For a year she took entire charge, with the help of Mary McClafferty, who had lived with us so long. It was no mean chore to maneuver that tall, big-boned man in and out of bed, no matter how thin he had become. I think Sophie's irritation saved her, sustained her in those last terrible months. "Harry always swore he'd take a pill when he got old and helpless, and finish himself off," she told me more than once. "We had an *agreement*. But now he never even thinks of it." If Harry had indeed demanded the lethal dose, I have wondered, since, whether Sophie would have administered it. No one could doubt her love for my brother, there had never been doubt of it. Yet there was in Sophie a steely attribute, something of the Medea that had always awed me.

Two years before Harry died, the American Bar Association voted to give him their highest award. Knowing of his condition, the lawyers invited Sophie to come to the banquet in New York City and receive it for him. She went, and on her return, put the

283

gold medal in Harry's hand. "I think he understood," she told me. "He closed his fingers on it and there were tears in his eyes."

One March morning in 1964, Sophie telephoned and said that Harry was dead. It was eight o'clock, and I drove at once to Merion. Sophie received me in the little room next to their bedroom. "I left our bed in the night," she said, "and came in here to sleep. Oh, I wish I had been with him!" She had a pencil in her hand and a slip of paper on which she had written something; she passed it to me. "It's for his gravestone," she said. "From Shakespeare. I've always known it was just exactly like Harry."

I looked down and read.

The day shall not be up so soon as I,
To try the fair adventure of tomorrow.

XVII

Coda. "Relating to those gone hence."

A PERSON reaches fifty at least before he cares about his ancestors. It was when Harry died that I began to think about mine. Perhaps, suddenly, I missed them. Somewhere in all of us there is an underground tide that lifts, carries us on. With me it had seemingly ceased to flow; a continuity, a connection was lacking. I walked into Harry's dining room and stood before the long wall where the portraits hung. Why, in all these years, had I never stopped to examine them? Here before me was Catherine Ann Shober, my namesake, painted by James Peale, *circa* 1812: a young girl with flowing auburn hair, holding a parrot on her wrist. The Peale brothers, I had heard, kept this bird in the studio for the contentment of posing children. Odd, that this radiant child turned into "Grandma Shober," the tiny, deaf old lady who dominated the household when Papa was a young man. . . . Here, beside the door, is Pa himself, with his nurse in daguerreotype, taken at Macao. The boy is perhaps seven and leans against the amah's knee; she wears a kimono. His bare young neck is thin, his silky hair flat above the high forehead. His ears stick out like Cecil's.

Papa's father hangs to his left. Sandwith Drinker, merchant captain, alert and healthy, a ship in full sail painted in the background. This is the grandfather who brought home our Chinese sofas and was a friend of Mr. Hukwa. . . . *His* father, Henry Drinker, at fifty-seven, in cutout silhouette, wears the Friends' black broad-brimmed hat. This Henry has a double chin; the mouth is drawn in and the figure portly — surely a contradiction in terms, considering his story? During the American Revolution Great-great-grandpa Drinker refused to fight and was thereby exiled to Virginia, carted out of town with some twenty other Quakers in full view of the populace; stones were thrown at them. A man who defies his neighbors and his government should be gaunt, bony; a well-fed protester is hardly credible. . . . Next to Henry on the wall his wife looks younger; she wears a fluted collar, her chin is a little sharp. This is Great-great-grandmother Elizabeth Sandwith Drinker, who kept a journal for fifty-eight years — the diary that my brother Cecil made into his book *Not So Long Ago.*

The wall blooms with Henry Drinkers. Somebody far back, labeled Henry the Scrivener. *His* grandfather, the one called Old Drinker, born 1680, inhabited a cave above the Delaware River, lived to be one hundred and two and had four wives and eighteen children. When they asked Benjamin Franklin, in France, how long the Americans lived, he said he couldn't tell until Old Drinker died. Old Drinker was no Quaker. He used to buy copies of King George III's more objectionable proclamations and make them into kites for his grandchildren and great-grandchildren to fly. I had read a piece about him, written in 1802 by the celebrated Dr. Benjamin Rush of Philadelphia, which said Old Drinker was a hearty eater to within a few days of his death, liked his hot toddy, and died "in a full assurance of immortality." And why not? Anyone who had such a good time alive is already half insured against oblivion.

"Americans don't talk about their ancestors," Papa had said once, and startled me. He must have meant, brag about them. These Henrys on the wall were nothing to boast about in a worldly sense — not famous, and only one even moderately rich. But they had vigor, and sinew. I felt better, looking at them. Harry, Jim, Cecil, Ernesta, Phil — all of us partook of this inheritance. What we did and thought was thereby conditioned.

From Elizabeth Drinker's diary:

SEPTEMBER 12, 1777. A part of Washington's army has been routed and have been seen coming into Town in great numbers; the particulars of the Battle I have not attended to; the slain is said to be very numerous. Hundreds of their muskets lying in the road — which those that made off have thrown down.

SEPTEMBER 19. Jenny woke me this morning about seven o'clock with the news that the English were near. We find that most of our neighbors and almost all the Town have been up since one o'clock in the morning. The account is that the British army crossed the Swedes-Ford last night and are on their way hither. Congress, Council &c. are flown. Boats, Carriages and foot pads going off all night. Town in great confusion.

SEPTEMBER 23. All the Bells in the city are taken away, and there is talk of pump handles and fire buckets being taken also. May we be strengthened and supported in the time of trial.

SEPTEMBER 24. Cannon placed in some of the streets. The report continues of the English approaching us, but I know not what to believe. The sign, over the way, of G. Washington taken down this afternoon. There is talk of the city being set on fire.

It was the third year of war, and Elizabeth's husband already exiled to Virginia. "H.D.," she calls him in the diary. She wrote from their house on Front Street above the river, at the northeastern edge of town. Elizabeth was alone with five children and the servants, though a continual flow of neighbors passed in and out all day. Nobody seemed to know where the armies were, nor could it be said that either side was winning. Pennsylvania was distracted by internal dissension to the point where General Washington had not been able to find a thousand recruits in a year. There is small doubt that local politics had much to do with the exile of the Quakers. The election of local assemblymen and the radical provisions of Pennsylvania's new constitution caused more violent feeling in certain quarters than the war itself. Instead of an upper and lower house, Pennsylvania's government had now but one legislative chamber — an arrangement that overrode the traditional safeguard of checks and balances. Many persons looked on it as an invitation to be governed by the rabble. Elizabeth Drinker was openly scornful; the diary refers sarcastically to the Pennsylvania Supreme Executive Council as "our present ruling Gentry." When Thomas Wharton is named president of the council she calls him, not Governor, but "Captain General," as if he were a pirate chief. From time to time the local Committee of Safety came to the door and demanded household furniture as reparation — blankets, leaden window weights for bullets, claw-footed mahogany chairs. "A valuable pair of large End-Irons, seized and taken from us by Philip Manse," wrote Elizabeth. In a town of twenty-five thousand, one knew everybody. When the peremptory knocking came at the door it was somehow worse to open to a familiar face, grown hard and mocking. Yet fines, requisitions, public humiliation — nothing would make the Quakers fight or pick up a musket. Down in Virginia they tied muskets to the bodies of fourteen Friends and forced them to march.

In the State House on Chestnut Street, the Pennsylvania Assembly had sat all summer directly across the hall from the Second Continental Congress. And now Elizabeth Drinker announced that Congress had fled the city. Actually they were headed for York to the westward, beyond the Susquehanna. Washington's army remained somewhere across the Schuylkill, no one knew just where. "The Americans," Elizabeth wrote, had taken up the bridge and cut the ropes to the ferry.

SEPTEMBER 25: It is now near 11 o'clock at night and has been raining for several hours, which I look upon as a remarkable favor, as 'tis said that tarred fagots are laid in several out-houses in different parts, with mischievous intent. The number of the English troops is not yet ascertained; some say 20,000, which I think is not very probable.

SEPTEMBER 26: Well! Here are the English in earnest; about 2 or 3 thousand came through Second Street, without opposition or interruption on the one side or the other. What a satisfaction it would be to our dear distant friends could they but be informed of it.

"Our dear distant friends" were, of course, H.D. and the Virginia exiles. I do not think Great-great-grandmother rejoiced because the British had come, but because they had been permitted to come quietly, with no fighting or killing. What the Friends desired above all was stillness, peace, loving-kindness; the words run through their written discipline. To me it is remarkable that the Drinkers came off as well as they did. H.D. was to remain in Virginia for nearly eight months; two of the Friends became ill and died there. Yet on the whole the exiles might have fared worse in Philadelphia, where Quakers were seized and paraded through town with fife and drum. One, young John Molesworth, was hanged on the Common "for spying." Later, the Quakers removed the body from the public grave to their own burying ground. Nor had it made things easier for H.D. and his friends that the secretary of the new Pennsylvania government was himself a renegade Quaker. Timothy Matlack had fought with the militia at Trenton and Princeton. True, he had been read out of meeting for running up debts and keeping bad company. But his power now was great; in his hands lay the fate of all professing noncombatants and non-Associators.

The congressional resolution which sent the Quakers to exile declared that certain persons had "uniformly manifested a disposition highly inimical to the cause of America." There followed a list of offenders: Joshua Fisher, Abel James (H.D.'s business partner), James Pemberton, Henry Drinker, Israel Pemberton — and so on. What seemed to anger Congress more than pacifism was the Friends' refusal to swear loyalty to Congress, to the State of Pennsylvania, or to an earlier pledge of the Associators not to trade with England. Just before Christmas of that year, the Quakers had put out a public declaration of instruction to all members of the Meeting: "Let not the fear of suffering, either in person or property, prevail on any to join with or promote any work or preparation for war . . . we exhort all who make religious profession with us, and especially our beloved youth, to stand fast in that liberty, wherewith through the manifold sufferings of our predecessors, we have been favored, and steadily to bear our testimony against every attempt to deprive us of it." A few months later another declaration appeared, signed by five names, the last and most conspicuous of which was, "Henry Drinker, Clerk of the Monthly Meeting for the Northern District." To the city fathers it was blatant, treasonable and they could not put up with it.

Again and again, before his exile, H.D. had been visited by members of the Committee of Safety, demanding that he sign or swear. Quakers simply would not swear to anything, or even agree to cooperate with the patriot party. "We do not make promises," they said mildly, and went their way. Even after seizure and arrest, the Quakers were offered parole if they would promise not to leave their houses and to "refrain from doing anything inimical to the United States of North America." The powers looked on this as lenient, considering the enemy was almost at the door. "Congress recommends it," the Pennsylvania Council wrote, "and we wish to treat men of reputation with as much tenderness as the security of their persons and papers will permit."

The Quakers would have none of it; a promise was as bad as an oath. And besides, why should innocent men bind themselves? When they had been four months in exile, H.D. wrote home that "Congress has said if we will subscribe a Test of Allegiance to them or some of them (wonderful condescension) then we may be released. How insulting!" Henry's name had been signed to most of the public protestations sent out by the Friends after their first arrest; he had indeed been named as one of "the most dangerous of the disaffected." Yet the Friends' protestations were not only eloquent but reasonable, couched in the honored terms of American libertarians since James Otis. Addressing the Pennsylvania Executive Council, "We would remind you," the Friends wrote, "of complaints urged by numbers of yourselves against the Parliament of Great Britain, for condemning the town of Boston unheard. . . . In the name then, of the whole body of the freemen of Pennsylvania, whose liberties are radically struck at by this arbitrary imprisonment of us, their unoffending fellow-citizens, we demand an audience, so that our innocence may appear and persecution give place to justice."

War, however, is no respecter of constitutional rights. The Philadelphia printer, John Dunlap, finally refused to publish any more Quaker protestations; he said his newspaper would be suppressed. The Friends found another printer and had their protestations distributed through the streets as handbills. In Philadelphia the Friends had been locked into the Free Masons' Lodge, just west of Second Street; at Winchester, Virginia, for lack of a jail they were confined to private houses and forced to "find" themselves, at exorbitant prices; the State of Pennsylvania had no intention of spending money on noncombatants. Winchester lay a hundred and seventy-five miles from home, a five days' journey and dangerously near the western border where, as the Friends reminded Congress, Indians had commenced hostilities.

A thick packet of letters exist, between Henry in exile and his wife Elizabeth. Henry's are pious, long, wordy. He is "a weak and unworthy Vessel." He prays that he may not capitulate to his persecutors, nor balk his testimony or flinch in the day of battle. He prays also "not to have a rancorous or unforgiving Temper of Mind." I think Great-great-grandfather's exertions to stand firm on the one hand while harboring peace and forgiveness on the other affected his digestion. He complains of "stitches floating about my Breast, a pain in my Head, a fullness and other indications that Bleeding is needful." Quite naturally he worries over the presence of British soldiers quartered in their Front Street house. To his sixteen-year-old daughter he sends admonitions: "My dear Sally, let me in great nearness and tenderness beseech thee to watch over thy words and actions every hour in the day. Avoid all impertinent curiosity, gadding unnecessarily abroad, appearing at the Front Door unconcerned and thoughtless, or mixing with light and unprofitable company."

Everything that Great-great-grandfather wrote was understated. Quaker discipline frowned on hyperbole; suffering must be endured with patience. What mattered was not subjection of the outer man but of the inner man, the spirit. H.D.'s letters home make no mention of hardships endured. The stoning of the travelers on the way down I learned from other sources, as also the fact that two of the exiles died in March: Thomas Gilpin, of what seemed to have been pneumonia, John Hunt some days after his leg was amputated (of course without anesthetic). "Sir," the surgeon said; "you have behaved like a hero!" There is no doubt that for H.D. the imprisonment and exile were greatly humiliating. From being a substantial merchant much respected in his city and state, at the top of local society, he had become an object of derision, to be stoned and cursed by his fellow citizens.

"All outward wars and fighting are unlawful," the Quakers said

— and preached and published the doctrine. The patriot party did not credit their good faith. To John Adams, the Friends were "hypocrites, endeavoring to raise the cry of persecution and give the matter a religious turn." Congress, censuring them, spoke of "Tories and others." The Friends were not Tories but belonged among the "others" — troublemakers who must be bundled off, out of the way.

H.D., forty-two years old, was in the flower of manly maturity. The portliness of the cutout silhouette had not yet overtaken him. It is impossible to doubt his sincerity. I am quite sure he would have laid down his life for his beliefs — though he would have done it altogether without flourish or style. H.D.'s letters from exile turn in upon himself, as though by taking thought he could bring the world to his way of thinking. "All outward wars and fightings are unlawful." Great-great-grandmother's letters in return are warm, loving; they do not stop for piety or soul-searching. Addressing her husband as "My dearest," she answers his questions, reassures him concerning the British soldiers in the house. The officers are mannerly. The others — "four great An-spachers — sit in the kitchen awaiting orders." She has had to put their cow in the washhouse to make stable room for the Britishers' horses. Also, the officers hold evening parties in the front room, with music, but on the whole they are well behaved. Elizabeth reveals a touch of worldiness not possessed by H.D. Perhaps it is the Sandwiths and Jervises coming out. Elizabeth's father and grandfather were Irish, from Dublin; her Great-uncle Jervis had been principal court painter to George II; also he was a friend of Alexander Pope and translated the whole of *Don Quixote* — a career as far removed from Front Street, Philadelphia, as if Uncle Jervis had been Khan of Outer Mongolia.

Elizabeth's letters to her husband have a cheerful, practical tone. She sends "an ounce of rhubarb and a small bundle of cardus," advising H.D. "not to make too free with purges." (H.D. had always been one for violent purges and bleeding.) To clean his pipe, Elizabeth recommends boiling for fifteen minutes, then wiping it dry. "My dearest," she writes, "can thee not alter thy old way of living in some measure, and instead of making water thy constant drink in this cold season, take a glass or two of good old Madeira, it might be of use to strengthen thy Bowels."

In April of 1778, with three other wives of the prisoners, Elizabeth journeyed out to Lancaster, where Congress now was sitting, to beg for the release of the exiled Friends. News of Gilpin's and Hunt's death had greatly distressed the Philadelphia Meeting, which heard also that the prisoners lacked medicine and other necessities, and that sickness was spreading amongst them. A petition was drawn up; the women who agreed to carry it, besides Elizabeth Drinker, were Phebe Pemberton, Mary Pleasants and Susanna Jones. They planned to travel in two wagons, with four horses and two Negroes riding postilion. Israel Morris offered himself as escort, declaring he had long had a concern to go before Congress on this business. The women accepted his offer on condition that he relinquish the notion of appearing with them before Congress. "We would by no means consent," wrote Elizabeth, "and he acquiesced. I wish I felt better both in body and mind for such an undertaking. May the Almighty favor us."

Their first ordeal was to get through the lines at Valley Forge, which they managed with considerable dispatch. At once, they requested an audience with the General. "It was not long before G. Washington came," Elizabeth wrote, "and discoursed with us freely, but not so long as we could have wished. We saw no more of him. He told us he could do nothing in our business further than granting us a Pass to Lancester, which he did."

Quite properly, the General left the fate of the Quakers to the Congress that had exiled them — an exercise known currently as passing the buck. The women resumed their journey to Lancaster in the April rains. At times they got out of the wagons and walked. "Climbed three fences to get clear of the mud," Elizabeth noted. "This day we forded three large waters; the Conestoga came into the carriage and wet our feet." Arrived at Lancaster, they were visited by none other than the secretary of the State Council, Timothy Matlack, politician, who called himself a Free Quaker. Elizabeth noted that "he undertook to advise, and perhaps with sincerity." The women remained at Lancaster for two weeks, busy and persistent, bringing their entreaties to such radical Pennsylvanians as George Bryan, Thomas Wharton, Joseph Read, David Rittenhouse. Elizabeth wrote that they all made "a show of favor, and appeared kind, but I fear it is from the teeth outward." Congress, with the whole business of a war on their hands, must have found the ladies an embarrassment. At any rate, after a fortnight of continual visiting and lobbying, the women heard one morning that their husbands were released. General Greene, indeed, remarked that had he been in Philadelphia last autumn he never would have arrested them in the first place.

Henry Drinker came home to Philadelphia unbroken by exile, determined as ever against war, and continuing to preach peace and quietude. On a winter's day of 1779, walking the street in his broad-brimmed hat, Henry was roughly handled by a group of militiamen. What he said or did is not recorded, but the men seized

him and took him to jail. Among the family papers is a poem in
H.D.'s handwriting, written from jail and addressed, "To my son
Henry Drinker — a dissuasion against too deeply resenting the
Wrong I suffer'd — written on the 12th of the 10th month 1779."

Doubt not, my Son, thy Father has his Feelings —
Infirmity is mine, I am a man
Beset with Foes within, more to be dreaded
Than those without . . .

The poem goes on to beg Christ's forgiveness, "in meekness and
lowliness of heart, beseeching by His grace to be led to patient
and retir'd stillness." Whatever H.D. had done or said when the
militiamen took him, he was deeply ashamed of his anger and
wanted his son to know it. Young Henry must not be led into false
pride at his father's having resisted instead of standing passive.

Nearly two years of war remained after H.D. wrote those lines.
With his inward struggles against resentment, the perpetual curb-
ing of temper, the setting an example in his own house and
abroad, one marvels that H.D. lasted out the war, and that the
stitches in his breast, the pain in his head and the "fullness" that
indicated "Bleeding is needful" did not finish him off sooner. He
lived to be seventy-four, his wife Elizabeth died at seventy-two.
After Yorktown and the Peace of 1783, all was forgotten and for-
given by the city of Philadelphia. H.D. found himself elected to
the Town Council and named a member of the distinguished body
known as the American Philosophical Society, founded by Benjamin Franklin in 1764, "For the Advancement of useful Learning,"
and still flourishing, with members from all over the nation.

In 1951, my brother Harry was elected to the American Philosophical Society; he kept his certificate of membership in a folder with H.D.'s, which bore the signature of Benjamin Franklin. Six years later Harry added my own certificate. When I saw the three together I wondered if, for Harry, this triple evidence took the sting out of our last name — or did it still rhyme with stinker? I told Harry it was a pity my name wasn't Henry, but even so I'd rather inherit Great-great-grandmother Elizabeth's spirit than her husband's — the pious, "passive," and mightily striving H.D.

What had my generation gained from them all, what had we lost and where lay their mark upon us? Does fate lie in the seed, or does one's future depend upon the ground where the seed falls? There is no answer to the questions. "Americans don't talk about their ancestors." Yet to remember them is partial answer. Henry the Scrivener, Old Drinker, Aunt Kate, Cecilia Beaux and the household on west Spruce Street. My parents, Harry, Cecil. . . . Now in the years of my age the sound of their names gives me strength.

Acknowledgments

This book is not spun entirely out of one person's memory. As with
all biography, help was sought from interviews as well as the records. Concerning my brothers Harry, Cecil and Philip, I needed
reinforcement from their colleagues in law and science. I wish to
thank Harry's law partners who gave generously of their time:
Thomas Reath, John Mulford, Lewis H. Van Dusen, Morris R.
Brooke, Henry W. Sawyer and Harry's secretary, Estelle Mallams.
Also Howard Lesnick, Professor of Labor Legislation at the University of Pennsylvania. Vexing problems about Harry's thematic
index of Bach's cantatas were untangled by Otto E. Albrecht, a
musicologist who sang with us for some thirty years. My old friend
Mary Melhado helped with my recollections of Bethlehem as it
was when we were schoolmates at the Moravian Seminary.

For the chapters on Cecil and Philip I am deeply grateful to Dr.
Jean A. Curran, whose excellent *History of the Harvard School of
Public Health* was made available to me in manuscript — a schol-

arly favor rarely met with. A few years ago, Dr. Curran asked Philip to dicate into a machine the recollections of his forty-two years at the Harvard Medical School and the School of Public Health. Persuading Phil Drinker to talk about himself is no easy accomplishment; the typescript of his tape reinforced my memory of what Phil had told me over the years. Cecil's colleagues and former students talked to me, some of them at length: Dr. Eugene M. Landis the physiologist, Stanley Cobb the neuropsychiatrist, whom I was fortunate to visit before his death in 1968. Dr. Cobb first met Cecil when they were residents together at the Peter Bent Brigham Hospital in 1914. Other associates and former students of Cecil's who enlightened me were the Doctors Francis M. Rackemann, Herrman L. Blumgart, William W. L. Glenn, James F. O'Neill. The enthusiasm with which they spoke, their generosity toward Cecil's uncertain temper, their statements as to his influence on their lives and of his talent as a teacher and laboratory worker strengthened my early conviction of Cecil's qualities. With Philip, still very much alive, the record was easier to come by. Theodore Hatch, Professor Emeritus of Industrial Engineering, talked to me, and the Doctors J. L. Whittenberger, Harriet L. Hardy, Francis D. Moore.

It is well known that scientists, unlike artists, do not work alone. I made a list of Cecil and Phil's collaborators as printed on the title pages of their scientific articles and books; the names were too numerous for me to mention in the body of this book or even here. Throughout the years I heard certain names spoken and often repeated: those that I remember or recognize are David L. Edsall, Alice Hamilton, Alfred C. Redfield, William B. Castle, Edward D. Churchill, Madeleine E. Field, Robert M. Thomson, John E. Enders, Donald L. Augustine, George B. Wislocki, Joseph

M. Yoffey, Constantin P. Yaglou, Leslie Silverman, Theodore Hatch.

Philip's son of the same name, an engineer, is Associate in Surgery at the Harvard Medical School — exemplifying the growing significance of the engineer in modern medical and biological science. Young Phil's current work on blood oxygenation with artificial lung membranes is, I am told, in a direct line with Cecil and Philip's work on respiratory diseases. A book published in 1969 by the Department of Surgery on *Post-Traumatic Pulmonary Insufficiency* has young Phil as co-author. One of his colleagues suggested the volume be dedicated,

To Cecil K. Drinker and Philip Drinker

1887–1956   1894–

Two Harvard Pioneers in the Application of Biological Sciences and Engineering in Respiratory Care.

I want to thank Edward Weeks of the Atlantic Monthly Press for warm encouragement and editorial advice; my secretary, Martha Sellers, for good typing and good nature through many years and many manuscripts. And lastly my friend Barbara Rex, whose literary criticism, greatly valued through six previous books, meant more this time I think than ever before.